Rosellen Brown
September 1962

In Defense of Ignorance

by Karl Shapiro

PERSON, PLACE AND THING

V-LETTER AND OTHER POEMS

ESSAY ON RIME

TRIAL OF A POET

POEMS 1940-1953

POEMS OF A JEW

In
Defense
of
Ignorance

KARL SHAPIRO

RANDOM HOUSE
New York

Acknowledgments

The author wishes to thank the following for permission to reprint the material included in these essays:

Beacon Press, Inc.—for selection from *I Wanted to Write a Poem* by William Carlos Williams.

The Bollingen Foundation—for the Foreword by C. G. Jung to the Richard Wilhelm–Cary Baynes translation of *The I Ching* or *Book of Changes*, Bollingen Series XIX, Bollingen Foundation, Inc.

The Brill Trust—for the material on page 250, which was taken from *The Basic Writings of Sigmund Freud*, translated and edited by Dr. A. A. Brill. Copyright 1938 by Random House, Inc. Reprinted by permission of The Brill Trust.

Les Editions du Chene—for selections from *Tropic of Cancer* by Henry Miller; and from *Tropic of Capricorn* by Henry Miller.

Farrar, Straus and Cudahy, Inc.—and Robert Graves and Faber and Faber, Ltd. for selection from *The White Goddess* by Robert Graves. Copyright 1948 by Robert Graves. Used by permission.

The Macmillan Company—and Mrs. W. B. Yeats and The Macmillan Company of Canada, Limited, for selec-

Contents

To the Reader

IT HAS never been my intention to write this book. For many years I have waited hopefully for someone else to write it—someone with more learning, authority, and literary competence than I have. This book, or a more judicious version of it, should have appeared a full generation ago, but we are still without it. The dictatorship of intellectual "modernism," the sanctimonious ministry of "the Tradition," the ugly programmatic quality of twentieth-century criticism have maimed our poetry and turned it into a monstrosity of literature. This criticism and the poetry it purveys have corrupted the curriculum of literature at every level in our schools and universities and have effected a complete blackout of public opinion in the art of poetry. An opposing voice will indeed seem quixotic; yet it may be the signal for a general assent.

These essays are addressed to the general public, to young poets and to teachers. The vast and well-organized army of critics will of course negate me; the intellectuals will drop their poses of serenity and hurry to defend their editorial castles. But poets, teachers, and public will, I hope, find comfort in these pages and once more take courage in the act of spontaneous judgment. One of the aims of this book is to <u>restore the respect of the ordinary reader for his own judgment—he who has so long been cowed and intimidated by the self-appointed guardians of Culture.</u>

Poetry is only the point of departure in these essays; once past the fortifications of modern poetry and criticism we should be able to perceive more clearly the intellectual dry rot of our age, for which the "moderns" have been largely responsible.

I make no apologies for the excesses of style and the extremes of opinion in this book. Against the hollow, impersonal voices of the official literati we must raise the sound of the living human voice. Only in this way can we restore the prerogatives of judgment to the reader and the right to create as he will to the poet.

About half of the chapters in this volume were delivered as public lectures under the Elliston Foundation at the University of Cincinnati in 1959. I wish to thank the trustees of the Foundation, and especially my friend Professor William S. Clark, for the opportunity to present my views to their large and generous audiences. A few of these chapters have already appeared as articles in various magazines. Others have been presented to audiences around the United States and in such remote places as Ireland, India and Japan.

KARL SHAPIRO

everything
we are taught
is false

In Defense of Ignorance

The Critic
in Spite of Himself

. . . a great deal of the best and most sensible criticism of any age is necessarily absurd.

RANDALL JARRELL

Randall Jarrell has had the last word on criticism. No one can improve on his blissful condemnation of the modern critic and the special languages and vested interests of criticism. No one has tried harder to curb some of the critic's wasteful activity. But whether he has done any good is hard to say; Jarrell is himself such a fine critic (at least when I can agree with him) that he may father a whole new family of critical minds. If he does, and if they are truly writers and not just "machines of sensibility," we may be able to see an end to the age of criticism, as he calls it. This is not very likely. We are indeed in the age of criticism and one can hardly put an end to the criticism without putting an end to the age.

I am one of that innumerable tribe of poets who was drawn into criticism at that tender age when one has published his first poems in a respectable place. I now look back on my initiation into criticism as something of a tribal investiture, for it was this ceremony that turned my hand to prose. As a writer of prose I eventually became an editor, which is to say a big brother to poets and critics. How many scores of young poets have *I* led by the hand into the kingdom of criticism. But I am not altogether sorry for it, any more than I am for my own initiation. Besides, there was nothing I could do about it. <u>We live in a time when every swan really dreams of becoming a goose, and does.</u> But my own hope has always been to make poets speak openly and judge freely, without regard for established critical canons.

Please do not think I am trying to fill you in on my autobiography if I resort to personal anecdote in these remarks. I am not averse to autobiography, even in criticism, and in fact favor it over the obscurantist and dehumanized styles which we associate with the Best Criticism. No one has ever referred to me as one of the Best Critics, but as it is an honor that I do not covet, it contents me to write the kind of criticism I do. This kind of criticism has its own very high goals, although it may not be recognizable as the thing we are accustomed to call literary criticism. It strikes me that my career as a critic is little short of fantastic, and I want to mention why, if only to point out the high place criticism has attained as a public or cultural function. I say my *career* as a critic—comical phrase—and not my criticism itself.

My criticism, and not my poetry, has carried me around the world several times, though I detest long journeys. I have lectured on *Leaves of Grass* in Dublin and in Calcutta, on William Carlos Williams in Hyderabad, on Edgar Lee Masters in Salzburg and on free verse in Tokyo. Last winter an admiral called me from the Pentagon to ask me to fly to the Antarctic, on three days' notice, to talk to our troops about modern poetry. As a critic I live in a Salvador Dali universe. As a poet I live in Lincoln, Nebraska. In addition to these voyages through time and space in behalf of criticism, all my jobs may be traced to my prose, though my poems may have had something to do with it. My first teaching job was given me, I am convinced, because of a lecture in which I took issue with George Saintsbury on seven or eight points of foot prosody. Looking back on this lecture, I see it as a kind of exercise in literary hypnotism in which I mesmerized myself as well as my audience.

I could go on listing the literary juries and such bodies on which I have served as critic, not as poet; the Foundations which have employed my critical acumen to help them get rid of their money; and even the publishers who have consulted me about new works of criticism in manuscript (I have usually advised no publication, only to receive the printed book a couple of months later).

You must be thinking what a gay life the critic leads—why, it's like a mixture of Lord Byron, Admiral Byrd, and V. I. Lenin crossing the Eastern Front in a sealed train! And it is. The life of the critic has long since taken the place of the life of the poet. There are no Byrons in the twentieth century; only poor bedeviled Dylan Thomases, who would rather crouch behind the decanter or dive from the Golden Gate Bridge than answer highbrow questions about their poems. Only those and the poet-critics, as some unfeeling lexicographer calls us. I wonder if it has ever occurred to the poet of our time that his audience prefers his criticism to his poetry because his poetry may be lacking in something? Is this possible? People, after all, are going to have literature in some form, and if criticism is all they can get, they will have criticism. We hear of no critics in Shakespeare's day: maybe one or two, but nobody who would be invited to address, say, a meeting of the National Council of the Teachers of English.

We must admit the sociological position which criticism has achieved in our time, while we are trying to wean our writers away from it. It is no accident that criticism occupies the place of honor among the modern literary arts. And it is no exaggeration to say that poetry is the weakest of the arts in the twentieth century because it is a criticism-ridden art—hardly an art at all. Criticism is an attitude of mind, not simply a method of elucidation. It is what remains when literature itself has begun to expire. Criticism flourishes when literature has failed; is not this tragically true even in the case of the individual writer? But this axiom would signify that twentieth-century literature is not the richly manifold art we tell ourselves it is. Is it time we re-examined modern poetry? Is it possible that modern criticism is only a handsome façade concealing a terrible poverty? Are criticism and poetry really one and the same in our time?

You will recognize that the position I take is that of the anti-intellectual, as sorry as the name may sound. My criticism has tried to be anti-intellectual from the beginning, although a couple of times I have been jockeyed into attacks on my own beliefs. What is an anti-intellectual? The best way to define it is through its opposite. An intellectual is a person who reduces all experience to abstract ideas. He need not be a writer, of course, or an artist of any kind. If an intellectual should come home and find his house in flames, he might rush into the burning building to save his manuscripts or his record player or even his children (for intellectuals are frequently men of action), but he will be thinking all the time of the complexities of megalopolitan life or of Euripides' *Medea,* or something of that kind. The intellectual cannot experience anything without *thinking* about it. It was the intellectual whom Lawrence loathed above all modern creatures, and Lawrence was right. The Spanish intellectual Ortega once made the penetrating remark that the intellectual is not necessarily intelligent.

Very likely I am not a true anti-intellectual, only a lowbrow highbrow. The true anti-intellectual would not be writing an essay against criticism (and I have written many), nor would he be quoting Ortega; he would be sure to avoid him. But it is virtually impossible for a twentieth-century writer not to turn into an intellectual. Every inducement will be held out to him to "philosophize" upon his experience, to abstract it and turn it into cold, calculating prose. "You have only to tell us how you wrote that poem," says the intellectual to the unsuspecting poet, "and we will pay your electric bill for life." The poet today is, as everyone is uncomfortably aware, the hostage of the intellectual. Intellectual, of course, is a synonym for critic. So the battle against intellectualism must be waged by people like me, in the hope that others may be spared.

The word *intellectual* has never taken root in America and to this day remains a foreign concept. This is curious when you consider that modern intellectual criticism, like modern poetry itself, is largely the invention of a few expatriated Americans. In Europe or in Asia the term *intellectual* is highly respectable; in America it still remains a term of derision. Modern criticism, however, has gone a long way to make the term and the thing respectable in this country, and it is the business of the anticritic to deride intellectualism wherever it raises its head. In Europe the term also refers to a social class and not simply to the individual. The Russians use the term as a class distinction. Marx used it so, as did his followers. The intellectual class is as much a part of Marxist society as the proletariat. And similarly, outside Russia, the European intellectuals form a class and hold hands across vast ideological chasms. For what they have in common is the reduction of social and historical experience to Criticism with a capital C (using that word in all its iridescent aspects at once). It amused me a couple of years ago to see two well-known literary critics, one a Catholic and the other a Marxist, dedicating their books to one another. No two writers could have less in common ideologically, but what they did have in common was Ideology itself. The modern critic has pulled criticism up by the boot straps to a position of cultural power which in the twentieth century is staggering. No wonder all those bright young men want to be critics, junior executives in the international culture conference of ideology. These intellectuals tell themselves and the world that they are responsible for the social, esthetic, and even spiritual "values" of the age. They are value experts all down the line. They have abolished the idea that esthetic values are established by works of art alone and that social and religious values—what colorless terminologies they have put in our mouths— are established by humanity, not by critics. Literary criticism hardly exists in our time; what we really have is culture criticism or theology ill concealed. The critic today uses literature only as a vehicle for ideas; he has bigger fish to fry than poets. The most insignificant book reviewer is really a social psychologist *in parvo*. Give him half a chance and he will turn into an Arnold Toynbee or an Oswald Spengler or an Ezra Pound overnight and regale you with theories of history that will make your head spin.

If what I have said is true, we are dealing with

a question of honesty. It is my contention that modern criticism is not honest, though it may be sincere. Its dishonesty results from its undying loyalty to generalities. I will give you an example. Ezra Pound in several places decries the poetry of Shakespeare because it does not fit his system of great books. This is typically the case with intellectual criticism. Pound knows as well as you do that Shakespeare is the finest of all English poets, but he must remain sincere to the system he has blocked out. He thus engages in a fantastic act of dishonesty. Eliot did the same with Milton and with dozens of other poets. Because of some theory Eliot had about the "musicality" of verse he forbade poets to read Milton. Eventually Eliot changed his mind, perhaps because his loyalty to Milton's puritanism finally got the better of him. Sincerity to the idea always takes precedence in the mental life of the intellectual, whether the idea comprises a total system or is some offshoot of one of the *isms.*

The honest critic has no system and stands in no dread of contradicting himself. And because he abhors systems he is in a better position to view a work of art in its wholeness and in its relations to other things. An essay like George Orwell's on Kipling is an example of honest criticism. Orwell rather dislikes Kipling and tells us why in clear English. Eliot, working from theory to fact, gives us a defense of Kipling. From what we think we know of the loftiness of Eliot's tastes this is something of a shock. Eliot admires Kipling by way of a typical act of intellectual dishonesty. He first tries to give the appeal of Kipling's kind of poetry a high-sounding name, in this case "ballad attention." Then he mentions in passing the more sophisticated forms in Anglo-Saxon, Welsh, Latin, Greek, Sanskrit, Persian, and Chinese, as if these languages have something to do with Kipling. To flatter his audience he talks about the "simple-minded," that is, people who didn't come to the lecture, and hides behind the mysteries of prosody to say something nice about "Danny Deever"! Eliot defending "Danny Deever" is a sight to behold; when he comes to the climax of the poem he says "the atmosphere has been prepared for a complete suspension of disbelief." The point is—I am not going to bog down in Eliot-on-Kipling or even Eliot—that Eliot is only *using* Kipling experimentally, in the best intellectual manner, as a guinea pig. Eliot is no more interested in Kipling than I am, but in his own ideas, such as "the willing suspension of disbelief," which Eliot adopted as one of his crucial ideas. The willing suspension of disbelief is almost as crucial to Eliot's criticism as Original Sin itself, but only one who believes in Original Sin (to paraphrase Eliot) will know what I am talking about. I don't happen to believe in it myself.

Milton is not good enough for the intellectualism of Eliot but Kipling is! The Uriah Heepishness of Eliot can almost make Kipling plausible, though not quite. Orwell, who is an honest fellow, though he got himself caught in Marxist intellectualism for a while, makes the simple observation that Kipling is a bad poet but that there are degrees of badness in poetry, just as there are degrees of goodness. Kipling, says Orwell, is a *good* bad poet. Eliot tried to arrive at something of the sort but ends up completely hamstrung in his own terminology. It is terminology that has made Eliot famous in an age of catchwords. That and Eliot's sincerity to his terminology. For Eliot does not talk about Kipling at all; he talks about Eliot talking about Kipling.

I bring up the matter of Eliot's criticism only incidentally here. What I am getting at is the difference between criticism and judgment. We have today the biggest and busiest criticism in the history of literature, but no judgment. The judgments we have are really precepts and are handed down from on high by Criticism. Most writers find out to their dismay sooner or later that the modern critic does not care about literature except as a bone of contention. To the critic, analytical or theoretical (one is bad as the other), a work of art is something that fits into a system or doesn't, and every new creation is a threat to already existing systems. It is not uncommon for the critic to complain of too much poetry in the world— if only there were!—and it is the critic who sees to it that there is only one poet recognized per decade, or whatever the quota happens to be. Modern criticism is highly orthodox, that is, based on exclusion. Nearly all such criticism deals with what it calls the elites. Now and then a Kipling is elected to the club, a writer who is admittedly rather common but who is orthodox at heart. This keeps the orthodoxy going and beefs up the blood stream.

The absence of judgment in modern criticism is beyond belief. Critics in fact no longer exercise judgment about literary works; they discourage it. They talk about poetry or fiction in terms of Myth or Symbol or Structure, anything at hand which can be intellectualized. The poem is only a conversation piece leading up to a discussion of the higher abstractions concerning society or religion. Originally, to be sure, the depersonalization of criticism was intended as a maneuver to attract attention to poetry, not to criticism. But very shortly the mightiest of tails began to wag one of the oddest-looking literary dogs ever beheld by man. Those of you who are exempt from reading modern criticism cannot begin to imagine the abdominous magnitude of this critical literature, even leaving out the textbooks and anthologies. The modern literary textbook is a thing to conjure with. Textbooks designed for the "understanding" or "exploration" of poetry have probably done more to warp the literary judgment of college students than the Collected Comic Books of the Twentieth Century. Because they are based on the "depersonalized" view of literature and life, they all tend toward the extinction of the faculty of judgment, one of man's most vital characteristics. My experience with students who have been subjected to these dry and terrible tomes, the very paper of which seems impregnated with lead, is that they are utterly and permanently stunned into literary insensibility.

Authoritarian criticism precludes judgment; this fact is too obvious to pursue. In place of judgment this criticism sets up two barriers to judgment. The first is the morass of concepts, the second is a list of approved works (in effect an *Index Expurgatorius*). By taking over the terms of ancient rhetoric, esthetics, logic, modern anthropology and psychology and even chemistry, the critic situates himself behind impregnable walls. So situated, he can completely ignore his real job, that of discriminating between works of literature, even in the simple way Orwell does with *good* and *bad* and *good-bad*. Naturally this is a great relief to the critic. The prolonged postponement of literary judgment also leads to the creation of a hothouse poetry, the poetry especially written for the critic. A frightening quantity of modern poetry is written to the criticism; it is hothouse grown, factory made. Such poetry may even become famous, if criticism takes a shine to it.

Inferior poetry of the past can also be made a touchstone: I am thinking particularly of the Metaphysical poetry and other kinds of poetry bordering on the freakish. John Donne gives the critic much more to talk about than, say, Robert Herrick; that is the criterion. Whether Donne is as good a poet as Herrick is never discussed. If you can impress students with how complex the mind of John Donne is, you need not mention any such crucial questions as how good a poet he is. Donne, of course, is better brain food than Herrick, and the modern critic and textbook author will put a hard thinker at the top of the list any time. It looks better to people like scientists, who do practically nothing but think. I judge Donne to be a good poet about on a par with Marianne Moore, a poet who writes well only when she violates the precepts laid down for her by T. S. Eliot. One of Hart Crane's worst poems, "Voyages," appears in every comprehension and exploratory textbook. Especially "Voyages II," which has an almost religious appeal to the modern critical mentality. Nothing is ever said about the bad writing in this poem, which ranges from the bombastic to the maudlin. On the other hand, Crane's *The Bridge,* one of the few modern poems worth reading more than once, was condemned by criticism almost before it was published. The critics said such things as American culture cannot afford such a subject, and other nonsense having nothing to do with poetry.

The matter of "understanding" poetry is too important to pass by here; and I would like to use an incident involving myself to make my point clear. Just at the time when I had published my first poems in a good literary magazine, and was highly elated at this recognition, I had to take an examination in "poetry comprehension." The examination was given in a school for librarians and was part of a very serious training program which would certify me to become a librarian. On the examination as a whole I received one of the best marks; in poetry comprehension I received the lowest. (Imagine what a book reviewer could do with that statement!) I was the only member of the class interested in writing poetry and the only one who read it almost to the exclusion of everything else. But I failed to comprehend poetry. I confess that I mention this incident with a certain glee. What was it I did not comprehend about poetry which was so simple to people who accepted poetry much as they did bibliography or cataloguing—a subject to be mastered cold? Obviously I was not reading poetry the way my classmates were. All of them did fine and comprehended in a split second, while I, the poet in their midst, went blank before the poems on the examination sheet.

That was many years ago and I still have not learned to comprehend a poem in the accepted manner. My students know—they are reared on understanding poetry, and hate it—and even some of the poets of my acquaintance are adept in this art. I look upon them with a fishy eye but I certainly do not begrudge them this skill or hobby, or whatever you want to call it. In my own case, I never think of reading a poem for what it "means" unless there is so little merit in the thing that there is nothing else to do with it. The examination-meaning of a poem is usually so obvious that it is hard to think about it at all. The opening period of *Paradise Lost* is one of the most extraordinary sentences ever written and worthy of the name of sublimity which Longinus gives to the creation in Genesis—what does it *mean?* It means that Milton has found the "poetry" of his immense theme, that he is caught up in the terror and splendor of his vision, which exists only in his expression of it. There is no way to say what these lines mean except by reciting them. They mean what they mean; they are their own meaning. The modern critic reads a poem backwards; he does not want to know whether the vision is achieved or how well; he wants to know what went into the pudding. He wants recipes. And how desperately the critic wants the student to believe what an awesome thing it is to compose a poem.

There is one more bit of private information I want to mention. Off and on for ten years I have been editing literary magazines of poetry and criticism. During this period I have had letters from nearly every living poet of note commending my judgment in the poems I have published. I am not sure what these commendations mean, but I take them at their face value; I weigh them against my distaste for poetry comprehension, and wonder. Can one be a good judge of poetry and a bad comprehender? Precisely. For the act of judgment in reading a poem not only precedes but encompasses comprehension (modern criticism to the contrary). Comprehension is documentation, nothing else. It is the learned appreciation of art and has only as much relation to the poem as the Appendix has to a history book. This is the way poetry is taught and criticized today, by internal documentation, and it is no wonder that the sense of judgment has atrophied. Once in a while, of course, documentation, or what is called analysis, is necessary, as when a painter says to the dealer, "Excuse me, sir, you have hung my picture upside down." This is when the critic pops up and begins to direct the traffic.

Modern Criticism is founded on a premise which I believe to be a profound fallacy. It commits this error consistently: it takes the words of a poem as words found in the dictionary, in the encyclopedia, and more likely in *The Encyclopedia of Social Science*.

Even if criticism advances some high-sounding concept such as "the auditory imagination," it still tries to keep poetry within the language, even in a literal sense. But poetry cannot be found in any dictionary; it is language in a state of becoming, language trying to escape its condition. Most poetry fails in this high venture.

The relations between the official language, the poetic language of a certain time and place, and the individual poet's language are purely diplomatic. The good poet's language is always at the periphery of the existent languages of his own tongue, from the vulgar dialects to the King's English. Language is his element and he moves through it in every dimension, apart from the dictionary meanings and the semantics of words. The poet uses language plastically, not semantically. The critic will devil you with principles like connotation and association and will even find poems to prove his case. If he can't find them, he will order them from the factory. <u>Ambiguity is one of the favorite principles of the modern critic, but this one has backfired rather badly, killing quite a few graduate students.</u> The critic sees the poem through the dictionary, as if the poet had taken the twenty-three definitions of *green* and used them all at once. But the way the poet uses *green* does not appear in any dictionary. (Incidentally, someone should analyze the dictionary, if analysis is the order of the day. The dictionary is a kind of large bad poem, or rather a fine piece of science fiction. And the card catalogue of the library is surely the most romantic epic of modern man. The greatest books defy classification completely. What is *Thus Spake Zarathustra?* Poetry, prose, philosophy, religion, cosmic science, business administration? Who knows?)

The same word used in a line of prose (and what is

prose?) and in a line of poetry is two entirely different words, not even similar, except to the eye. Further, the same word used by two different poets becomes two different words. The meaning of the word depends on the poem in which it occurs, not on the dictionary or on *The Golden Bough*. It is in its degenerative phase that poetry moves into lexicography, into meaning that you can look up and find. It then becomes the poetry of verbalization, of wit, of cleverness, of cultural allusion, of metaphysical metaphor, and finally of philosophic abstraction, after which it dies. You will find this well illustrated in the modern anthology. Worse, you can trace this process in the writing of a dozen of the most prominent intellectual poets. A healthy poet uses the dictionary like a phone book; he looks up a number and then dials it; and that is only the beginning. The intellectual poet takes the number down, forgets that it leads somewhere, and begins to do the numerology of the Second Coming of the Messiah. This is known as the poetry of the Tradition, with a capital T.

"She utters senseless sounds, through fever of her love," says a Hindu poem describing the love of Krishna and Radha. It is these senseless sounds which are the "words" of poetry.

> Ah, Sun-flower! weary of time,
> Who countest the steps of the Sun, . . .

cries Blake in one of the most beautiful lyrics ever written. (I use the word *beautiful* although it is forbidden by modern criticism.) It is hard to explain to the critic that one of the key words of this poem is *Ah!* The letter *O* is the first letter of the poetic alphabet; *Ah* may well be the last. What sounds does Radha make? What is the meaning of *Ah!* If we knew we would not need poetry at all, for the poet does not use words in any sense already known. He uses words in spite of their meaning. Criticism always and necessarily talks about poetry in retrospect, in the language of recollection. But poetry itself projects into the unknown of language and of all experience.

Literature is always at a greater disadvantage than the other arts when it comes to criticism; it is simple for the critic to pretend that the poet's words are also his. In school all but the very brightest students are taken in by this shell game. A real test of critical ability is to have a critic criticize a work of music or a painting. Even Grove's *Dictionary* doesn't contain the musical equivalent for ambiguity. Eventually of course the critic would invent the terminology he wants, even if he had to hire Mortimer Adler to write a whole new *Syntopicon*.

Insofar as criticism is a branch of philosophy we should leave it alone. The poet and the poet-in-us-all have no business hanging around philosophy. But where criticism touches literature we must be on our guard. A criticism of concepts is the more pernicious because it atrophies the judgment and prevents the free play of opinion. Opinion is a mass prerogative, not a matter of personal fiat by some *soi-disant* Dr. Johnson. I admire endlessly the patience of the twentieth-century audience, considering what it has had to put up with in poetry and criticism. The intellectual critic considers its audience stupid and says so. I consider the audience polite to the exploding point. But the audience has contented itself with the quietest type of revenge known to literary man: it has refused to buy the books. The critic has retaliated by cramming the textbook with unreadable and dishonest prose and factory-made poetry and shoving it into the curriculum under the title of Contemporary Literature. The modern anthology is even worse,

being only a sugar-coated textbook with photographs
of the poets, all taken in 1935. In profile.

Perhaps philosophy would do well to take criticism
back. Let us leave the esthetician in quiet to do whatever it is the esthetician does. As for the critic, let
him get back to the lost art of judgment, if indeed it
is an art and not just an instinct. The business of
criticism is discrimination, pure and simple. Analysis
belongs to science and to psychology, which is practically a science. It has nothing to do with literature,
nothing to do with literary discrimination, nothing to
do with the use of poetry. I am exaggerating a little
but not much. An honest nonconceptual critic will
sometimes analyze a poem, as certain professors used
to do in Spain when the peasants came to have a poem
of Lorca's interpreted. But this was an act of kind-
ness, not a philosophical *tour de force*. The professional critic depends heavily on the kind of poem
which is said to have various "levels" of meaning. Of
course there are such poems and some fine ones, but
they are in no wise a touchstone of art. The true critic,
it seems to me, has an obligation to affirmative judgment; I would go so far as to say that we cannot get
a true work of criticism which has a coil of negative
emotion lying at the bottom of it. A work of criticism
may become a work of art only when the critic is in
love with his subject and is carried away by it, exactly as the poet is carried away by his. Think of poor
A. E. Housman, who spent his critical life gnawing
away at the dreary Latin poet Manilius, whom Housman himself looked down upon. To what end?
Housman admired Propertius, not Manilius; what per-
version of intellect drove him to spend thirty years on
a poet who meant nothing to him?

The chances of relegating criticism to its proper
place in the scale of things, as the most tentative and

least tried of the arts, are small at the moment. There is already a generation of critics in America and in England (the Anglo-Saxon countries) trained in the special highfalutin of analytical criticism. If they were only a literary faction it would do no harm, but a large number of them are teachers of literature who spread the gospel of impersonality, depersonalization, objectivity, and so forth. They write criticism themselves and even teach classes called "creative." They are the backbone of the big literary quarterlies, the liberal weeklies and even the commercialized book review of the Sunday papers. In short, they are in office. Judgment, the total and immediate perception of a work of art, is ruled out of court. Taste is unknown. An artificial demand has been created for criticism but the natural demand for poetry is nowhere encouraged, except where the poet meets the critic on the critic's terms. Criticism has set up a soundproof wall between poetry and the audience. It keeps poetry incommunicado and talks to its audience only through the *gobble-gobble* of critical prose. And it invents reasons for acting as interpreter. We seem to have forgotten that the reader in Dante's age knew what Dante was referring to; the poetry of Dante was in the language of the newspaper of his time—had there been one. Homer's audience didn't have to consult Bulfinch's *Age of Fable* to find out what Homer meant. We in the twentieth century seem to think that those Greek and Italian audiences must have been almost as learned as Sir James Frazer; we seem to accept the fact that we cannot understand the poet unless someone tells us what he means. Thus has poetry become a part of criticism and a phase of pedagogy.

The critic begins with the premise that the audience does not understand. This is the premise that keeps him in business. But the concept of understanding does not apply in the first place; and secondly, the audience "receptivity" is the only valid receptivity there is. There is indeed a kind of poetry that needs rehearsal with the audience before it can be performed, but this is by no means the best poetry. In any case, poetry is for the audience to judge. The word *audience* is anathema to the modern critic and signifies in his mind popular art and a menacing mob or rabble. The critic prefers his own hand-picked audience of critical trainees and a few students who are on the road to criticism. How puzzled all those critics were when hundreds and thousands of completely uninformed students and even just ordinary people with two ears flocked to hear Dylan Thomas. What had happened!

But the critics had their inning, too. The largest gathering so far recorded to come to hear a poet-critic came to hear T. S. Eliot in Minneapolis. Of course he was not reading poetry; he was talking about the "Frontiers of Criticism." Right on the frontier. So where Thomas had his thousands, Eliot had his ten thousands. Minnesota has changed since the days of Sinclair Lewis, if it can muster a criticism audience the size of a regiment. Eliot ended the lecture with the nervous remark that maybe criticism has become "too brilliant" in our time, but the speaker left no one in doubt as to the role of the critic, to elucidate poems and to *correct* taste.

Culture poetry, which is what modern poetry is, can be precisely described in every way. We know its forms, its psychology, its subject matter, and even its aims. It has a definite and limited number of themes, a prescribed method of composition, as well as a set formula for comprehension. Under the bad and obscurantist writing of criticism and its textbooks, under the weird confusion of the anthology, we find everything laid out neatly. The atmosphere of modern poetry is that of the hospital, of criticism that of the dissecting room. The patient is never expected to recover.

If we posit two types of poetry, culture poetry and just *poetry*, the first type is that which attempts to explain culture. It can do this in the manner of the Metaphysical poets, who were troubled by scientific knowledge and who wished to compete with science; by rewriting history according to a plan; by tracing the rise and fall of a particular belief, and so forth. Culture poetry is always didactic, as indeed most modern poetry is. It is a means to an end, not an end, like art. Culture poetry is poetry in reverse; it dives back into the historical situation, into culture, instead of flowering from it. And there it remains to enrich the ground for criticism.

It is true that anything can be turned into poetry, even Culture (horrid word). But who has written the poetry of "culture"? Certainly no one in our time, unless Rimbaud. There are passages in Ezra Pound which come close to the "poetry" of money and also the poetry of Mandarin civilization; but on the whole the *Cantos* form a dreary epic of history which never gets off the ground. Sometimes I begin a course in modern poetry with the poem called *"Une Charogne"* by Baudelaire, one of the most vicious of "modern" poems and a true culture poem. Baudelaire attacks the Romantic conception of love (for the culture poet is forever on the attack). He takes his girl to view a female corpse, a carrion lying in a lascivious position and being eaten by maggots. "And that is what is in store for you," observes the poet to his beloved.

> *Et pourtant vous serez semblable à cette ordure,*
> *A cette horrible infection,*
> *Etoile de mes yeux, . . .*

> And you too shall be like this filthy excrement,
>   This horrible infection,
> Star of my eyes, . . .

The word *ordure* is particularly juicy. In the preface
to his poems Baudelaire announces that Paris is a
center radiating "universal stupidity." Stupidity is one
of the favorite words of culture poets, for modern
poetry prides itself on its intelligence, if nothing else.
How intelligent this poetry really is, is another question.

Baudelaire's poem and Yeats' "The Second Coming"
seem to me two of the best examples of modern cultural or criticism poetry. In his poem Yeats predicts
the coming of the Antichrist and even dates it.

> Surely the Second Coming is at hand.
> The Second Coming! Hardly are those words out
> When a vast image out of *Spiritus Mundi*
> Troubles my sight: . . .

It is one of the stagiest of Yeats' poems, about a third
of which are culture poetry. But "The Second Coming" is one of the favorites of the age, as far as *correct*
taste goes, and it is fine to *elucidate* in a classroom.
Yeats was a poet of genius who wandered into the
culture camp and never got out. People who have not
been indoctrinated with modern criticism have no
difficulty discriminating between "The Second Coming" or "Byzantium," famous textbook pieces, and
something like "Easter 1916," in which Yeats finds the
poetry of modern Ireland. But of course if we used
literary discrimination instead of intellectual analysis
we would have to lop off quite a few boughs from
the sacred oak of culture.

Modern poetry outside English is somehow less
pretentious about its use of culture, with the excep-

tion of a few poets like Valéry. One can see a simplicity, even in translations, in the works of such poets
as Rilke, Lorca, or Cavafy, who have as much to say
about the past and its mythology as Pound, Eliot, and
Yeats. Cavafy, the twentieth-century Greek poet, who
in some respects is the first poet of our age, has more
to say about the past than even the famous Pound-
Eliot-Yeats triumvirate, but he never forgets that he
is a poet and not a sociologist.

In the religion of modern poetry the Trinity is composed of Pound, Eliot, and Yeats. All three men are
provincials, the two Americans being Europeans by
adoption. Cultural expatriation is a deeper thing than
taking up residence abroad. The most salient act of
literary sabotage committed by Pound and Eliot has
been their immolation of Walt Whitman. Whitman is
the only American poet we have ever produced who
deserves the name of greatness, if we must use such
an undiscriminating word as *great*. The shameful and
dishonest denigration of Whitman alone should re-
duce the critical authority of Eliot and Pound to zero,
and eventually will. The "Song of Myself" is known
throughout the world, but not in the United States,
as one of the chief poems of world literature. It is
more than that; it is one of the most inspired works of
art of man. But modern criticism looks the other way,
just as it is inclined to do with Shakespeare. The only
nice thing Pound can find to say about Whitman's
poetry is that it is not in iambic pentameter. Eliot
cannot even say that. Whitman does not fit into the
culture program and must be ruled out. One of the
reasons why Eliot calls D. H. Lawrence *ignorant* must
be Lawrence's honest love and admiration for Whitman. A really cultured poet can't see anything in
Whitman but an embarrassing use of grade-school
French.

What we call modern poetry is in reality a brief moment in twentieth-century literature, buttressed by a few godfatherly names like Baudelaire and John Donne. The ruling intellectuals themselves are wary of the word *modern* and put it in quotation marks. They do not want to be left behind when the century is over. But modern poetry, with or without quotes, is an actual thing, a small body of poetry and criticism written circa 1915-25. This was the decade that saw the publication of "Prufrock," Valéry's *La Jeune Parque*, Eliot's *The Sacred Wood, The Waste Land*, Pound's *Mauberley*, Fenollosa's essay on the Chinese written character, Yeats' *The Tower*, Laforgue's *Derniers Vers*, Stevens' *Harmonium*, Cummings' *Tulips and Chimneys*, Marianne Moore's *Observations*, Hulme's *Speculations*, Joyce's *Ulysses*, Richards' *The Meaning of Meaning*, Ernest Jones' *Essays in Applied Psycho-Analysis*, and Pound's *A Draft of XVI Cantos*. Herein lies the whole canon of modern poetry or a fine glimpse of it, and these are the works that dominate literary thinking even today. Yet during the same period were published such works as the poems of Hopkins, William Carlos Williams, D. H. Lawrence, A. E. Housman, Rilke's *Duino Elegies* and *The Sonnets to Orpheus*, Wilfred Owen, and Thomas Hardy. The intellectuals are heavier in criticism; the non-intellectuals, however, produced such prose as Williams' *In the American Grain* and Lawrence's *Studies in Classic American Literature*, which will probably be read long after the *Speculations* of T. E. Hulme, and *The Sacred Wood*, or so I hope.

This is not to say that there were two camps or teams of poetry circa 1915-25 such as Classicists and Romantics, although the intellectual faction calls itself "classical," with characteristic immodesty. But in the first list there is a definite factionalism, the formation of schools, manifestoes, programs of action, and the eventual election to all the cultural boards and committees which reach down through literary society from the royal academies to the Midwestern college town. We cannot imagine D. H. Lawrence at an international culture meet, nor the shy proud Rilke. When Rilke finally became famous in Paris, the French were very disappointed in his salon behavior. He didn't act in the least like the Messiah of intellect or what the sociologist calls in his unbeautiful patois, a "culture hero."

Changes of taste are brought about by critics. The history of art is brought about by critics, while art itself goes on at an entirely different tangent from criticism. It is not the public that changes taste; the public is the victim of it, as much in literature as in millinery. A healthy literary audience comes into view when criticism is removed. Painting is flourishing today because of the relative absence of art criticism and the healthy exercise of judgment. There is a huge population of amateur painters, people who do not aspire to become famous artists but who love to paint. This is the true audience for the dedicated painter. The same is true of contemporary music. But there is no comparable audience of poets, only a grim little army of poet-critics grinding out mean little stanzas under the gooseneck lamp. And for every poem there are ten critics poised over their typewriters, waiting.

What is the remedy against criticism? There isn't any except the creation of new poems which will divert attention away from intellectualism and toward the work of art itself. Nonparticipation is the only rule; no criticism against criticism will do much good, even the kind I am presenting here. We must create a stoppage of meaningless critical work, simply by ignoring it. And we must not force new poems. If poetry is again to grow it must choose its own time. The condition of poetry in America today is similar to that in Russia; the creative spirit is not free; it is dictated to from above. Russia has government control of poetry; we have official criticism at the helm which determines the standards of work, directs the organs of expression, controls the fellowship foundations, and even reaches into the curricula of schools. The only opposition to this state of affairs comes from a self-styled literary Underground. But this Underground plays directly into the hands of the critical police of letters, being itself only a negative version of culture poetry. It is mostly the form of small life found under stones. But at least it is alive. Elsewhere, whatever real poetic talent is available is probably unaffiliated and hides in stunned silence writing its books.

It is necessary to demolish the great empty Bastille of criticism, if only as a symbol of rebellion against it. Our whole conception of literature is by now so overgrown with notions of society, history, religion, and government that we are in a fair way to smother our writers. I do not want to go into the grisly recitation of the lives and deaths of our modern poets, the suicides, alcoholics, and mental cases, except to say that there is a connection between these tragedies and intellectualism. The textbook explanation will give you an equation of poet-versus-society, poet-in-the-industrial-world, poet-and-Original-Sin, or some such thing. I do not agree, but think rather the equation should be poet-versus-criticism, poet-versus-intellectualism. The intellectual tries and sometimes succeeds in converting his own sociological hysteria into what he is pleased to call a mask. He "depersonalizes" so completely that he escapes even himself. The honest poet has no such defenses and is made a prey to the

Here Shapiro says that poetry should be childlike. (Not retired?)

bombardment of ideas from all sides. Unless he has a strong psychic constitution he will sooner or later crumple under the pressures of Criticism. The intellectual will fortify himself behind the barricades of Tradition and Orthodoxy; the honest poet will find no asylum. The intellectual considers his "exile" at an end when he has established himself in society, at the top. The honest poet knows that he is a member of no society, past, present, or future. It is a sad thing to see poets dissipating their talents in culture criticism and city planning. With what a sublime disgust Rimbaud turned his back on all that and marched off into Abyssinia. Rather a slave trader than an intellectual; that was his message. It was not society he spat on; it was modern poetry.

It has taken me twenty years to break away completely from modern poetry and modern criticism, which I consider to be one and the same thing. Being a teacher has helped me immeasurably to see how pernicious this poetry and criticism really are and how destructive they have been to poetry and the faculty of judging poetry. Being an editor has helped me see what has happened to the craft of writing in our time, to witness the essential dishonesty of the modern critic, the dearth of taste, the misuse of understanding as a criterion of appreciation, the shameful muzzling of the audience, and the seizure of poetry by culture theorists. If this sounds like a new evangelism, I apologize, but I look at it that way. Actually, I wrote down all these views as long ago as fifteen years. That was before I had read criticism seriously or become involved in criticism myself. In the interim, my taste has been "corrected" by the intellectuals several times, and indeed they have done their best to educate me. During the notorious Bollingen Prize incident in which a jury of poets and critics gave this famous award to the *Pisan Cantos*, I was almost nudged into voting for Pound myself. Giving that honor to Pound was an act of intellectual arrogance which has no parallel in literary history. Several of the poet-critics in the group made it quite clear to me that they had no use for Pound or the *Cantos* but that they were honoring the *skill* of his controversial book. Eliot had popularized the term *autotelic*, which made it possible for critics to ignore the views of the poet, however unsavory, while commending the technique. Thus, the intellectual critic has it both ways: he can dictate to society about its ills and he can regard a poem as a pure exercise of language, at his convenience. It is another major paradox in modern criticism, bridged in this case by flimsy concepts having to do with change of "sensibility," etc. No scholar has been able to reconcile the fundamental contradictions in Eliot's criticism, any more than one can reconcile Pound's Confucianism with his Fascism.

The practice of criticism is today universal. Taking Western literature as a whole in the twentieth century, the dominant poetry is English; it is not French or German or anything else. Even in those parts of the Orient where there is a contemporary literature of any kind, the dominant poetry is English. Extraordinary as it sounds, this is true in India and in Japan. I have been told by Japanese poets that the most influential poet in Japan today is—T. S. Eliot! This dominant English poetry, however, is at bottom American, or rather the poetry of certain Americans of the little moment of 1915-25: Pound, Eliot, Cummings, Stevens, Tate, and others. The combined poetry and criticism of these men, of this brief period, constitute what we know as Modern Poetry and Modern Criticism. The approach of this poetry is cultural, even sociological, and embodies one or another world-view of art, of esthetics, of politics, of history, and of the ethical bases of human society— all the mistaken approaches to the art of poetry, in other words.

In taking control of the cultural situation the poet-critic has had to accomplish two almost insuperable aims. The first was the neutralization of judgment. By relegating the natural faculty of judgment to the lowest rung of the critical scale of things, he has been able to usurp judgment and arrogate it to himself. The "correction of taste" has superseded the normal, free exercise of taste by the public. Normal opposition to works like *The Waste Land* and the *Cantos* of Pound was defeated as long ago as a generation; and constant reinforcement of the so-called "classical" position has prevented any new voicing of opinion. The disappearance of the poetry audience is a direct consequence of this maneuver. In place of a poetry audience we have today a criticism audience. The actual poetry audience, which is potentially as large as the population itself, has had to betake itself to cellars where it can listen to poetry of some kind in an atmosphere of desperate spontaneity.

Criticism is always the latest and least reliable of the literary arts, the renegade and the spoiled brat of letters. Criticism has an almost congenital tendency to degenerate into something else, anything it can think of—psychology, esthetics, anthropology, politics, or theology. It is the true black sheep of the literary family. The modern phase of criticism encompasses all the "sciences" of culture, but there is virtually no *art* of literary criticism in the twentieth century. In espousing theory and divorcing judgment or discrimination, criticism has set itself a task which has nothing to do with poetry or the arts and everything to do with the misuse of art as an instrument of social value.

What then is the role of criticism? The answer is that *a good work of criticism is a work of art about another work of art.* Anything short of that is failure. I have made no reference to scholarship. I revere scholarship, but no scholar I ever heard of has made the claim that scholarship is art. We need good literary scholarship more than ever today, scholarship based upon honest judgment and not mere intellectual exercise. We may even need good estheticians, but this I cannot vouch for. But the critic who considers himself a man of letters should humble himself before literature and compose his essays in the same spirit of happy dedication as the poet or the novelist. Only the other day I received a new anthology-textbook on the essay, half of which was devoted to chapters called "Mass Culture" and "High Culture." This is the way we are training our students—to be culture scientists, not writers.

The absence of good criticism today is a simple indication of the absence of the audience. The war waged against what modern criticism calls popular art has deprived literature of its only soil. There can be no refined art without popular art, even bad popular art. In the absence of popular and folk art and primitive art we get only an artificial hieratic art, art in the laboratory. Modern painting is a healthy art because it has brought into it all the elements of the folk, the primitive, and the popular. A good bit of the calligraphy of modern painting is based on the comic strip and the commercial poster. Modern poetry is a sickly and desiccated poetry because it has cut itself off from elements of daily life and has relied on sociological texts and specially approved classics. "Popular" in the minds of Pound, Eliot, and Yeats signifies debased, when it should signify the raw material for poetry.

In these remarks I have used the word "modern" in

a sense which I hope will clarify it at long last. It is a synonym for "ideological" or "cultural" and it applies more to poetry, and the poetry circa 1915-25, than to painting or music or even fiction. It was during this period that Eliot and the "classicists" captured poetry through criticism and even tried to do the same with fiction! For in 1921 Eliot, as chief strategist, announced that the novel was over and done with. The novel, we were told, "ended with Flaubert and James." Of course he was using the word "novel" in some special intellectual sense and as a maneuver to establish James Joyce as the prototype of a new kind of novelist. Fortunately the maneuver failed and the novel was not killed off. It is only recently that criticism has moved in with all its forces to deal with fiction as it has dealt successfully with poetry. But it is too late. Poetry remains the only casualty of modern literature, but it is the most crucial casualty.

Having said all this, I might be expected to conclude with some words of advice to the poet and to the critic of good will, but I have said enough already. Quite obviously, poet and critic must draw apart, and beyond this I have no message. For poets to band together in groups is always fatal; history has a tendency to bury poets in threes. Poets venturesome enough to set up a "school" of their own only offer a large target for critical gunnery practice. Even the individual poet who commits himself to prose must have a care; the critic will always tackle the prose as an excuse to avoid committing himself about the poetry. Coleridge, who deserted poetry to become the father of modern criticism, is the ideal of a dozen or more modern poets of talent who abandoned poetry for criticism. It is one of the literary tragedies of our time.

There is little hope of rescuing the critic who is

already mired in ideology and culture. But it is the poet I have in mind when I point to the saurian prose of Eliot, the vulgarity of Pound's essays, and the narcissistic rhetoric of Yeats.

I think the poet will find, once he has turned his back on criticism, that his quarrel with "society" will evaporate. Imagine not having to write poems about the Just City or to make definitions of Culture or to fret like poor Baudelaire about reducing the traces of Original Sin. No more theology, no more economic systems, no more psychology of the depths, not even myth-making or the decline of the West! What a vacation for poetry! "But what else is there to write about?" cries the modern poet, dropping his *Explicator*. "You don't expect me to write about the birds and the bees, or flowers, or *people!* That's all been done, ages ago!"

Yeats speaks somewhere of the fascination of what's difficult, and we all agree, but add: the difficult isn't the only thing that's fascinating. We do not find the difficulties of modern poetry and modern criticism particularly *intelligent* difficulties. Why make a fetish of difficulty-for-difficulty's-sake? Is there no fascination for what's beautiful, or what's unknown, or what's innocent? Or are these things only the province of the "ignorant"?

T. S. ELIOT: *The Death of Literary Judgment*

THERE IS NO passable essay on Eliot at this time (about A.D. 1960) and little chance of there being one. As far as the literary situation goes, nothing could be more useful today, but the literary situation has seen to it that this essay does not exist. The very idea of a summary of Eliot's writings seems a kind of blasphemy, or an act of unpardonable rudeness. For the Literary Situation (whatever that ecclesiastical expression is supposed to mean) is largely Eliot's invention, and for that reason it is all but impossible to discuss. Eliot is untouchable; he is Modern Literature incarnate and an institution unto himself. One is permitted to disagree with him on a point here or a doctrine there, but no more. The enemy at Eliot's gate—practically everybody—searches his citadel for an opening and cannot find one. Eliot has long since anticipated every move; he and his men can prevent ingress or exit. Eliot resembles one of those mighty castles in Bavaria which are remarkably visible, famed for their unsightliness, and too expensive to tear down. Life goes on at the bottom; but *it* is always up there.

The question of Eliot as the chief obstacle to poetry today may not be a real question; it may be precisely the kind of imaginary question which Eliot himself brings up in his writing. Insofar as one tries to deal with it, he is simply playing Eliot's game, with all the odds against him. I do not myself consider the question real, but I know of no way to discuss the ultimate value of Eliot's work without first discussing the exploits of his straw men. Eliot's reputation and the antagonism to it may both be false. I propose in this essay to show both the reputation and the opposition to it in another light. That there is something of value in Eliot's poetry and Eliot's criticism is quite possible, even from my pessimistic point of view; though the valuable portion is miniscule and is much different from what has been supposed.

Eliot is both the hero and the victim of a historical predicament. And he himself is as much the author of that predicament as "history" itself. Eliot created a literary situation deliberately; he and his "situation" are fabrications, and very plausible fabrications at that. In other words, Eliot invented a Modern World which exists only in his version of it; this world is populated by Eliot's followers and is not a reality. The Eliot population consists of a handful of critics and professors and a few writers of Eliot's generation, though one would think, reading modern criticism and teaching from modern literary textbooks, that there really is a kingdom of Modern Poetry in which T. S. Eliot is the absolute monarch and Archbishop of Canterbury in one.

You will be thinking that I am using metaphorical language and am attempting to work up a nice critical discussion, the subject of which is the overestimation of T. S. Eliot. I am saying something quite different, namely, that Eliot exists only on paper, only in the minds of a few critics. <u>No poet with so great a name has ever had less influence on poetry</u>. At no point in the career of Eliot has there been the slightest indication of a literary following. For example, W. H. Auden, for a decade or so, set patterns for poetry which were followed by thousands of new poets all over the world. Dylan Thomas did the same, as did Wallace Stevens. Neither Eliot nor Pound ever had any such effect on their readers or on young writers. Eliot's "influence" is confined purely to criticism. Insofar as Eliot has enjoyed a *poetic* influence, it lies outside literature entirely and is what can only be called a "spiritual" influence. This spiritual influence is itself calculated and synthetic; and insofar as it fails as a true influence, it removes Eliot's one and only claim to literary power. But here he does not entirely fail.

To deal with Eliot outside the literary situation which he has invented, means to deal with his poetry head-on. It means passing judgment upon it as good or bad poetry or, in some cases, as not poetry at all. But how is one to look at Eliot, if not from his own viewpoint? There is the rub. Eliot has arranged matters in such a way that criticism of his own poetry is impossible.

Eliot has written a small body of poetry which is sacrosanct; he has written his most favorable criticism about poetry which is like his (namely Pound's); and has surrounded both with a full-scale esthetic-social doctrine. What I would like to do is to draw attention to Eliot's poetry—for that is the heart of the matter. For those who do not instinctively and spontaneously reject this poetry, I suppose some form of argument is required. Perhaps this essay will be of some assistance to them. I have in mind students primarily, those who are given Modern Poetry as gospel; I also have the young critic in mind, and also teachers and scholars. Poets do not need these remarks. I have met hundreds of poets in my life but not more than one or two who entertained the reverence for Eliot which they find in the textbooks. As most poets are not intellectuals and are the opposite, they are always stunned by the intellectual pretentions of Eliot and are at a loss to deal with them.

Eliot's preparation of the historical ground upon which he would found his position was the territory of all literature—excluding the Chinese, which was the preserve of Pound. He did not, evidently, intend a personal seizure of intellectual power; Eliot's famous humility testifies to his uneasiness in the face of overwhelming success. His irrational and subservient association with Pound also points to a genuine desire to refuse intellectual leadership, or at least to share it with others.

There was, it appears, a need for an Eliot about 1910. Eliot arrived on the literary scene at the point of vacuum; and he filled this vacuum which literary Nature abhors. Such at least is the accepted view. What is probably nearer the truth is that Eliot appeared at a time when the vitality of the audience was low; and when this is the case, criticism pours into the void. It is the critic in the guise of poet that we have to deal with, not a new kind of poet. For it is criticism which is the twentieth-century substitute for poetry.

The Historical Situation which Eliot exploits under the banner of Tradition was in the beginning the Educational Situation. It was local and Anglo-American, a defense of the Gentleman's Education. I put it vulgarly because that is the way it was. Too many writers have commented on Eliot's fears of being taken for a provincial for me to add my comment.

These fears, however, are part of the New England heritage—the worst part—which leads the New Englander to become the Old Englander. Eliot's early life and work follow an almost hypnotic pattern; one might call him that pseudo-American, the type which finally won New England from the immigrant and gave it back to "history." The cultural dryness of New England was a by-product of this attitude which Eliot exemplifies even better than Henry James: that of relating America to New England, New England to England. Eliot was simply retracing the path back to Europe, exactly as Pound did, and as so many of our nineteenth-century writers tended to do, all but those specifically American.

The criticism of Eliot and Pound has blighted enormous literary areas, as far as we can tell.

The critics who helped establish Eliot were no less instrumental than Eliot himself in opening the frontiers of the cultural territory. Eliot with his palaver about the Tradition could gather in the entire Indo-European world, leaving North Asia and Africa to his senior. I do not want to go into the story of Eliot's critical rise to fame, but to illustrate what I mean I want to point to two literary critics who from every indication should have become his strongest foes; instead of becoming foes they were easily engaged to take his part in the high venture of Modern Poetic Culture. They are Edmund Wilson and F. O. Matthiessen.

Edmund Wilson may be fairly described as a critic in every way the natural opposite of Eliot. In his early estimate of Eliot in *Axel's Castle*, probably the first work to install Eliot in a high position in the literary mind, he pointed out almost every serious defect of the poet: his "fear of vulgarity," his intention to "depersonalize" literature, his overintellectuality, his obsessive imitativeness, and so forth. Wilson described Eliot as the Puritan-turned-artist and expressed the fear that the extravagant praise of Eliot on all sides would perhaps unbalance literary judgment, as of course it did. What then attracted Wilson to Eliot? *It was Eliot's influence on literary criticism.* Wilson walked straight into the trap which Eliot had baited for all humanists and run-of-the-mill men of letters. Eliot had written so high-mindedly about the literary past and so dolefully about the present that Wilson was taken in. He even began to praise Eliot's prose style—probably the worst prose style in the history of the English essay, as well as the most personal. What attracted the budding critic Wilson was, of course, the keenness of intelligence, the range of ideas, the feel of authority, and the sense of History. Also, a hopeful critic like Wilson was on the search for a poet to praise, and Wilson thought he had found him. Meanwhile Wilson was popped into the Eliot oven to be turned into a nice little, right little gingerbread man. Fortunately, he escaped, but that chapter does not belong to our chronicle.

F. O. Matthiessen's relationship to Eliot is even more extraordinary than that of the humanist critic who gazes in fascination at the Puritan-turned-artist. Matthiessen, I think, felt the same attraction for New England that Eliot did, the one coming from the West Coast, the other from the Midwest. To the critical and historical mind of Matthiessen, Eliot must have seemed an incarnation of American history. But Matthiessen had some adjusting to do in his own thinking in order to place Eliot in the same high position that Wilson had. He acknowledged his indebtedness to Wilson and also to I. A. Richards, the man who tried, and almost succeeded, in driving the poetic mind into the test tube. Matthiessen could not agree with Eliot's philosophy, his religion, or his politics, and yet he felt he must adulate Eliot! The result was his book on Eliot in which Matthiessen disdains the kind of criticism that deals with the poet's "ideas" and praises the kind of criticism that deals with the "forms." This book, *The Achievement of T. S. Eliot,* was published during the height of the Depression and at a time when Marxism was strong in the United States. Matthiessen was perhaps the most intensely engaged political mind among the English professors of his day, and a leftist; *yet he chose to cut himself off from the politics of Eliot's poetry and criticism to talk about the "forms."* This was a split that Eliot had invented for himself and which Eliot evidently kept from being fatal in his own life by various makeshifts of criticism. The false dualisms set up by Eliot between art and social action are symptomatic of the insanity of much modern criticism. In any case, it was Eliot's attractive formulation of these dualisms that neutralized so many critics and led Criticism itself into a squirrel cage where it still performs so brilliantly for its own amusement. Even Eliot's most favorable critics have never been able to resolve his major contradictions, which are central and irreducible conflicts rising from a false view of art as a function of history and culture, and a twisted attitude toward human nature.

Eliot's criticism is not "one thing" and his poetry another. They are one and the same. Herein lies the only unity of his work and of his "sensibility." This unity has been achieved coldly and ruthlessly, on paper. It has only as much relation to life as books can have: experience in Eliot is always and necessarily literary experience. All other experience is vulgar, with the possible exception of the religious experience, which is Eliot's escape hatch. His poems are therefore illustrations of the various stages of his "position," just as Pound's poems are illustrations of Pound's politick. Pound is not interested in poetry as poetry but in demonstrating what poetry is for. Eliot is above pedagogy, being closer to philosophy than to history. But the unifying element in Eliot is theology: and it is not inaccurate to describe Eliot as a theologian gone astray. The difference between Eliot's respectability and Pound's notoriety lies here as well. The frequent violence of Eliot's feelings is overlooked because of the "religious" context. Both his verse and his prose are held together by the main strength of certain theological abstractions. Eliot shows a positive hatred for originality and in fact condemns it in every manifestation; originality is irresponsible freedom to him. It is for this reason that he consigns Blake to limbo while hanging on to Pascal for dear life. Blake, says Eliot, is home-made religion. Eliot stays within the shadow of his theological law, which shelters his politics, his religion, and his esthetics.

How then is one to deal with his poetry without bringing in such terms as "mythic form," the "objective correlative," the "auditory imagination," the "dissociation of sensibility," the "Tradition," and fifty or sixty other concepts which are supposed to explain his poetry to us? The answer is by dealing with the poetry as poetry, as if Eliot had never published a single line of critical theory or laid down a single law or set up a single guidepost to "correct" taste. Ignore the criticism, if possible. Eliot's criticism, like all literary criticism, has a place in the seminar room in the philosophy department; let's keep it there. How it ever got out is a biographical question which we will leave to anyone daring enough to violate Eliot's fiat against biography. I take it that Eliot is mainly responsible for the modern taboo against literary biography, one of his less publicized fields of propaganda.

In another section of these notes I have made a distinction between criticism and judgment. The strategic purpose of Eliot's criticism was to prevent judgment; that is the purpose of the criticism which he gave birth to (called the New Criticism), to replace judgment by theory. Eliot's own judgment is seldom shown, governed as it is by precept. His intellectualization of feeling and taste led him to such twisted judgments as the praise of Kipling and the execration of Whitman, the approval of Donne and the disparagement of Milton, and to pronouncements such as "the novel died" on such and such a date. One of Eliot's followers, taking a suggestion from the master, writes a long, seemingly "objective" account of the weaknesses of the poetry of D. H. Lawrence. Lawrence had committed the horrible sin of expressing his own feelings in poetry. Instead of following "the discipline of a rationally constructed imagination," Lawrence *expresses*. If only, this critic complains, Lawrence had learned to use "controlled hysteria" like Eliot. And so forth. ("Controlled hysteria" strikes me as an accurate description of Eliot's poetry from an amateur psychology point of view, but the critic in question, R. P. Blackmur, egregiously takes Eliot's tightly buttoned-up pathology to be the normal state of affairs for poetry.)

To Eliot and Pound, with their provincial and educated horror of the unlettered and the spontaneous, the idea of a large or mixed audience was unspeakable. Throughout the criticism of these two leaders of modern taste the audience is constantly defined as a danger to the *status quo*. Pound, for example, in making up his booklist for converts to his criticism is even suspicious of the ballad. He cannot explain to himself that the ballad may be and probably is the product of the "unliterary" mind; he distrusts Shakespeare for the same reason. Eliot's own plays, of course, are addressed to a good sound upper-middle-class audience, British preferably, even though a couple of his dramatic works have a popular appeal. Eliot must get quite a chuckle out of that.

In discussing Eliot's or Pound's idea of the audience (or what they would call the *function* of literature, in their strangely mechanistic language) one runs into the old danger of bogging down in points of doctrine and definition. It is no exaggeration to say that Eliot's criticism contains a definite plan of action, leading from a theory of poetics to political philosophy and covering all the intermediate stages. I will come back to this matter in my remarks on Yeats and Pound and their part in the religion of modern poetry. As far as the audience is concerned it is enough to say Eliot and Pound have not really had one—Eliot not until a few years ago, Pound never. The public has consistently rejected all of the poetry of 1915-25 from the beginning and has ignored both the poetry and its scales of values. In the voluntary withdrawal of the audience, the critics have created an academic audience, that is, a captive audience. The true audience, when it is allowed to grow, may of course reach all levels of appreciation from the lowest to the highest; it is ever the job of the poet to address himself to the present *condition* of the audience and to the language of that audience. Eliot and Pound have both attempted to find the language of their time: both have failed miserably and have succeeded only in constructing parodistic copies of the language. (This is the cogent argument of William Carlos Williams against both poets.)

Eliot's style of deliberate plagiarism is the first
symptom of failure to locate the language—in his
case a lifelong admission of defeat. Modern poetry
is macaronic because, in fact, it is not linguistically
modern at all. It is high time we related the Pound-
Eliot antiquarianism in ideas to the antiquarianism
of their styles. Pound uses more archaisms than the
Poet Laureate of Florida.

I am going to deal with only a sample of the
most typical and celebrated poems of Eliot's, from
"Prufrock" through the *Quartets,* trying to *judge* these
poems as if Eliot had never written any criticism. I
judge them from the point of view of writing, on the
assumption, which is to me a certainty, that all
English-speaking people can appraise their worth as
English poetry. This is the way poetry has always
been read—without criticism or in spite of it. I disregard, as far as possible, Eliot's talk about the form
of this and the form of that. I am confident that my
judgments of these poems as poetry, not as sociology
or esthetics, is extremely close to the judgments of
nearly all readers of modern poetry who have not
been conditioned by the criticism.

"The Love Song of J. Alfred Prufrock"—this is
probably Eliot's best poem and is a little masterpiece
of its kind. It is highly unoriginal in content and in
style, based as it is on the rhythms, the attitudes, and
sometimes the very lines of minor Symbolist poets like
Corbière and Laforgue. Rhythmically it is the most
successful of Eliot's poems, possibly because it was
conceived as a dramatic unit. The meter is varied
within the conventional English line, and the rhyming
is superb. There is every indication that at the time
of composition (age twenty-three) Eliot still took
seriously the customs of English prosody and was
trying in earnest (i.e., without irony) to develop this

technical side of our poetry. The general tone of the poem is that of polite sophisticated ennui, an essay in self-mockery. The literary allusions in the poem, not counting the epigraph, are of the most obvious nature. This poem does not offend on the side of Culture. The epigraph from Dante purportedly throws a special light on the meaning of the poem; it is the epigraph which critics talk about most and which teachers teach. This quotation is gratuitous, a meaningless decoration; later it becomes the actual method of the Eliot poem. The difficulties of the poem, which are intentional, are not insurmountable, say, to a reader quite conversant with poetry tending toward the baroque or self-conscious. "Prufrock" is a poem *about* self-consciousness. The split personality of Prufrock creates the chief obstacle to a first understanding of the poem. The other primary difficulty is imagistic, but this is also the main virtue of the poem. The famous opening image of the evening prostrate "like a patient etherized upon a table" is one of the most brilliant examples of the poetry of exhaustion; very possibly it is a variation of Baudelaire's statement that the sexual act is like a surgical operation. Eliot's poem, however, is humorous rather than vicious and develops a kindly pathos to the very end. The imagery of the poem is all related to suggestion, a watering-down of the extreme suggestiveness of "effect" of poets like Mallarmé and Poe, and is, in fact, a retreat from official Symbolism. (Eliot would already be conscious of all the "historical" possibilities of his "position.") "Prufrock" is a masterpiece of a "period," the high point of Eliot's poetry. It is a true poem and also an experiment in criticism. It is a true poem by virtue of a personal content, which we can only guess at, for Eliot is always more sensitive about the autobiographical than any other writer

I know of. But many things in the poem point to the so-called objectification of experience; even after Eliot airs to the public his problem of the personal and the impersonal, Life versus Art. The figure of Hamlet in "Prufrock" he finds particularly expressive of his own dilemma, even though Prufrock disclaims a true identity with the Prince. But Hamlet is the figure who makes an art of indecision. Indecision leads to thinking things over, soliloquizing, becoming an intellectual. Eliot's poetry all turns to talk. As it goes on through the years it becomes nothing but talk, and talk about the kind of poetry that comes closer and closer to talk. Technically, the poem prefigures all the criticism, with its debates about the personal and the impersonal, the more and more "objective," the great struggle toward "unified sensibility" and what not.

Eliot's failure as a poet is his success as a critic. Prufrock as a character is of no intrinsic interest but he is of high *literary* interest to all. In this poem Eliot has remained close enough to a human footing to make poetry out of a personal complex of crises, private, social, and intellectual. Had he written nothing else he would be remembered for this masterly little poem.

The "Portrait of a Lady" is also a young poem, written apparently at the time of "Prufrock." The "Portrait," however, is not a textbook piece; it is too much of a love poem. It is not as good a poem as "Prufrock," actually, because it has the tone of adolescence rather than the tone of a prefigured worldliness, as in "Prufrock." In the "Portrait" the woman is made fun of; she is wiser but inferior to the young Eliot; the poem leaves the reader nothing much to dwell upon except its excellence of execution. It appears to be one of Eliot's many exercises in tone.

The epigraph in this case is a falsification. Eliot takes three lines from Marlowe's *The Jew of Malta,* the meaning of which he distorts for his own purpose. The lines are these:

> Thou hast committed—
> Fornication: but that was in another country,
> And besides, the wench is dead.

These three lines are actually part of a long involved dialogue; two people are speaking, not one. Eliot does not mean to convey that only one person is speaking, but he must for convenience gloze over the sense of the play. Eliot exegetes can retrace the quotation and explain that a friar is accusing the traitorous Jew, Barabas, of a series of crimes and that the Jew is evading answering; in the same way the Eliot in the poem is evading answering the questions of the woman. Psychologically this kind of thing can become so involved that everything reverts back to the meaning of the *quotation.* This is the crux of the Eliot poem, as we all know: how does the quotation fit the poem? Very shortly the matter is reversed and the question becomes: how does the poem fit the *quotation?* The beauty of the "Portrait" testifies to Eliot's residual interest in the poem, not in its possible intellectual overtones; the quotation (virtually a misquotation) also indicates the poet's concern about what he writes rather than what he quotes. But the quote is also a loophole for the meaning of the poem, permitting Eliot to evade his meaning or permitting critics to elaborate it.

In both of these poems Eliot displays a mastery of sound and rhythm which marks the poet of genius. The rhyming is dazzling, a mixture of shock (the use of near-comic pairs such as Pole-soul) and the much more subtle effect of nonrhyme, such as we find in

"Lycidas." It is almost, but not quite, apparent that Eliot at the beginning of his career is playing the weary virtuoso. But this is not sufficient, either for Eliot or for the literary scene. There is not much to be gained by becoming another Anglo-American Laforgue.

The remaining poems of this early style are even more "French" than the longer ones, but more satisfying evidently to Eliot. "Preludes" introduces the typical sordid furniture of the Eliot world, a Baudelairean rather than Laforguean world. The poem is a series of images evoking despair and disgust. The popularity of the poem comes from its seriousness, the transference from youthful, well-educated ennui to a genuine, if not very thoughtful, revulsion for all those people "raising dingy shades in a thousand furnished rooms." Eliot here imports the clichés of nineteenth-century French poetry about the wickedness (i.e., mediocrity) of the modern city. "Rhapsody on a Windy Night," a much more convincing poem, dramatizes and symbolizes the horror of the city. Eliot has already found the Culture of the modern city; by simply recording its images (a broken spring in a factory yard, a morsel of rancid butter, the toothbrush hanging on the wall) he evokes a cultured response—the response of the *avant-garde* reader to society. It is assumed, without having to say so, that the modern city is a degeneration of the Past. *Now he knows what to say*: the housemaids have "damp" souls; people await the evening paper for want of something better, the old order changeth and Cousin Nancy has taken to smoking; the poet is quietly rejecting both the present and the immediate past—the American past.

The first really literary poem comes in this phase also. (I use the term "literary" opprobriously.) "Mr.

Apollinax" marks the new Eliot; the Greek epigraph becomes an integral part of the poem, an explanation of it; and there is no attempt to provide links from the reader's experience to the cultural cues. The meter begins to break and the rhymes are now artfully coarsened (afternoon-macaroon). Mr. Apollinax is something of a pagan oracle to Eliot and a Priapic figure, but not to the Boston professors who entertain him. The poem is inferior to the "Rhapsody" in every way; it is already a culture poem and an exercise in footnoting.

Eliot's reputation to a large extent is based upon the poems of this early period, and rightly so. "Prufrock," "Portrait of a Lady," "Preludes," and the "Rhapsody" are among his best works. Of these "Prufrock" is head and shoulders above the rest and is sufficient to justify Eliot's claim as one of the most gifted twentieth-century poets. At the same time it is extremely close to *vers de société,* as the first reviewers were aware (and first impressions are generally valuable in literary criticism), while the other poems mentioned are almost mannerist in their attention to theory and precedent. These are true weaknesses and Eliot is evidently conscious of their defects, the proof being that he deserts these forms for new ones.

In the next phase we find the majority of the poems in pedantic and ironic quatrains. There is one attempt at a "major" form, as the critics say, in the poem "Gerontion," and there are several poems in French, which certainly cannot be judged as English poems. The quatrain poems introduce Sweeney and various minor characters in Eliot's pantheon. In this group there is also the extraordinarily crude antichurch poem named "The Hippopotamus," one of those surprising lapses of Eliot's which almost equal his good poems in number. Equally crude is the embarrassing anti-Jewish poem "Burbank with a Baedeker," a typical utterance of the modern "classical" school. Eliot's anti-Semitism, which I am not going to discuss, is connected with his view of American commercial wealth: Bleistein is "Chicago Semite Viennese" and he is described in disgusting physical detail. It is interesting to note that as Eliot's feelings become more violent and shocking the epigraphic matter becomes more talky and deranged. The quotation affixed to this poem is a hodgepodge of a French poem, a Latin motto, something from Henry James, something from Shakespeare, something from Browning, and something from Marston. It is as obscure as the quatrains are clear. The Chicago Shylock and the British baronet with a Jewish name have taken back Venice, according to this culture lyric. Stylistically and otherwise there is little virtue in the piece.

Stylistically there is little or nothing of value in all the quatrain poems, "Sweeney Erect," "A Cooking Egg," "Whispers of Immortality," "Mr. Eliot's Sunday Morning Service," and the famous "Sweeney Among the Nightingales." In these poems Eliot is exploring the possibilities of character symbols; most turn out to be mere caricatures and do not appear again. Sweeney survives as a representation of Eliot's dim view of modern man. Eliot tries humor in the poems, if humor is the proper word (a highly polysyllabic bumbling kind of pseudo-British joking); and this he alternates with scenes of horror and disorder made ironical by the propriety of the meters. The close of the "Nightingale" poem is said by critics to mark a high point of nobility, why I am not sure, unless it is that Eliot leaves off "Rachel *née* Rabinovitch" and switches to Agamemnon and the Convent of the Sacred Heart. These closing lines, if indeed they are serious, are cheap rather than noble and so poorly articulated that they can barely be pronounced. These poems show a drastic falling-off from the poet's earlier work. (I have said nothing of the complexities of cultural allusion in these poems; most people know them and accept them as part of the rocky road to modern poetry.)

"Gerontion" is usually placed high among Eliot's works; but it is not much better than "Mr. Apollinax" and is in fact an extension of that poem in its manner. In order to escape a derivative Symbolism, Eliot has settled on the borrowing of quotations. Without a knowledge of the sources the poems sound more or less unified; the quotations themselves remove some of the author's responsibility for what the poems say. Eliot was here working out a method for a kind of poem which would implant certain ideas and images in the reader's mind, almost as if Eliot himself had nothing to do with the poem. The use of quotation without reference has a further advantage: it creates a specialized class of readers; I am quite serious when I say that Eliot is here providing texts for a new academic faculty. In the same way as Pound he is trying to solve an educational problem. But "Gerontion" is also a personal catechism of the poet's religious hopes and doubts and is part of his spiritual autobiography. Its best feature is the rhetorical accretion of the same grammatical form and the use of meaningless but suggestive names. The theme of the youthless-ageless man, which is Eliot's one contribution to symbology, is advanced again, as in all his earlier poems. There is in "Gerontion" a careful propaganda for Eliot as a symbolic figure, the poet deep in thought, seated among the ruins of the ages, longing for a salvation which will suit his intellect as well as his desires for spiritual comfort.

The Waste Land is the most important poem of the twentieth century, that is, the one that has caused the most discussion and is said by critics to be the culmination of the modern "mythic" style. The poem, by Eliot's own admission, is a collaboration with Pound. Pound edited it and removed a third or two thirds of it. The "continuity," we can assume, is therefore the work of Pound, who abhorred continuity in his own more ambitious poetry. As everyone knows how to read the poem or can find out by visiting the nearest library, I will say nothing about its meaning. I will speak rather of the success and the failure of the poem. That it is lacking in unity is obvious (assuming, as I do, that unity is a literary virtue). Any part of *The Waste Land* can be switched with any other part without changing the sense of the poem. Aside from the so-called "mythic" form, which is worthless and not even true—for Eliot misread James Joyce's *Ulysses* when he saw it as a parallel to Homer—the underlying unity of the poem is tonal and dramatic, exactly as a Victorian narrative poem would be. Eliot tries to conceal this indispensable literary method by mixing languages, breaking off dramatic passages, and by dividing the poem into sections with titles. But what really keeps the poem moving is its rhetoric, its switches from description to exclamation to interrogation to expletive, sometimes very beautifully, as in the passages beginning "Unreal City." The straight descriptive passages are weak: "A Game of Chess" is one of the dullest and most meretricious of Eliot's writings, indicating his own dissatisfaction with that kind of verse. The dialogue, on the other hand, is generally good. The best moments of all are the image passages, where the images are set in dramatic tonalities: "What the Thunder Said" is the finest of these. The very worst passages are those which are merely quotes; even Eliot's most abject admirers can find no justification of the last lines of the poem, with its half-dozen languages and more than half a dozen quotations in a space of about ten lines.

The Waste Land, because of its great critical reputation, not because of any inherent worth it might have, is one of the curiosities of English literature. Its critical success was, I dare say, carefully planned and executed, and it was not beyond the realm of possibility that the poem was originally a hoax, as some of the first readers insisted. But hoax or not, it was very shortly made the sacred cow of modern poetry and the object of more pious literary nonsense than any modern work save the *Cantos* of Pound. The proof of the failure of the "form" of this poem is that no one has ever been able to proceed from it, including Eliot himself. It is, in fact, not a form at all but a negative version of form. It is interesting to notice that in the conventional stanzas of the quatrain poems Eliot is more personally violent and ugly about his own beliefs; in his unconventional style the voice of the poet all but disappears and is replaced by characters from his reading.

The emergence of Eliot's piety in "The Hollow Men" and in *Ash Wednesday* takes the form of self-disgust in the one and self-pity in the other. "The Hollow Men" is in every way a better poem than *The Waste Land,* though the parodistic style again enforces a poverty of statement and language which become the marks of self-imitation in Eliot. *Ash Wednesday* is probably even more laden with gratuitous quotation than *The Waste Land,* but its ecclesiastical imagery and richness of music give the poem a beauty which the poet can finally accept as beauty. Eliot here luxuriates in the emotions of piety and sur-

render which seemed shameful to his Puritan soul
in a purely human situation. The Eliot-God equation,
once he has made the daring step, gives him an in-
tellectual-emotional balance for the first time in his
career. After the publication of this poem, Eliot's
former work seems more of a piece and his future
work is all laid out for him, everything from church
pageants to Christmas-card poems. The *Ariel Poems*
are relatively simple and almost narrative. The rest
of the poems are shelved under "fragments," minor
pieces, and unfinished experiments. Eliot's career as a
poet virtually comes to a close with *Ash Wednesday.*
After that there is criticism, theology, and drama. The
Four Quartets is the only attempt at what modern
criticism calls a "major" poem—meaning a poem
that deals with Culture wholesale. The *Quartets* were
hailed by the Eliot critics as his crowning achievement; actually they are evidence of the total dissolu-
tion of poetic skill and even a confession of poetic
bankruptcy. Eliot is quite open about this in the
Quartets.

The *Quartets* are Eliot's bid to fame as a "philosophical poet." In it he expounds his metaphysics,
his poetics, and his own place in the scheme of
things. All of this is quite legitimate and not at all
surprising; what is disturbing about the poems is
their commonplaceness, their drabness of expression,
their conventionality, and, worst of all, their reliance
on the schoolbook language of the philosophy class.
Eliot has traded poetry for the metaphysical abstraction, as in *The Waste Land* he had traded narrative
for "myth." This development is psychologically consistent, a descent from French Symbolism to Metaphysical complexity-for-the-sake-of-complexity, to pas-
tiche, to the myth-science of *The Golden Bough,* to
philosophical abstraction without poetic content. It all

ends in the complete abandonment of poetry. When he comes to the drama in earnest he knows, of course, that he must use human language and he begins a new ascent into literature and the voices of poetry. But the *Quartets* lie at the bottom of the literary heap. All the so-called lyric sections, with one or two exceptions, are written with such disregard for the ear that one cannot associate them with the Eliot of "Prufrock" or the "Rhapsody." "Garlic and sapphires in the mud/ Clot the bedded axle-tree" is typical of this diction devoid of both image and music. Eliot, who used to condemn poets like Tennyson for what he called crudeness of feeling, here shows an insensitivity toward language which is marvelous. The more prosy passages are even voided of that kind of poetry which rises from the use of imagery or sound. As for the philosophical development, it fails to reach a state of poetry, and it may fail as philosophy—of this I am no judge. The much-quoted third section of "East Coker" about everyone going into the darkness, even people in the Almanach de Gotha and the Stock Exchange Gazette, is possibly the best passage of a long, very bad piece of writing; one feels that here there is an acceptance of the badness of the writing, as if good writing no longer held any meaning for the poet. The "lyric" section that follows contains a stanza ("The whole earth is our hospital/ Endowed by the ruined millionaire. . .") which in its vulgarity of thought and expression is hardly superior to "Only God can make a tree." For the rest there is a kind of narcissistic figure of the aging Eliot lolling through the poem, the climactic Dante imitation in "Little Gidding," and finally the magnificent passage "Sin is Behovely, but/ All shall be well . . ." Unfortunately these glorious lines are not Eliot's but are one of his borrowings. In general, the *Four Quartets* appears to be a deliberately bad book, one written as if to convince the reader that poetry is dead and done with. We should remember Eliot's lifelong interest in the final this and the final that, and at least entertain the possibility that the *Four Quartets* were intended to stand as the last poem in the Great Tradition. Eliot and Pound have both shown themselves capable of such arrogance.

I have now said all the wicked things I can think of about Eliot and it remains at last to say something favorable. At the beginning of these remarks I mentioned one phase of Eliot's work in which I regard him as a true poet and a man of rich spiritual insight. While I cannot feel that Eliot has contributed anything to the spiritual advancement of our age, I am convinced that he tried. But why is it that his own poems are rubrics rather than works of art? What are they for? What are they trying to say? Is it really all just sociology, reactionary politics, bitterness, spite and despair? I think not. I have spoken of the apparently deliberate erosion of his great gifts, leading to the final desertion of poetry. And I have touched on Eliot's lapse into religion. Here is a capital puzzle for the critic.

My solution to the puzzle is this. The motivating force in Eliot's work is the search for the mystical center of experience. This search in his case has been fruitless and increasingly frustrating. Eliot's entire career is a history of his failure to penetrate the mystical consciousness. He begins as a youth with Symbolism when it is already a dying religious-esthetic *mystique*. He moves from Symbolism to the Metaphysical poets of the seventeenth century. (Neither the dictionary nor modern criticism explains what it is that interested Eliot in these poets, for it certainly

was not extreme metaphorical technique or what the
textbook calls the conceit.) Eliot was fascinated by
the Metaphysical poem because it is virtually a
demonstration of prayer. Nearly all the Metaphysical
poets were Divines, men deeply troubled by the new
scientific knowledge. What Eliot studied in their
poetry was the possibility of fusing sacred with secular knowledge in poetry. Metaphysical poetry lies
close to absurdity because it is premised on this peculiar dualism. We recall also that Eliot associated the
fairly recent French poet Laforgue with the English
Metaphysicals, for at one time it seemed to Eliot
that a keen enough wit might serve as a key to the
door that refused to open. But neither Symbolism nor
Metaphysical sacred poetry offered a way to Eliot,
even when he tried a fusion of the two. Third, he attempted secular mythology as a way to penetrate the
mystical consciousness. It was in this phase that he
wrote *The Waste Land,* a poem which is a jumble of
sacred and "profane" myths, adding up to nothing.

Meanwhile, both Eliot and Pound had discovered
T. E. Hulme, whose essays provided written authority
for them both, in different ways. Every major doctrine
of Eliot's can be found in Hulme's *Speculations,* the
most basic the one that relates fundamental Christian
doctrine to a theory of society and a theory of poetics.
Hulme formulated for Eliot the attack on Romanticism and the attack on mysticism (for the Romantic
and the mystical are always related, while the Classical and the orthodox are related in their ways, at least
in the critical mind). Hulme pointed the way for
Eliot to orthodoxy in letters and to ritual and dogma
in the spiritual realm. I consider Hulme's book as the
Mein Kampf of modern criticism and a thoroughly evil
work; and it was Eliot's undoing. For after the assimi-

lation of Hulme, the rest is elaboration. Except for one thing: the search for the mystical center of experience goes on. Eliot worries it in Dante, in the Hindu scriptures, in St. John of the Cross, and in Julianne of Norwich. But poets of more recent vintage who come closer to mysticism infuriate Eliot, and he pours out his scorn on Blake, Lawrence, Whitman and our own Transcendentalists. Yet it is eternally to Eliot's credit that he does not fake the mystical (as he seems to accuse Blake of doing) and it is also to his credit that he does not relapse into magic and spiritualism, as Yeats did. It appears that Eliot is not even acquainted with estericism; at least he does not even seem to be conscious of the esoteric meaning of the Tarot, which he uses in *The Waste Land* for "fortunetelling."

The failure to achieve mystical consciousness (which indeed is one of the rarest achievements in mankind) drove Eliot back to metaphysics proper and to religion proper. This in my view is the great failure of Eliot. Eliot ends up as a poet of religion in the conventional sense of that term. And once having made the religious commitment he tried to visualize a religion-directed society; he thus becomes an official of the most conservative elements of society and a figurehead for all that is formalized and ritualized. Yeats' fascination for the Byzantine betrays the same spiritual conservatism, as does Pound's fascination for the corporate state and the leadership principle. And Eliot ends his quest with his caricature of the modern poet-priest or psychiatrist-priest who alone has power to allay the Eumenides. Witch-hunting runs through Eliot from beginning to end.

Eliot is a poet of religion, hence a poet of the second or third rank; he is a thoroughgoing anachronism in the modern world, a poet of genius crippled by lack of faith and want of joy. I believe in Blake's proverb that "the road of excess leads to the palace of wisdom." Had Eliot ever set foot on that road he might have been as great a seer as Whitman or Rimbaud or even Dylan Thomas.

EZRA POUND: *The Scapegoat of Modern Poetry*

> . . . the goat shall bear upon him all their
> iniquities unto a land which is cut off; and
> he shall let go the goat in the wilderness.

ANY WAY you look at it, writing about Ezra Pound
and his poetry is an unpleasant business. It is unpleasant for his friends and fellow travelers, who
must either by-pass or explain away the various
Pound scandals; just as unpleasant for his ill-wishers
and critics; and unpleasant as well for the scholars,
book reviewers, and historians of the age who find
him looming up menacingly from the card catalogue.
Pound is not the kind of writer who once did something wrong and can now be forgiven in the mellow-
ness of time. It is hard to forgive him because everything he did wrong he insists was right. He is
righteous about his wrongness; he forces his worst
upon us wherever we meet him, and there is no
escaping it.

People who try to minimize Pound's sins, errors,
and crimes are simply playing a game that Pound
himself refuses to play. Critics who would like to
shelve the ugly side of Pound's poetry for its virtues
are also playing a game that Pound refuses to have a
hand in. Of all the modern didactic poets there is

none more didactic than this one, none more "topical," whether the topic is religion, politics, war, or money and banking. Eliot hopes that his readers will distinguish between his poetry and criticism, but Pound demands a thorough identification of his prose with his poetry. They are one and the same, all a single immense prose-poem supposedly covering in time all the known civilizations in all their main ramifications. The size, scope, and style of this prose-poem raises the most embarrassing question of all about Pound, which I am going to express my opinion about. This question is whether Pound is insane.

The question of whether Pound is insane is, properly speaking, none of our business. Many poets and artists have been, or have been adjudged, insane and have spent terrible years in asylums. But we who are readers and lovers of poetry are not doctors and it is not within our scope, except out of human sympathy or curiosity, to dwell upon an artist's worst moments or periods of life. What does concern us is whether the poet's *poetry* is insane. If it is, and we as readers should be able to tell that, then we must treat it as such, as the work of a sick mind, or, sometimes, a dangerous one. I have read Pound's poetry all my life, carefully, with pain and with pleasure, and I know that his poetry is anything but insane. People who have termed it so may know a good deal about insanity but they know little about poetry. One of the chief defects of Pound's poetry, in fact, is that it is too *rational*, forced, and wanting in imagination. Insofar as we can reconstruct the character and intellect of a man from his writings, we can get a fairly whole portrait of Pound. I will be sketching that portrait for you, and you will see that he is a perfectly normal, though badly frustrated, fellow American. He is, in fact, a well-known American type, the provincial overexposed to the guidebook.

But leaving the question of insanity aside, there is also the question of the social dangerousness of Pound. Pound is, or rather wants to be, thought dangerous, but it appears that the danger is now a thing of the past. Eliot, if anything, is a much more dangerous element in society than Pound. He is more persuasive, highly respectable, a better strategist, a theologian, a modernist, and a gentleman saint. No one that I ever heard of has been seriously influenced by the theories of Pound—except Eliot! But Eliot's danger period has also passed; in any case, his job has been done; he has put literature back in the Reference Room and has apologized for his youthful indiscretions about the lower races and popular governments. Eliot today is the kindly Greco-Judaic-Christian gentleman who made good. There is an almost touchingly comic element in the Pound-Eliot team, their spats and undying loyalties to one another, their division of the empires of literature into East and West; but there is a good bit of pathos as well.

The chief difference between Pound and Eliot is one of intelligence. As far as poetic talent goes, Pound sometimes seems the superior poet; but as far as the I.Q. goes, Eliot is head and shoulders above his teacher. In the case of writers like these two, we must speak of intelligence because they make us consider their minds, their ideas, and their opinions, and not simply their poetry. They make a cult of Intelligence. Dylan Thomas, for example, makes no pretenses about his intelligence, and it is hard to tell whether he was or was not a man with a good thinking apparatus. That Eliot has a fine intellect we all somehow agree; it is his chief claim on our attention. Eliot even talks about the importance of the intelligence in such a way that it seems an attribute comparable with poetic artistry. It is one of his tricks of strategy. Following this mode of criticism, W. H. Auden writes an introduction to the poems of Tennyson warning the reader that he must not make the mistake of considering Tennyson intelligent. Auden (mimicking the tone and manner of Eliot) says: "He had the finest ear, perhaps, of any English poet; he was also undoubtedly the stupidest." According to "modern" criticism, Tennyson is unintelligent or stupid because he did not develop a fine critical sensibility. Those are Auden's words. One could wish that a fine critical sensibility (whatever that is) would prevent a critic from calling a poet like Tennyson stupid, if only for the sake of common decency. On the other hand, I am tempted to call Ezra Pound stupid, but in this case I think even Pound's best friends might agree.

The question of the intelligence of the artist is one of those phony questions which have been brought to the fore in our time by critics like Eliot, Valéry, and Auden. Once we begin to debate this question we are in the Dismal Swamp of criticism. It is an endless and irrelevant question, like art and homosexuality, or art and science—questions which belong anywhere but in literature. Was Mozart intelligent or "stupid"? Critics sometimes point out the "stupidity" of Beethoven, based on the laborious evidence of his notebooks. Beethoven was slow, Mozart quick as a flash, but "stupidity" somehow seems the improper term for so great a genius as either. I think we should consider the intelligence of the artist within the framework of art. It is meaningless to call Tennyson stupid while complimenting him on his excellent ear. Ear *is* to a great extent what poetic intelligence means; not "critical sensibility" or a sense of history, and so on. What annoys Auden about Tennyson is that Tennyson had not read sociology or thought deeply enough about Original Sin. (I will deal with this quirk in Auden's thinking in another place.)

But when the poet makes a boast of intelligence like Pound and is defended at the last ditch on the grounds of his *ideas,* and is elevated by T. S. Eliot as the most important critic of the age—what are we to do? For Pound has chosen to be the "poet of ideas" (grotesque and unbeautiful phrase), and it is as a poet of ideas that we have to accept him. The ideas in Pound are not only explicit, they are magnified, repeated and spelled out in block letters. No poet in history has boasted so loudly of what he believes; none has tried harder to convince, without trying to please. So, discussing Pound's intelligence is something one would almost rather not do: it is like taking candy away from the baby.

I have called Pound the scapegoat of modern poetry. This is true in a very real sense. Pound is famed for being the teacher of modern writers: of Eliot, of Joyce, and of Yeats. This reputation, while it is the kind of exaggeration that approaches falsehood, is true in the legendary sense. Yeats must have used Pound in order to avoid certain mistakes which Pound insisted upon making. And to Yeats, Pound must have seemed a voice of the future. Joyce could have learned nothing of consequence from Pound; and Eliot, who evidently learned a very great deal from him, still developed in a direction that seemed to Pound seditious. What all three got from Pound was not so much inspiration as the sanction to use the "poetry of ideas." In return, and possibly out of a sense of guilt, Pound was overpraised, especially by Eliot, without whom Pound's reputation would probably be no greater today than that of, say, Richard Aldington. Eliot's defense of Pound and his wild encomiums are also a self-defense. Eliot has had to bear the brunt of all of Pound's mistakes, poetic, esthetic, and cultural. There is a kind of haggard nobility in Eliot's support of his mentor and friend. But it bears looking into.

There are two large classes of "ideas" in Pound's work; one has to do with works of poetry (his esthetic), and the other with social ideas. The second category comprises whatever he has to say about philosophy, science, history, ethics, and economics. All of the ideas in the second class are exposed, in the worst sense of the word. They are vulnerable. They are vulnerable because they all relate back to source works, other books. This throws Pound into an arena where readers of any description can have a go at him. Purportedly Pound makes connections between his various interests, such as economic theory and esthetics, and this becomes one of the worst burlesques of poetry we know of in modern literature: in Eliot's case, we have a different, more sophisticated element at work. But we cannot understand Pound without Eliot, or Eliot without Pound. One is the wide-awake, cautious scholastic; the other is the wild, noisy, system-crazy Yankee who demands to be a prophet, at any expense. My own sympathies are much more with Pound than with Eliot; and this is the case with William Carlos Williams also, who is revolted by Pound but who is always ready to go bail for him. Eliot uses Pound, not for his own advantage but for the advantage of the intellectual position. There is in Pound something which appeals to every American writer—it is the super-European drive and the blundering arrogance that goes with it—and there is also the provincial snobbery. It is the snobbery that appeals to Eliot, the bluster that makes him cling to Pound as an American-in-exile and a displaced European at once.

In speaking of Pound's career we should keep in mind that this man was almost a contemporary of Henry James and Mark Twain—that he was born in the twilight of American literature. Pound has been busy in literature for half a century.

Pound started out as a young poet and scholar who was not appreciated in the America of about 1905. Having behind him a tradition of cultural expatriation and discontent, he thought he would assail England. But Pound was not really for England—he was a Romance-language scholar, not an "Anglo-Saxon man." In England he was the type of belligerent European-American we know so well through our literature. He married an Englishwoman named Shakespear and left for the Continent. Pound became European editor of Harriet Monroe's *Poetry* until he could no longer stomach her Americanism. He then became a one-man literary movement—but there is no point in recapitulating all this. The only fact of interest about Pound's *biographia literaria* is that he managed to capture the esteem of such poets as Eliot and Yeats, though almost no others.

Pound's ideas are neither very complex nor very extensive. In the first place he is without religion and practically without a *mystique* of any kind. He is a rational poet, a humanist *manqué*, if one needs a name for him (though not many humanists would claim him). Pound's humanism is, of course, a bookish variety and derives from the periods of art and poetry he admires. The eighteenth century is about as far as he wishes to go in time, Jefferson and Adams being the main political figures he admires from our own past. The Italian Renaissance and similar periods in China are his two main focal points. In the twentieth century he tries with miserable results to equate Jefferson with Mussolini; and Mussolini he even compares with Christ. His worship of "the Boss" of course is partly born of spite, but it contains rational elements also. Mussolini's paternalism and economic program somehow recall Jefferson in Pound's mind. That Pound could not recognize the Chicago-gangster quality of his hero is typical of the humorlessness and childishness of Pound's political ideas. This is the poet who will spend his life writing an epic of world history and culture and who is claimed by Eliot as his peer. As far as a social order goes, Pound has a vestigial idea of a kind of hierarchy based upon the good-ruler-art-patron equation; very likely it is this simple notion which led him to a study of Oriental history. Confucius provides what basis for an ethical-social order there is in Pound's world; Chinese calligraphy and the imagistic character of Chinese writing help convince Pound that an interest in clear definitions leads directly to good government. Finally there is Pound's own economic system, which according to his view could stop war, balance all national economies and bring about something like a terrestrial paradise. His precedents for this belief are a few non-usurious banks tried out here and there in history. Evidently the greatest crime Pound can invent in his world ideology is the crime of Usury; and it is because of Usury that he devotes a good deal of his prose and poetry to imprecations against capitalism and the Jews, whom he associates historically with *Usura.*

Pound's lifelong problem has been to establish an equation between poetry and society, between the esthetic and the politick. The nexus is economics. Good economic system and good ruler equal civilization. That is the whole story. His solution is not convincing even to his adherents, and the best of it is based partly on the sayings of Confucius. Pound acts out the pathetic drama of Modern Poetry, that of trying to make a place for the poet in the modern world by re-making the world. It is in this phase that Pound's so-called insanity has been brought to the attention of nonliterary folk. It is his air of conviction rather than any series of acts or writings which has struck the bystander as lunacy.

This brings us to the most unaccountable paradox of all in Pound's writing, that of his own style as the exemplum of precision in language and in ideas. If it is the high responsibility of the poet to clarify the language, as the good ruler clarifies economic life, then certainly we should expect the poetry of Pound to execute this service. But instead of clarity and pre-cision we get an epic poem which not even scholars can read without long study. Recently the University of California published an index to the *Cantos* with seventeen thousand references to names, dates and other factual information in the poem. Certain refer-ences could not be solved even by the editors; nor would the author lend a helping hand! Clarity, evi-dently, is not as simple a matter as telling someone what you mean. But the *Cantos* are supposed to be case studies of the economic-esthetic failures of all civilizations, and the quantity of data available is, of course, sizable. The style of the poem represents the brave and hopeless attempt to carry over into poetry all the sad prose of History. These case studies are documented by the use of large image groups. For instance, Ovid's *Metamorphoses* is used to denote change, Dante to denote punishment, Homer to de-note the brave exile, etc. This is pretty much what Pound means by the ideogram method—giving one image or anecdote or document after another to build up the total ideogram.

In looking at the vagaries of Pound's various styles

Pound's state of affairs

we must not lose sight of the fact that he is a Modern, that he is one of the poets who flourished around 1915-25. We must remember his proximity to the James Joyce of *Ulysses*, Eliot of *The Waste Land*, the heyday of the little magazine, and so on. The *Cantos* are an anachronism, or rather a historical phenomenon of a certain decade of long ago. While Eliot abandoned the fads of the twenties, Pound did not. The method of the *Cantos* is precisely the method of *The Waste Land*. Had the so-called mythic method, with all its artificiality, proved successful, we may be sure Eliot would have hung on to it. No other poet has profited by this "form," and only Pound would not give it up. The reason he did not give it up is that he was still searching for the meaning of the form. The *Cantos* are a series of experiments that failed; they are almost scientific in their exhaustive persistence. But this hysterical search for "form" is the chief characteristic of modernism.

If anyone needs proof that there is no form to the *Cantos* he can take Pound's word for it. When the poem was three-fourths finished (1939) Pound wrote to an American poet: "As to the *form* of the *Cantos*: All I can say or pray is, wait till it's there. I mean wait till I get 'em written and then if it don't show, I will start exegesis . . ."

As with the poetry of Eliot, we must look closely before we can find a point of departure to discuss the poetry of Pound. Pound is even more permeated with his own criticism than Eliot, though fortunately almost nobody reads Pound's prose. But Eliot is also intertwined with Pound's poetry and in fact has misled the entire literary world as to the worth of this and that poem and in the total assessment of Pound's work. Looking, for instance, at Eliot's introduction to Pound's *Selected Poems,* a book which every twentieth-century poet will have a copy of, I can see how all of my own early ideas about Pound's work derive from Eliot. I am sorry to revert to Eliot this way, but that is where all the arrows point in modern criticism. And this is Eliot on his favorite subject—Pound. Here Eliot is making some mysterious remarks about Pound and Whitman which are supposed to show why Pound is the better poet. Eliot says that Whitman's originality is spurious as well as genuine. Whitman, says Eliot, speaking of Whitman's poetry, was "a great prose writer," and his originality "is spurious insofar as Whitman wrote in a way that asserted that his great prose was a new form of verse." But Pound, he goes on to say, is original (Eliot slyly changes the subject while he seems to be talking about versification). "Now Pound is often most 'original' in the right sense, when he is most 'archeological' in the ordinary sense." . . . "One of Pound's most indubitable claims to genuine originality is . . . his revivification of the Provençal . . ." Anyhow, in this typical shell game of Eliot's, the pea under the shells is the word "original."

The poems in *Personae* (1909) are nearly all bad, full of the worst "romantic" and sentimental affectations and the most archaic English. Pound has never really stopped being archaic—it is another of his inherent weaknesses—and even in the late *Cantos* when he becomes moved he drops back into the *thee's* and *thou's* and *hadst's* of old. This becomes painfully ludicrous when he is *theeing* and *thouing* about money, as in the much-quoted Usury *Canto*:

> Usura slayeth the child in the womb
> It stayeth the young man's courting
> It hath brought palsey to bed . . .

Pound sentimentalizing over usury in Quakerish English is almost too painful to read. Many of the *Per-*

sonae poems are translations or adaptations, nearly all in the pre-Raphaelite manner and different from late Victorian verse only in their reliance on the erudition of the student of Romance culture. A few of the poems are still repeated in anthologies, for instance the "Sestina: Altaforte," which is appealing in its loudness—"May God damn for ever all who cry 'Peace!'" Pound's good effects are frequently based on volume of sound. The *theeing* and *thouing* are also forms of loudness, as in the translation of Leopardi, where he also uses "ye" as a half-colloquialism, half-archaism for the second person singular. These may be details but they spoil any quality of the poetic Pound. Pound so far fails to achieve a style and covers up its absence with a mixture of noise and gimcrackery. Even the pretense of a rich tradition underlying the poems is dissipated by all the flailing around on the surface.

Ripostes (1912) and *Lustra* are different and contain the best of Pound's poetry, the best of his experiments and the best of his "translations." Except for a few passages in the *Cantos,* all that is good in Pound as a poet is represented in these collections. Significantly, one of the books is dedicated to William Carlos Williams. It is in these poems that Pound produces his best epigrammatic verse; the translations and adaptations are still uneven, as they will remain, not so much in their incorrectness but in their failure to convey the quality of the originals. His chief defect is trying to invent a diction which he cannot achieve; throughout his life Pound plays with dialects in all languages. His use of dialects in English is poor and one can assume they are not much better in Old French, Latin, Greek, or Chinese. Sometimes Pound claims to write in what he calls the American language, with results that few Americans can recognize.

His translation of Confucius' *Ta Hio, The Great Learning,* is subtitled "Newly Rendered into the American Language." In this work he renders the Chinese for "make it over" into

"Renovate, dod gast you, renovate!"

Great chunks of the *Cantos* are composed in this pidgin. But in *Lustra* (1916) Pound reaches his best style, possibly because he begins to write about himself (this is also true of the *Cantos;* the *Pisan Cantos* are the best because they are so personal). Many of these poems are on the subject of Pound's "exile" and the sorrows of the artist. They are not very important and they are badly dated but they are honest and clear and to a degree dramatic. If one compares them with poems of the same period by Lawrence, Sandburg, John Gould Fletcher and especially Williams, one will see that Pound is doing the same thing as these poets, almost as well. As for the epigrams and translations from the *Greek Anthology* and such sources, Pound is about on a par with Horace Gregory's *Catullus,* which is saying a great deal. Gregory has done *Catullus* better in English than anyone else in our time. Pound, however, is not content to be a mere translator, because he is always teaching some lesson about history or civilization. Consequently, even his translations have a queer evangelistic ring. His haiku are neither better nor worse than all such Japanese forms in English. English being what it is and Japanese being what it is, the haiku seems destined to sound silly in our language. The general tone of all these poems is that of the world-weary college instructor who writes tweedy poems about the burden of being so horribly well educated. "O God, O Venus, O Mercury, patron of thieves,/ Give me in due time, I beseech you, a little tobacco-shop, . . ." [anything] "save this damn'd profession of writing, where one needs one's brains all the time." One feels for Pound, trying so desperately to justify his existence with such verses. The fact is that Pound has not yet found anything to be heroic about except Romance languages; he is still innocent, still a poet, though the most bookish one we hear about.

The *Cathay* poems (1915) are also at his best level and form the only group of complete poems Pound ever wrote. Chinese was the making of Pound, not in the misleading sense that Eliot means when he says *ex cathedra* that Pound is the "inventor" of Chinese poetry for our time. This is not it at all. Pound's discovery of Chinese poetry was good for Pound but for no one else. As Eliot says, the poems are paraphrases. They lead not to China but to Pound, and that is valid for Pound and for us. Pound can here write complete paraphrases because he is out of Europe, out of America, out of a literature which presumably nobody knows except a few functionaries at the British Museum. It was about this time that Pound wrote conspiratorially to a young lady that it was good for a writer to know a certain large body of knowledge which nobody else did. Any large body of knowledge would do as long as it was more or less unknown, even to experts. China was to be that knowledge for Pound. Parenthetically, I must make mention of the *Letters* of Pound, which like his poetry are almost devoid of human substance, character, and relationship. Pound is a littérateur, even in his letters; the letters are meticulously offhand, each one a specimen for future publication. There is no question about it. Poor James Joyce's letters are human, all too human, with his broken glasses and failing eyesight and poor wages; Joyce poured all his artistry into his novels and stories; but a letter to him was a letter. Not so with Pound. A letter to Pound is a document for the ages, even if it refers to having his shoes half-soled or varnishing his floor.

Let us glance now at the poem *Hugh Selwyn Mauberley,* which Eliot has nominated as a great poem, "genuine tragedy and comedy," etc. Eliot introduces *Mauberley* as a great poem in his typical manner: his opinion worms its way into a discussion of versification, of all things, in which Eliot guffaws that "I only pretend to know as much about versifying as my carpenter knows about woodwork . . ." He does and he doesn't; you can never quite pin Eliot down. Anyhow, *Mauberley* is a great poem, according to Eliot.

Mauberley is a miniature of the *Cantos;* it has all the defects and only a couple of suggestions of the virtues. No one but T. S. Eliot, and that for his own reasons, would ever call it a good, much less a great poem. It has the kind of skill which we associate with putting a full-rigged four-masted schooner, with people on deck, inside a bottle. But there is nothing to be gained by making fun of a very bad poem and the only reason for mentioning it at all is that it has been called a great poem by the critic who has the greatest authority in the twentieth century. There is no question that the poem would never have reached publication, much less "greatness," had it not been for the critical hoodwinking of the Eliot-Pound team. In addition to calling the poem great (as if that weren't enough) he calls it the most advanced portion of what is a textbook of modern versification. Eliot's snide references to versification lead one in two directions: (a) that there is really no such thing as versification for Serious Poets (this is the meaning of his remark that he knows only as much about versification as his carpenter knows about woodwork), and (b) that versification is the real key to the esotericism of poetry.

Actually, Eliot is right on both counts: he knows nothing about versification, even though like all good natural poets, it comes naturally to him. He is also right that successful rhythms lie at the bottom of any successful poem. And he is wrong about *Mauberley*, which is a childish work of versification, as well as being a childish work of intellect. In charity to Eliot, one must say that his loyalty to Pound is magnificent.

Hugh Selwyn Mauberley does have some sections which are good poetry: Part IV about the World War, Part V, and the envoi to Part VI. The rest is student poetry which every teacher of Creative Writing sees at least once in a semester, the weighty and deliberate display of what and how much the author knows, put into "poetry." This is not meant as a joke: it is an exact description of *Mauberley*, which is such a poor little poem that one turns away from it with a blush. Everyone, that is, except T. S. Eliot. The poem is a literary critique and an autobiography, very cryptic supposedly, but in reality a ponderous summation of the literary mistakes of the author. It contains such juvenilities as the rhyming of Τροίη with *lee-way* and the pun of the Greek τίν' with the English *tin;* it contains all the Baudelairean platitudes about modern commercialism and the failure of the Esthetes, all decorated with Pound's linguistic cartouches and pseudo-British harumphing ("Dowson found harlots cheaper than hotels"), all dedicated to a farewell to Style. There are even little provoking pseudonyms in epigraphs, a variation on the more grim headnotes of Eliot's poems. Nowhere is there the faintest note of Versification or Style or anything that would hold the attention of anyone but a close friend. In a very biographical sense the poem is, among other things, a confession of hopelessness. The cry is against "the faint susurrus of his subjective hosannah" of whatever Dowsons and Lionel Johnsons that Pound was plowing under. He himself would not succumb to that. But my sole point here is to remind the reader that this is a poem which Eliot has made a standard of form and content (evidently) of the modern canon. There is little proof that anyone, even Eliot followers, has been convinced by this pronouncement of Eliot's; and yet the record is there, one of the larger stumbling blocks of modern criticism and modern poetry.

The big poem of the "Age," however, is the *Cantos,* the modern poem *par excellence,* and I want to relate this big poem to the shorter ones and to the criticism by Pound.

First, there is no form, plan, or subject matter of the *Cantos* except the reading matter of the poet. There is a very simple proof that Pound himself did not know what "form" he was using when he began the epic. The first versions of the *Cantos* which appeared in *Poetry* magazine are quite intelligible and almost confessedly written in the manner of Robert Browning. Immediately after these attempts he began the final version which we know. There are ponderous books written about the form of the *Cantos* and it is of interest to note that the obscurity of the criticism is in a direct ratio to the difficulties of the poems. The difficulties of the *Cantos* are, as I have said, entirely encyclopedic and linguistic, and not structural. With a good reference work at hand one can piece together the main names and dates; with a half-dozen foreign dictionaries one can make real headway; with the Pound Index all difficulties evaporate, except those having to do with the relationships in the poet's ideas. Even these are not insurmountable; as all of the poet's ideas are derivative, based upon other books, one has only to compare him with the originals. The only really deep water Pound ever enters is Confucianism; but Confucianism, compared with, say, the Hermetic philosophy of Yeats or the religious symbolism of Eliot, is child's play. The so-called obscurities are then the obscurities of the pedant and the obscurities of pedantic rhetoric, plus certain profundities inherent in the quoted works. The most original canto is the one which is a malediction against Usury; it is, sadly, the high point of the whole poem. As for the form, Pound is still looking for it; he says so himself.

Critics of Pound, pro and con, have paid him the highest compliments as adaptor and translator. Here lies his strength. As the *Cantos* begin with a translation of a translation, the entire work is a rewriting from language to language of the documents, literary and historical, which the poet tries to organize into a pattern. The use of bits and pieces of other languages is often of great beauty; and the method itself offers possibilities for originality, although the limitations are obvious. Pound also develops a prosody for the poems, which more than anything else suggests a unity. The prosody is an approximation of the Greek heroic dactyl: the most common rhythmic figure through the poem appears in a line like

> And then went down to the ship,
> Set keel to breakers, forth on the godly sea . . .

This is an excellent device, lending itself to some of the properties of modern speech. But it fails to achieve a standard for all the levels of diction and foreign languages the poet uses. Eliot's versification is nearly always a variation of standard iambic, and it is no surprise to see his later dramatic verse falling back into a weak iambic line. Pound's verse is stronger because he reverses the iambic from the beginning, thus opening the way for new forms such as Whitman invented. But Pound is more conservative than Whitman or Williams and falls back on "Greek" rhythms, where Whitman took as his model the English of the King James Bible and the idiom of America. Whitman's free verse is therefore more natural because it is English, not Greek.

But the fatal weakness of Pound's *Canto* style is his inability to relate one passage or "ideogram" or "image cluster" with another. His usual device is simply to use a conjunction at the beginning of the line (there are passages of great length which rely on this weakest of all English structures of grammar. The weakness, however, is inherent in the material; there is no way to relate it because the relations are arbitrary, chaotic, and without design). There is no vision or ideal central to the *Cantos*, only a tangle of data, prejudices and galvanic twitches of emotion. One would think a poem of this kind would plunge into the universe of philosophies, theories, and systems of knowledge which fill most libraries; but Pound has very little of even this kind of intellectual interest. American that he is, he is so bowled over by facts and statistics that he hardly ever pauses to consider the relevance of his data.

Let us keep in mind the place of Eliot in the appreciation of these poems of Pound. It is impossible to separate Eliot from Pound just as, according to Eliot, it is impossible to divide Pound's criticism from his poetry. "His criticism and his poetry, his precept and his practice, compose a single *oeuvre*," says Eliot. They are the least dispensable body of critical writing in our time, he continues, underlining *least dispensable*. Let us glance hurriedly at this least dispensable body of criticism. Incidentally, Eliot warns against quoting Pound out of context, but it is hard to find the context in these jottings. Pound's criticism is no more than a series of maxims repeated over and over again and illustrated with threats and imprecations— all designed to show that poets are the most important people in history. For example: "A civilization was founded on Homer, civilization not a mere bloated empire." This saying supplies the rationale for the poetry of Pound.

"It is as important for the purpose of thought to keep language efficient as it is in surgery to keep tetanus bacilli out of one's bandages." "Efficient language" of course is Pound's way of trying to make poetry as respectable as science.

Or again: "Great literature is simply language charged with meaning to the utmost possible degree." This is a good definition of poetry as far as it goes. Pound makes his definition in order to talk about those who are inventors and those who are masters and those who are "diluters" of language. The only point of interest here is that <u>Pound is trying to invent categories of poetry which can then be applied to a curriculum of books.</u> The language of poetry is also broken down into categories; the three divisions of lyric, image, and idea-poetry imply a theory of psychology which Pound never states.

Pound's simplification of literature and history is convenient for him. Poetry, he tells us, is a science, just as chemistry is a science. Bad art is inaccurate (unscientific) and is therefore immoral. I am not sure how he makes the jump from "inaccurate" to "immoral," but he does. On this basis he can relate a civilization which he dislikes with the art he dislikes. Thus democracy, a form of government which went to pot after the death of Jefferson or thereabouts, would give rise to such degenerate poetry as *Leaves of Grass*.

"Most important poetry has been written by men

over thirty," he announces as he approaches his thirtieth birthday. The Eliot-Pound war against the poetry of youth and what they call Romanticism is an attempt to show people that poets can sit at conference tables as well as the next man.

"The disease of the last century and a half has been 'abstraction.'" This is one of Pound's better directives, and makes him, in practice, a better poet than Eliot.

"There is no use talking to the ignorant about lies, for they have no criteria," says Pound, speaking of the hideous "lie" that poetry is made to entertain.

Pound's feeling on poetry to entertain

"The twenty-three students of Provençal and the seven people seriously interested in the technique and aesthetic of verse may communicate with me in person." No comment.

"I do not think the rhyme-aesthetic, *any* rhyme-aesthetic, can ever do as much damage to English as that done by latinization in Milton's time and before." Pound rails against Milton's style but he himself invents a whole new polyglot on the analogy of the Chinese written character!

"A sound poetic training is nothing more than the science of being discontented."(!)

"Democracies have . . . always fallen, because humanity craves the outstanding personality." ". . . there should be definite subsidy of individual artists." These are platitudes, of interest only because of the connections Pound makes between the effect of art on history, the basic premise of his work, unprovable and in any case unexplored by Pound.

"The British public liked, has liked, likes and always will like all art, music, poetry, literature, glass engraving, sculpture, etc., in just such measure as it approaches the Tennysonian tone. It likes Shakespeare, or at least accepts him in just so far as he is

'Tennysonian.'" While intended to be a cute remark, this denotes Pound's contempt for nearly all things British. Speaking of America and her view of the artist he says: "America has not yet realized that never in history had one of her great men abandoned his citizenship out of shame." This is in praise of Henry James and is also an explanation of Eliot's contempt for his native land, as well as Pound's.

These few quotations I have taken from Eliot's edition of Pound's essays, the introduction to which announces Pound's critical supremacy in our time. I have not combed the essays for their worst but for their typical ideas, the ones that appear over and over again in the *Cantos*. On what ground Eliot considers his colleague a great critic it is hard to say. One of the most curious facts of modern poetry is that Pound has had followers such as Archibald MacLeish, men who are in direct opposition to Pound's atrophied political and social views but who use Pound as a symbol of their own literary plight. In looking at such poets we must come to the dismal conclusion that they have been infected by the belief that the poet is the handmaid of History. It was this self-important attitude that led to the infamous Bollingen Prize award to Pound in 1948, when under the leadership of Eliot, a group of his followers presented a prize to Pound (at that time under indictment for treason) in the name of the Library of Congress. I was myself a member of that group and narrowly escaped being pressured into voting the prize to the *Pisan Cantos*, which among other things, contained Pound's wildest anti-American and racial outbursts (by that time fused into the same thing). Eliot's criticism had by 1948 so far penetrated the critical mentality of his followers that they dared ignore the plain English in the poems for what they called their magnificent artistry. The insults in the *Cantos*, curiously, are quite clear English, so clear that much of it is given in dots and dashes, which every schoolboy would delight to fill in. One of the judges even informed me sanctimoniously that the award to Pound was a great act of piety, a remark which I am still puzzling about after all these years.

Everything I have thus far written about Pound I have written with a feeling of lassitude and distaste. I do not want to write about Pound; I do not think he is worth my time or yours, but as you can see, there is no escaping him even now. I hope that this essay will help remove Pound from the position of prominence in which Eliot has placed him. I am also aware that all Pound adherents will immediately discount everything I have said about Pound on the grounds that I am a Jew. This is not the place to deny such a motive: I am dealing with the poetry and prose of Pound and not with Pound's ethnological prejudices. It happens that these prejudices occupy a large place in all of Pound's writings and that they are inescapable.

Everything about Pound seems to sum itself up in the photograph that appeared in the papers a few months after his release from the prison asylum. There was Pound back at his home in Rapallo, arm outstretched in the Mussolini salute! Charlie Chaplin couldn't have been more true to life.

I would like to close with an apology and a summary.

The apology is for continuing to hammer away at Eliot. This is tiring, I know, but it is the crux of the matter. I will continue to deal with Eliot wherever he rears his critical influence, and that unfortunately is practically everywhere. I have no apologies for my remarks about Pound himself because I consider him an effect rather than a cause. Actually, I have been gentle with Pound; if you don't believe me, pick up one of his books of criticism, or his pamphlets on economics, or his broadcasts for the Axis, or the *Cantos* themselves: you will see how criticism works with no holds barred and with flowing introductions by the Possum himself, as Pound calls Eliot.

By way of summary: Pound and Eliot meet on the grounds of Education, if that is the right term. They begin as students, one of philosophy, the other of Romance literature. Both are poets and expatriates, anti-American and antidemocratic. The one becomes a monarchist, the other a Fascist. Both gravitate toward orthodoxy, the one toward a national church freighted with tradition; the other toward a ritualism of culture without religious sanction. Both construct theories of literature out of opposition to individualism, "freethinking" and what they label Romanticism. Both center their attention throughout their careers not on poetry nor on belles-lettres nor on literature proper, but on the function of these things in a controlled society. As late as 1940 Pound and Eliot are worrying about the Ideal Curriculum to save civilization via the American university student. They even try to enlist George Santayana, aged about eighty at the time, to lend respectability to their project. What project is this? Is it only Pound's poor old booklist of Homer, Dante, Ovid, and Confucius, which he thinks will save the world because it leaves out Virgil and Milton? Very likely it is no more than that.

But to Pound the great curriculum is the *Cantos,* a manual for princes, as it were, a compendium of history and culture morphology, as well as guidebook and a bibliography, as well as an exposé of Judaism and Christianity, the New Deal and the vocabulary of the American Army.

Eliot's part in these schemes has been more frivolous and irresponsible than Pound's, for Eliot knows better. With Pound the scheme to save civilization with a poem is true-blue evangelism and rather poetic to boot. Pound at bottom shares that American optimism which, when it goes bad, attempts to destroy itself in a wholesale negation of everything that can be tagged American. We recognize in Pound that peculiar buffoonery of the frontier American, the intellectual dandyism of the tourist abroad, and the enormous wasted energy of the crank.

How much of Pound's worst can we attribute to the solemn encouragement of T. S. Eliot? How much to reckless journalism? How much to criticism itself, which disdains so haughtily to talk about anything except the poem *in vacuo*?

And yet under it all one feels a flow of sympathy, a kindliness, and a sorrow for Pound. He is such a storybook American, a stereotype, and a scapegoat certainly. And when you come right down to it, there is something lovable about the old man.

W. B. YEATS: *Trial by Culture*

I

Modern Poetry as a Religion

A CLEVER FRENCH CRITIC once said the nineteenth century began with the poetry of religion and ended with the religion of poetry. This saying sticks in my mind; it is one of those epigrams which would be fascinating for somebody to document and even write a book about. One can see the plan of strategy at once: the nineteenth century begins in France with the Romantic Catholicism of Chateaubriand and ends with the poet-priests Mallarmé and Valéry. It begins in England with the religious mysticism of Blake and Wordsworth and ends with the poetic high seriousness of Arnold, Pater, and Yeats. Even in America the equation works, with the poetic mysticism of Emerson and Whitman turning into the cultural priestliness of T. S. Eliot. Anywhere you look, in fact, it appears that "poetry of religion" resolves into the "religion of poetry."

The trouble with epigrams like the one I mentioned is not that they are false but that they are misleadingly true. And when we analyze such a saying, which is made in good faith certainly, we find that it is not an answer after all but only a new question to be solved. It is an elegant question, and it is hard to resist answering.

The question is whether modern poetry has metamorphosed into a religion. And the answer is: Yes. But then one must define both "modern poetry" and "religion," a tedious business. But like most poets, I have thought about this matter a great deal, and have what I think is a passable answer.

In the first place, "modern" poetry is not synonymous with contemporary poetry. Modern Poetry to my mind refers to a group of writings of about one decade, say 1915-25, and comprises all the works which we refer to mentally when we use the term Modern.*

"Modern" poetry is a school, a literary philosophy, with definite and precise aims, all of which have been enunciated boldly by Pound, Eliot, Yeats, and their associates and followers. This philosophy, called "Classicism" in the textbooks, has its own poetics, its own esthetic, and its own world-view. That it has fathered a new pedagogy and a new criticism every sophomore is dismally aware. Modern Poetry is the official poetry of the twentieth century in all English-speaking countries. But properly speaking, it is not a religion; *it is a surrogate for religion.* If we could digest this extraordinary fact, we would have the key to Modern Poetry as a "religion."

Let us look at three or four of the chief Moderns ("Classicists") in relation to religion: Pound, Eliot, Yeats, and Stevens. Stevens sets poetry apart from and above religion. Yeats gingerly dissociates himself from religion, while pursuing occult and mystical studies. Pound comes no closer to religion than an Oriental ethics permits; Christianity he X's out. Eliot

* See page 25.

alone makes a specific religious commitment. But at
the same time, all four poets observe one or another
version of the central religious doctrine of Original
Sin. It is at this point that Modern Poetry differ-
entiates itself from "Romantic" poetry, whether by
Whitman, Blake, Lawrence, or Williams. It is also at
this point that Modern Poetry becomes anti-American
and anti-twentieth century. All four poets adulate the
Tradition, accepting the "fall" of man from Civilization, and an esthetic Ideal which is capable of rein-
stating the artist as the carrier of Civilization. All four
are anti-Humanist (therefore politically pessimistic).
All are anti-"Rationalist" (that is, anti-Science).

Modern Poetry (still using the famous decade as
the point of reference) recognized the failure of Symbolism, the poetry-religion of the late nineteenth
century. It is for this reason that Symbolism is used
sparingly, if at all, by our quartet. We note that Eliot
takes off not from Mallarmé but from Laforgue, for
Symbolism is already bankrupt when Eliot picks it up.
Pound denigrates the great Symbolists for the same
reason. Yeats remains closer to Symbolism, as Stevens
does in a more superficial manner, but neither is a
"purist" in the Mallarméan sense. (It is curious to see
Eliot use the line from Mallarmé about Poe in which
it is said that Poe purified "the dialect of the tribe."
Eliot has no admiration for Poe but pays his respects
to dead Symbolism in that manner.)

Symbolism in the hands of the French lay close to
a proper religion. The Symbolists believed that poetry
through symbols apprehended the secret meanings of
the world. Symbolism failed as a religion because of
its divorce from the commonplace. A bona-fide religion must have a pyramidal base and not merely an
apex. Symbolism finally led to its own defeat through
its own idealism; it virtually parodied itself out of

existence in such works as *A Rebours, Un Coup de Dés,* and even in the tragicomic life of Oscar Wilde. When the movement collapsed, poetry found itself once again on the street.

It has always struck me that Eliot's use of Laforgue is somewhat counterfeit. Laforgue did not mean what Eliot meant by Banality, for instance. To Laforgue banality was a phase of the landscape. To Eliot it is a religious miasma of some kind, related to spleen, accidia, and so forth. Nevertheless, our four poets all recognized the new attraction of the commonplace, the "antipoetic." Their object was not to exalt the commonplace but to explore it as a cultural site. Eliot's empty lots and sputtering lamps all point to the "fall" from civilization. Yeats has it in a perfect epigram in which God takes (not Eve) the spinning jenny out of the side of—Locke. No French Symbolist would have come that close to the history book. Yet Symbolism was a profitable failure for the Moderns. Pound knew that poetry must, according to his lights, descend to history and even politics, and he taught Yeats this message. Eliot's religion is, in fact, a *descent* from Symbolism to a lower plane of poetic endeavor; for religion in Eliot is just another name for Civilization.

Modern poetry claims a moral prerogative which is in effect a religious prerogative; but it does not claim it in the name of religion. Modern poetry claims a moral prerogative in the name of Culture. It is this Culture which is the substitute for religion and which is the cement of Modern Poetry.

There is, of course, no secret about the aims of the culture religion instituted by Modern Poetry. This poetry began, to be sure, as a poetic movement, or a series of poetic movements, such as a new "Classicism," Imagism and so on; it then became a theoretical educational revolt, the more conservative motto of which was to "correct taste." The correction of taste led to a full-scale re-examination of history. <u>It is very important to remember that with Pound, Yeats, and Eliot it is not the history of poetry or of literature that matters, but history itself.</u> Poetry is actually secondary to anthropology and sociology in the writings of Eliot and Pound. Yeats alone tried to escape from this culture revolution with his head; but his own later poetry is much contaminated with cultural theorizing and historical prophecy.

In what seems an innocuous statement in *Notes Toward a Definition of Culture* Eliot says: "The dominant force in creating a common culture between people each of which has its distinct culture is religion." Even so, he spreads his definition of this culture to include the "legacy of Greece, Rome, and Israel." In other words, it is not simply Christianity which the poet must transmit, according to Eliot, but the whole cultural complex of the Western past. <u>This Culture, supposedly derived from religion, is larger than the religion and subsumes it. Culture is therefore the chief business of the poet, his religion in fact.</u>

It is my opinion that Eliot scamps the relationship between Culture and religion, despite his own churchly affiliations. It would be unfair and pointless to accuse Eliot of exploiting religion for the purposes of literary ambition, but even a casual look at Eliot's religious view reveals that it is much more eclectic than the European tradition calls for. The chief object seems to be not religion for its own sake, or even for Eliot's sake, but for the sake of civilization, for Culture. Eliot approaches mysticism from time to time but retreats hurriedly into metaphysics. He quotes the mystics but is not on good terms with them. The mystics are too original, unmanageable, and "homemade," as he says of Blake. Yeats, however, is a better example of the Modernist withdrawal from religion into some cultural substitute. In Yeats' case it is magic and occultism which are the cultural substitutes for mysticism.

Yeats begins an essay on magic with these words: "I believe in the practice and philosophy of what we have agreed to call magic, in what I must call the evocation of spirits, though I do not know what they are; in the power of creating magical illusions, in the visions of truth in the depths of the mind when the eyes are closed . . ." And in three doctrines, he adds: that many minds can flow into one another and reveal a single mind; that our memories are part of the Great Memory of Nature herself; and that this great mind and great memory can be evoked by symbols.

This credo represents only one of the phases of Yeats' occultism, but it is one which he never rose above. Yeats' use of magic is closer to primitive science than it is to mysticism. There is in all spiritualist and theosophical activity an element of spite, based on the envy of modern science and its triumphs. Even Blake's cry that "Sir Francis Bacon is a Liar" partakes of this bitterness against rational science. Blake, however, appears to be more of a true mystic or gnostic than Yeats. Mysticism and magic are two different things, and it is on the latter inferior level that Yeats rested.

We should remember that in the great decade of Modernism, magic in such forms as spiritualism and theosophy reached its greatest popularity among artists and intellectuals; and that it was in fact an acceptable convention of the poet. Eliot's use of the fortuneteller in *The Waste Land* is a very *topical* allusion. Rilke himself indulged in spiritualism, even though he was aware that greater powers lay in him-

self than outside him. (". . . my greatest, my most
passionate wonderment lies with my own achievement . . . and with certain movements in Nature
rather than with any mediumistic occurrences, however much they have stirred me on occasion.") But
Rilke knew enough as an artist not to enter the lists
against Science or to fight battles for Culture. Neither
Blake nor Yeats made a distinction between mysticism
proper and magic. We gather from this fact that both
poets were exploring the possibilities of a cultural
mystique, a *mystique* lying outside religion and outside modern rationalist science.

I take it that the failure to distinguish between
mysticism and magic in Modern Poetry is deliberate
and strategic. Religion is not a primary force in modern civilization and some substitute for religion must
be found. So reasoned the Pounds and Eliots and
Yeatses and Stevenses. Mysticism proper was therefore suspect; it lay at the very heart of religions. The
mystical must therefore be intellectualized in some
manner. Stevens took the most tentative path, that of
employing the minor techniques of Symbolism and
doodling with a theory of the Imagination. Imagination is the Providence in this version of the culture
religion of the Moderns. It is probably because of
Stevens' relatively perfunctory view of a total Culture
poetry that he was not "recognized" by Eliot, Pound,
and Yeats. "The poet is the priest of the invisible,"
says Stevens in his notebook, but he goes no further.
To do so would be to encourage the sweeping Romantic outlook of, say, Shelley. We cannot understand
the anti-Romantic bitterness of Stevens without taking into account his fear of mysticism proper.

Yeats' scrambling of mystics, alchemists, theos-
ophists, neo-Platonists, and so forth, is his attempt
to steer clear of both religion and philosophy. "Sci-

ence" of course is his avowed enemy, but so are clericalism and orderly philosophical speculation. Occultism was to Yeats what anthropology was to Eliot —an instrument for fashioning the culture religion. It is commonly said about Yeats' interest in the magical that it helped him perceive his poetic images, or something equally silly. Yeats himself is responsible for that interpretation of *A Vision* and of most of his culture poetry. In reality, *A Vision*, like the notes to *The Waste Land*, the *Notes Toward a Definition of Culture*, or Pound's book on *Kulchur*, is a highly programmatic, even political work. The occultism suddenly jells into a practical psychology and ethics, providing not "metaphors for poetry" as the spirits whispered to Yeats, but a full-scale commentary on socialism, democracy, famous periods of history, and great men. The object of the book is to help create the cultural climate in which the poet can again take up the robes of authority, dethroning rationalism and clericalism. Everyone who loves poetry forgives Yeats this book, although it would be foolhardy to overlook its dangers.

All Modernists, including Eliot, agree unanimously that Pound is the father of the Culture religion of Modern Poetry. And Pound certainly makes no bones about it. He proposes to lay down a "system" and does. It is a way of life, an *Anschauung* dealing with man and with nature. God, significantly, does not come into the system. Pound's anti-Semitism and anti-Christianity, by the way, are his version of the poetic liberation from religion. (I should think that Catholics would complain more about the *Cantos* than the Jews.) Pound is almost charming in his arrogance about the founding of the culture religion— "these are notes for a totalitarian treatise and I am in fact considering the New Learning or the New

Paideuma . . ." What this New Learning is everyone knows by now: a full-scale culture revolution in which the end justifies any means at hand, "ideas in action," and the rest. But in the long run Pound turns out to be the weakest link in the cultural chain. Eliot's commitment to him, Yeats' acknowledgments and the tacit approval of the New Critics (students of the New Paideuma) all throw a strong light on their own motivations as culture religionists. It does no good to brush Pound off as old Assen Poop, as Williams calls him; he remains the figurehead of the religion. Eliot does not miss an opportunity to defend him in every phase.

Eliot, however, is the key to the religion of culture. Eliot is the only Modern of any consequence who decided to take the risk of religion. Pound was furious; it was almost as much of a betrayal as Jung's branching away from Freud. I do not pretend to know the ins and outs of Eliot's spiritual biography, for it is a labyrinth. But the most interesting thing about it is that it appears to be a highly suspect commitment and may be no more than an intellectual stratagem to capture confidence. When Pound calls him the Reverend Eliot he is very nearly letting the cat out of the bag; evidently Pound refuses to believe that his prize pupil has really turned respectable.

Eliot's sanction of religion is a parallel to Pound's cultural sanction of Fascism. Religion to Eliot is primarily a social question, and not a *mystique*. It is a dismal crutch for a society he detests. In Eliot's words: "As political philosophy derives its sanction from ethics, and ethics from the truth of religion, it is only by returning to the eternal source of truth that we can hope for any social organization which will not, to its ultimate destruction, ignore some essential aspect of reality." The term *democracy* (says Eliot) "does not contain enough positive content to stand alone against the forces that you dislike . . ." Notice how easily democracy becomes almost incompatible with God in this little recital.

Eliot's cultural development may be sketched in this manner. He begins as an uneasy Symbolist; he knows something is wrong with Symbolism, and that it has not worked. He approaches religion in the typical manner, by negating it (at a time when negating religion is an anachronism). The negation is also typical in its dual anti-Catholicism and anti-Semitism. He then explores the possibility of a relativistic mythology, thus flattering the more rationalistic of the mythologists and anthropologists, such as Sir James Frazer. This is the famous "mythic method" and it is so overwhelmingly a *succès d'estime* that Eliot is suddenly elevated over and above Yeats and Pound and becomes the living incarnation of Modernism. He has now earned the authority to proceed on his own, and it is at this juncture that he makes his extraordinary conversion to the Church of England. It is extraordinary in every respect: the last decision anyone would expect from a twentieth-century American intellectual and poet. Now, with religious authority behind him, and with historical tradition at his side, he begins the elaboration, not of his poetry but of his criticism. He even seems to defend Humanism, though it is a brand which Eliot calls *pure* Humanism.

By fixing his spiritual authorities and antecedents, his literary references and forebears, he manages to rewrite English poetic history, resurrecting the forgotten Metaphysical poets, burying the Romantics and Victorians, removing Walt Whitman to a footnote, and so forth. Finally, departing from Church of England orthodoxy, he scans the mystics. Any suspicion of parochialism is therewith removed, and he is now free to take up his real job of pronouncing about world culture. He becomes in his own lifetime a culture god. This is not the place to delve into the school of literary criticism of which Eliot is godfather. The New Criticism is one of the more noxious by-products of the culture religion and it is too large a subject for me.

Before the coup d'état of the culture religion, readers of poetry tended to think of it as a "secular" art, or a refined amusement, an expression of the national or of the individual psyche. That is, there was at the beginning of the twentieth century very little doctrinaire agreement about the nature and the uses of poetry. Eliot began by explaining the uses of poetry and the uses of criticism, as Pound had begun with his great blast about a total cultural upset. But by 1925, poetry was no longer "secular"; neither was it "religious," nor philosophical, nor rationalist. It had found a way to compete with every other form of intellectual activity: by pronouncing a curse on the century and everything it stood for; by plunging back into the past and "making it new"; by removing the arts from the people and returning them to the classroom; by promulgating new theories of the Imagination, of the State, of the "sensibilities," and of the *Spiritus Mundi*. Systematically this culture faction eradicated as best it could any influence by D. H. Lawrence, William Carlos Williams, Blake, Walt Whitman, and all other "Romantics" and humanists. It ignored the great poetry being written on the Continent by Lorca, by Rilke, by Cavafy (a much finer "traditionalist" than either Eliot or Pound).

It would be interesting to speculate upon the narrowly "Anglo-Saxon" character of this religion of culture, but I had best not go into that. Suffice it to say that this religion has all the earmarks of puritanism at its worst. Its bitterness, its sense of exile from one or another homeland or paradise, its strong theocratic flavor, its sanctimoniousness, its hatred of spontaneity, originality, and freedom, its insistence on orthodoxy —these are all symptoms of the puritanical hatred of poetry and its cynical abuse for purposes of power.

II

Only a few years before his death Yeats paid a visit to Ezra Pound at his home for the purpose of seeking advice about a play he was writing. Yeats had been troubled by loss of creative power and he thought he would see what Ezra would have to offer as an oracle. The anecdote has been repeated now and then for its anecdote value, but no one seems to have taken it more seriously. But the fact that Yeats went to the trouble to print the story as a note to one of his books signifies, to me at least, that Yeats was finally washing his hands of the American panjandrum. Here are Yeats' own words:

A year ago I found that I had written no verse for two years; I had never been so long barren; I had nothing in my head, and there used to be more than I could write. Perhaps Coole Park where I had escaped from politics, from all that Dublin talked of, when it was shut, shut me out from my theme; or did the subconscious drama that was my imaginative life end with its owner? but it was more likely that I had grown too old for poetry. I decided to force myself to write, then take advice. In 'At Parnell's Funeral' I rhymed passages from a lecture I had given in America; a poem upon Mount Meru came spontaneously, but philosophy is a dangerous theme; then I was barren again. I wrote the prose dialogue of *The King of the Great Clock Tower*, that I might be forced to make lyrics for its imaginary people. When I had written all but the last lyric I went a considerable journey, partly to get the advice of a poet not of my school who would, as he did some years ago, say what he thought. I asked him to dine, tried to get his attention. 'I am in my sixty-ninth year,' I said, 'probably I should stop writing verse. I want your opinion upon some verse I have written lately.' I had hoped he would ask me to read it but he would not speak of art, or of literature, or of anything related to them. I had, however, been talking to his latest disciple and knew that his opinions had not changed: Phidias had corrupted sculpture, we had nothing of true Greece but Nike dug up from the foundations of the Parthenon, and that corruption ran through all our art: Shakespeare and Dante had corrupted literature, Shakespeare by his too abounding sentiment, Dante by his compromise with the Church.

He said, apropos of nothing 'Arthur Balfour was a scoundrel,' and from that on would talk of nothing but politics. All the other modern statesmen were more or less scoundrels except 'Mussolini and that hysterical imitator of his, Hitler.' . . . He urged me to read the works of Captain Douglas who alone knew what caused our suffering. He took my manuscript and went away denouncing Dublin as 'a reactionary hole' because I had said that I was re-reading Shakespeare, would go on to Chaucer, and found all that I wanted of modern life in 'detection and the wild west.' Next day his judgment came and that in a single word 'Putrid.'

Then I took my verses to a friend of my own school and this friend said, 'Go on just like that. Plays like *The Great Clock Tower* always seem unfinished but that is no matter. Begin plays without knowing how to end them for the sake of the lyrics. I once wrote a play and after I had filled it with lyrics abolished the play.' Then I brought my work to two painters and a poet until I was like Panurge consulting oracles as to whether he should get married and rejecting all that did not confirm his own desire.

Now this seems a lengthy and uncalled-for footnote from the poet who in 1935, when this was penned, was probably the most revered living poet in the world. We notice the graciousness of Yeats' manner even in this footnote and his sly Swiftian style ("Then I brought my work to two painters and a poet until I was like Panurge. . .") but underneath the story and the style we are aware that Yeats' blood is boiling. Because of the little insult or because of the long, slightly unsavory association with Pound? It is hard to tell. But the fact that Yeats ever wandered into the Pound orbit at all is one of the more disturbing facts of modernism.

Yeats takes his place along with Eliot and Pound as the third of the triumvirate of Modern Poets who have made the Modern canon respectable. But Yeats was never happy in the company of either. He had a barely concealed contempt for Eliot and he used Pound as a kind of antithesis of his own being. But the fact remains that Yeats is part of the club.

People generally agree that there are several Yeatses: the youthful romantic poet of love and the Celtic twilight, the Yeats of Ireland reborn, the Yeats of the Hermetic societies, and finally the Yeats of world culture. These appellations are grotesquely crude but in effect they give the well-known departments of Yeats' writings. And they are somewhat related. The love poems are also folklore poems to a degree; the patriotic poems of the Irish revolution are also part of the folklore idealism and part of the esoteric explorations simultaneously; and the Culture poems are the final effort to project the subjective personal Yeats, the national Yeats, and the magus or alchemist Yeats into the figure of the seer of history. It is in this final phase that Yeats writes his occult book *A Vision,* in which he contends that he will adapt the symbolic and mythological techniques of Swedenborg and Blake to an interpretation of history, "historical movements and actual men and women." So here is Yeats acting precisely like Pound and Eliot. Yeats is a poet of true genius and not a mere opportunist, but he's off to make a sociological ass of himself all the same. And with much the same results as we have already seen.

I would like to run through one poem of each of Yeats' main phases as a way of seeing him as a whole. If my observations are right, this bird's-eye view of Yeats should lead us to a complete sketch of him. In any case, Yeats cannot suffer from critical myopia on my part; he is too good a poet; he even escaped the condemnations of Ezra Pound. But did he escape the blandishments of the culture religion? That is the question.

Here is the young poet nostalgically in love with the old Celtic Ireland before he knows much about the mysteries of the Irish past. He takes a song he has heard a few lines of from a peasant woman, and he rewrites it. The poem is the famous and pretty song "Down by the Salley Gardens" and was printed as long ago as 1889. The book it appeared in contained several pieces of the same exquisite lyric quality which were to make Yeats famous long before the intellectuals arrived on the scene. What Yeats did with the poem was typical of his gift for changing the sense of a line by using an unusual sense of a word. The original song read "Down by my Sally's garden my love and I did meet"—this version evidently being something of a bawdy song. Yeats changes the proper name Sally to the word *salley,* meaning willow.

> Down by the salley gardens my love and I did meet;
> She passed the salley gardens with little snow-white feet.
> She bid me take life easy, as the leaves grow on the tree;
> But I, being young and foolish, with her would not agree.

In a field by the river my love and I did stand,
And on my leaning shoulder she laid her snow-white
    hand.
She bid me take life easy, as the grass grows on the
    weirs;
But I was young and foolish, and now am full of
    tears.

What Yeats was doing here besides writing a lovely
song was to find and modernize some of that poetry of
the past of his country which had evidently died out.
This was Yeats' first concern as a poet and a true one:
to discover his poetic identity. Forty years later he
was using the identical technique to write the modern poem " 'I Am of Ireland,'" which is one of the best
of all Yeats' poems. Now here, too, Yeats has had
his material given to him, he says, by someone else.
He himself never went to the trouble to immerse himself in the old languages, or that is my understanding.
And I dare say there is a clue here to all of Yeats'
later difficulties, obscurities, and pretenses, namely,
that he never gave himself to that Ireland at all and
was afraid of it. The Irish poets take their pride in
Yeats but they know after all that he is Anglo-Irish
in letters. Yeats virtually exiled himself to England off
and on throughout his life. When we remember that
Yeats' life spans the high moments of the struggle for
independence and that Yeats wished to be the spokesman for Ireland, we have the making of a rich conflict. The biographers have handled these questions
well; but I see in Yeats' English-Irish ambivalence the
thing that made him a prey for the Pounds and the
Eliots, men without a country. Most important of all,
Yeats never developed completely away from his early
Irish "Celtic" romanticism. It was still the Holy Ireland, not of St. Patrick but of the pre-Christian reli-

gions. Yeats, of course, spent almost as much time combating the official religions of Ireland as he did writing poetry. This is the poem " 'I Am of Ireland' ":

> *'I am of Ireland,*
> *And the Holy Land of Ireland,*
> *And time runs on,' cried she.*
> *'Come out of charity,*
> *Come dance with me in Ireland.'*

> One man, one man alone
> In that outlandish gear,
> One solitary man
> Of all that rambled there
> Had turned his stately head.
> 'That is a long way off,
> And time runs,' he said,
> 'And the night grows rough.'

> *'I am of Ireland,*
> *And the Holy Land of Ireland,*
> *And time runs on,' cried she.*
> *'Come out of charity,*
> *And dance with me in Ireland.'*

> 'The fiddlers are all thumbs,
> Or the fidddle-string accursed,
> The drums and the kettledrums
> And the trumpets all are burst,
> And the trombone,' cried he,
> 'The trumpet and trombone,'
> And cocked a malicious eye,
> 'But time runs on, runs on.'

> *'I am of Ireland,*
> *And the Holy Land of Ireland,*
> *And time runs on,' cried she.*
> *'Come out of charity,*
> *And dance with me in Ireland.'*

Yeats puts a note on this poem telling that he heard a bit of it from someone who told him it was from a fourteenth-century Irish dance song. One would assume as a certainty that Yeats would have at some time made a mad dash for all that old Irish literature which, we are told, is still unexplored, still untranslated, and which only the post-Yeats poets are beginning to get at. Why did Yeats avoid it and yet saturate himself in spiritualism, theosophy, neo-Platonic cabalism, and finally cyclical theories of history? I think the answer is apparent. Ireland wasn't big enough for Yeats, even mythologically. But in " 'I Am of Ireland' " he is beckoned to come "out of charity," too late, and can do no more than cock a malicious eye. The voice of pagan Ireland never held Yeats the way the poetry and mysticism of Bengal held his friend Tagore. The difference between them is the most vital one possible between two such similar poets: Tagore accepted the mystical content of the folk poetry of Bengal; Yeats rejected the mystical content of the Irish tradition while hanging on to the superficies of the "supernatural" (ghosts on the stair, the wee folk, ectoplasm, etc). There is a lifelong silliness about Yeats' preoccupation with magic which he himself contributed to by not ever quite believing in it; and in the end it weakened his whole structure of thought. Not that the esotericism is inherently weak— it is not; it is one of the most powerful elements of literature, though we are seldom led to literature via the occult. But Yeats dallied with it; he was hangdog about it, or "literary" or affected, as the case might be. He was expelled from one Hermetic society for breaking the discipline; he was rather cavalier about the leaders of magic of his day, though he was in it up to his ears.

I seem to be getting ahead of the early Yeats in mentioning the Yeats of "'I Am of Ireland,'" but these phases of Yeats do overlap and recur. Here next is Yeats of the Irish revolution, which is his best phase of all. Possibly a fourth of all Yeats' poems deal with modern Irish history and nearly all of them are of the highest caliber of that type of topical verse which almost invariably defeats itself in time. What is it about Yeats' patriotic poems that keeps them readable long after so much other "political" poetry has died? The best answer is that Yeats wrote them; second, that they are not patriotic but that they deal with a more or less imaginary Ireland, Yeats' Ireland. This is an Ireland compounded of Irish mythological heroes, national heroes, literary and political, and personal acquaintances; Yeats' Irish poems all have a closely personal quality; an intimacy which is born of a common cause. And Yeats always managed to extract the dramatic and the heroic from the scene; he was a dramatist and a hero in his Irish political poems, inside and outside the scene at once. Yeats sees the poetry of the rebirth of all Ireland through the firing of a few shots. The most trivial and meaningless persons have become transformed through the Easter Rebellion and the Civil War; Ireland itself becomes a symbol of tragic and noble power in the modern world. Here is a piece of the stirring poem "Easter 1916":

> Too long a sacrifice
> Can make a stone of the heart.
> O when may it suffice?
> That is Heaven's part, our part
> To murmur name upon name,
> As a mother names her child
> When sleep at last has come
> On limbs that had run wild.
> What is it but nightfall?
> No, no, not night but death;

Was it needless death after all?
For England may keep faith
For all that is done and said.
We know their dream; enough
To know they dreamed and are dead;
And what if excess of love
Bewildered them till they died?
I write it out in a verse—
MacDonagh and MacBride
And Connolly and Pearse
Now and in time to be,
Wherever green is worn,
Are changed, changed utterly:
A terrible beauty is born.

I doubt whether any other poet of the English tongue
in the twentieth century could have pulled out all
those stops without making a mockery of the poem:
everything is in it, from mother and childhood to
God, England, Ireland, and the names of four of the
revolutionaries who were shot by the English, including MacBride who took Yeats' beloved Maud
Gonne away from him. But instead of a shambles we
get a ringing elegy and something like a battlecry.
Yeats has managed to put together a vision of the old
listless Ireland and the new, with the sixteen dead
men as the metamorphosis and himself as the seer; a
wonderful performance.

So far so good. But when Ireland has become a
contemporary reality and even a national literature
has been brought into being, largely through the
efforts of Yeats, when the cause is won (or as much
won as it can be), what then? Was Yeats ever really
concerned about the political Ireland as much as he
was about the "magical" symbolic Ireland?

There is something indeterminate about Yeats' interest in magic and the occult. That he belonged to

various Hermetic and spiritualist and theosophical societies off and on from early youth we know. What we are not sure of is whether Yeats was a believer or an experimenter. I am inclined to think the latter. His entire performance as a magus from beginning to end smacks of the literary. The interest itself seems to have grown from the reaction against the modern commonplace world, and is a plunge back into that age when science and alchemy were still undifferentiated. Yeats' distaste for modern scientific progress was another thing that drew him toward Pound. Yeats also shares with Pound a distaste for religions of any description, but he takes religion seriously enough to want to be heretical about it. In the poem "The Magi," Yeats shows the Wise Men slipping away from the revelation of Christ and the "turbulence" of the crucifixion to the pre-Christian vision of some Dionysian mystery. In this poem, too, one can see the rather violent sexual preoccupation of Yeats.

Now as at all times I can see in the mind's eye,
In their stiff, painted clothes, the pale unsatisfied ones
Appear and disappear in the blue depth of the sky
With all their ancient faces like rain-beaten stones,
And all their helms of silver hovering side by side,
And all their eyes still fixed, hoping to find once more,
Being by Calvary's turbulence unsatisfied,
The uncontrollable mystery on the bestial floor.

So with all Yeats' poems that touch the religions: he will preserve the symbol, if he can, but not the form of a belief. It is really striking the way he skims over the surface of religion:

I asked if I should pray,
But the Brahmin said,
'Pray for nothing, say
Every night in bed,

"I have been a king,
I have been a slave,
Nor is there anything,
Fool, rascal, knave,
That I have not been . . .

For an oversimplification of Hindu homiletics this goes pretty far, unless we keep in mind that Yeats is probably not even thinking about religion but about the kind of reincarnation which can be used to explain historical data. Everything in Yeats' esoteric activities points to a search for a plan of history. As a religious agnostic and poet he must gravitate toward one or another system of symbols to explain cause and fate, personality, great events, creativity, himself in the cosmos, and so on. I find Yeats' solutions always charming and brilliant and disappointing; he seems unnecessarily driven to patent a system; his system after all is not much more convincing than Pound's view of history.

Yeats is a modern "Classicist" by virtue of his emphasis on the civilized and the aristocratic. Civilization is the touchstone. He defines it: "A civilization is a struggle to keep self-control, and in this it is like some great tragic person, some Niobe who must display an almost superhuman will or the cry will not touch our sympathy. The loss of control over thought comes towards the end; first a sinking in upon the moral being, then the last surrender, the irrational cry, revelation—the scream of Juno's peacock." Yeats' fear of the mystical revelation weakens him as a poet; and the irrational and the popular become identified in his mind, as in the mind of Pound, with demagoguery, the decline of the West and what not. What he has to say about his extraordinary sonnet "Leda and the Swan," though it may be one of those critical irrelevancies which we are accustomed to nowadays, signifies that Yeats had very little inspiration for poetry outside his historical speculations. These are his words: "I wrote 'Leda and the Swan' because the editor of a political review asked me for a poem. I thought, 'After the individualist, demagogic movement, founded by Hobbes and popularized by the Encyclopedists and the French Revolution, we have a soil so exhausted that it cannot grow that crop again for centuries.' Then I thought, 'Nothing is now possible but some movement from above preceded by some violent annunciation.' My fancy began to play with Leda and the Swan for metaphor, and I began this poem; but as I wrote, bird and lady took such possession of the scene that all politics went out of it . . ." The rape of Leda by Zeus in the guise of a swan resulted in the birth of Helen, the symbol of perfected female beauty and the cause of war. Yeats seems to be asking for some violent annunciation or rape, "from above," as he puts it.

> A sudden blow: the great wings beating still
> Above the staggering girl, her thighs caressed
> By the dark webs, her nape caught in his bill,
> He holds her helpless breast upon his breast.
>
> How can those terrified vague fingers push
> The feathered glory from her loosening thighs?
> And how can body, laid in that white rush,
> But feel the strange heart beating where it lies?
>
> A shudder in the loins engenders there
> The broken wall, the burning roof and tower
> And Agamemnon dead.
>   Being so caught up,
> So mastered by the brute blood of the air,
> Did she put on his knowledge with his power
> Before the indifferent beak could let her drop?

Lucky for this poem, Hobbes and the Encyclopedists and the French Revolution are nowhere to be seen. But Yeats uses the poem as the frontispiece to one of the sections of *A Vision*, the work said to have been dictated to his wife by spirits and taken down by her in a species of automatic writing. *A Vision* is a "system of thought," in Yeats' words, that would leave his imagination free to create as it chose and yet make all that it created part of the universal history. All history is fixed upon a lunar wheel; the individual human personality as well as historic and cosmic events can be plotted according to the twenty-eight phases of the moon. The wheel, its phases, and the gyrations of great and small events make an understanding of past civilizations and their mythologies possible; more important, in the case of Yeats, they make prophecy possible. Yeats took a dim view of the chances of our scientific civilization to survive; he envisioned a new terror abroad in the world which he likened to the Antichrist. He wrote poems to that effect but his prose from *A Vision* is even more explicit; this was written in 1925:

It is possible that the ever-increasing separation from the community as a whole of the cultivated classes, their increasing certainty, and that falling-in-two of the human mind which I have seen in certain works of art is preparation. During the period said to commence in 1927, with the 11th gyre, must arise a form of philosophy, which will become religious and ethical in the 12th gyre and be in all things opposite of that vast plaster Herculean image, final *primary* thought. It will be concrete in expression, establish itself by immediate experience, seek no general agreement, make little of God or any exterior unity . . . Men will no longer separate the idea of God from that of human genius, human productivity in all its forms.

Unlike Christianity which had for its first Roman teachers cobblers and weavers, this thought must find expression among those that are most subtle, most rich in memory; that Gainsborough face floats up; among the learned—every sort of learned—among the rich—every sort of rich—among men of rank—every sort of rank—and the best of those that express it will be given power, less because of that they promise than of that they seem and are. This much can be thought because it is the reversal of what we know, but those kindreds once formed must obey irrational force and so create hitherto unknown experience, or that which is incredible . . . it may grow a fanaticism and a terror, and at its first outsetting oppress the ignorant—even the innocent—as Christianity oppressed the wise . . .

This passage is laden with obscurities, of course, but it is clear that Yeats envisions a turn of the wheel of history which will mean the end of our era. "A decadence will descend" he says; and the new era will bring its stream of irrational force. "I imagine new races . . . each with its own Daimon or ancestral hero . . . history grown symbolic, the biography changed into a myth . . ."

In all of which I detect overtones from T. E. Hulme, Eliot, and especially Pound. But primarily the theme is Yeats' own and goes back to his earliest years when he dreamed romantically of a world made perfect for love. As Yeats matures, this passion for the earthly paradise expresses itself in the extreme symbol of Byzantium. Yeats looked upon Byzantium as next to Heaven. "I think if I could be given a month of Antiquity and leave to spend it where I chose, I would spend it in Byzantium a little before Justinian opened St. Sophia and closed the Academy of Plato . . . I think that in early Byzantium and maybe never before or since in recorded history, religious, esthetic, and practical life were one . . ." This then is the ideal, that absolute stylization and depersonalization of experience which we associate with the Byzantine mosaic but of which Yeats sang so fervently:

O sages standing in God's holy fire . . .

To the aged Yeats, the cold fire of the impersonal mosaic was an answer to the unquenchable passions of the flesh. In fact, what keeps Yeats lively and interesting to the very end of his poetic life is this intensity of conflict between body and soul which he could never resolve. The jaunty Crazy Jane poems are a record of that conflict also. Yeats was a Puritan as much as Eliot and Pound; in the Irish Senate he once made a speech defending the divorce laws. Later he felt guilty about it—it was hardly the kind of thing to come from the leading poet of the land—but there you have it. In Byzantium everything is fused together, in Yeats' fine phrase, "into the artifice of eternity."

Altogether, Yeats poses one of the central questions of the modern Classical poet, of which he is one of the gods. That question is also Eliot's question and Pound's question, namely, what is the position of the poet vis-à-vis history? From my point of view, I consider the question unreal and not worth the asking. If the self-consciousness of this attitude and the pompousness of it did not utterly defeat Yeats, that can only be because his genius never completely deserted him even throughout his intellectual soul-searchings. But it is my opinion that Yeats will always remain pretty much a poet of his time, because of his commitment to the historical role. The burlesque magus and spiritualist do not add to his stature; they detract from it; all the pronouncements about history and historical types are so much doodling in the margins of his mind. The poetry itself becomes affected; while the idiom steadily increases in subtlety and beauty, the feeling becomes more violent, turning against himself. Yeats could not make peace with age in any aspect; his central image becomes that of "this caricature," decrepit age tied to him "as to a dog's tail." Even that simple wisdom of reconciliation with age is denied him. That Byzantium symbol is a desperate remedy, no remedy at all. That vision of history is hardly a great vision after all but more of a travesty of the great cosmic systems of emanation which he had borrowed from the Hindus and the Neo-Platonists. The flaw in Yeats is his narrowly conceived idea of civilization; Yeats is quite eighteenth century in the long run. He loved Blake, but did he really learn anything from Blake? It appears not. There is no marriage of heaven and hell in William Butler Yeats—save in Byzantium. Think of the Byzantine mosaic and then try to set beside it the flowing angelography of Blake's pen. There is a complete divergence of imaginations.

The key with Yeats is the word "civilization," the alpha and omega of his culture philosophy. And civilization apparently is—Byzantium. Little wonder that Yeats, a scant generation after his death, is considered a master craftsman of the poem, and nothing else.

The Retreat of W. H. Auden

I DOUBT WHETHER any man living has read everything published by W. H. Auden, probably the most prolific poet-critic of the twentieth century. Not only the quantity but the range of Auden's writing is the most extensive of any contemporary poet's; what is more remarkable, everything he writes is readable. The luxuriance of the Auden bibliography, even in his mid-years, recalls the Victorians, who provided not only the high literature of their time but the popular literature as well. Auden, however, is not popular, any more than T. S. Eliot is popular. Like all Moderns he has eschewed popularity.

The Victorian analogy is a fair one. There is in the quantitative Auden as in the ideal Auden a comfortable paternalism and a sense of cultural responsibility which dates back to the days of Herbert Spencer, Thomas Huxley, and the great novelists who wrote—who must have written—eight hours a day for decades. There is a pervasive and convincing pastness about Auden's writing which always leaves me wondering whether he really is a twentieth-century man or one of those creatures flung over the time barrier by a nineteenth-century time machine.

Auden is probably the most *English* poet since Thomas Hardy died in 1928, the year Auden published his first book. Internationalism has never sat on him well; nor has Americanism (Auden has camped out in America for many years); he is indeed the chief ornament of English letters in the twentieth century. But English poetry is to this day largely "nineteenth century" compared with American or French or Spanish poetry.

In calling these remarks the *retreat* of W. H. Auden I am not referring to the fact that Auden was in his early days a Marxist and is today a poet more involved with theology than with anything else. The fact is that Auden was never as much interested in the social revolution or in religion as he was in psychology; it is Auden's fascination with psychological behavior that makes him readable, charming, and, it may be, lasting. The retreat of Auden is the retreat from poetry to psychology, an almost total sacrifice of the poetic motive to the rational motive. We shall see that Auden is as great a schoolmaster as Pound, though a much more kindly one. Auden is truly a civilized, rational poet (if these are not contradictions in terms), the last of a long line of illustrious "new-classicists" and the father of contemporary poetic style. There is in him nothing of the visionary or the seer, everything of the conversationalist and the classroom wit. Auden, moreover, is an intellectual through and through, and poetry to him is a species of talk. The retreat of poetry into talk, which Auden has made a respectable poetics, is part of the canon of Modernism.

There is no point, in a brief essay of this kind, in trying to sort Auden out into phases, styles, genres, categories of ideas, allegiances, and what not. My aim rather is to determine to what extent Auden takes poetry seriously; and if he does not, what view of it he does hold.

There is one minor matter I would like to dispose of first, namely, the relationship between Auden's earlier social revolutionary poetry and his present-day theological poetry. Readers of Auden have been greatly disturbed (a) by the conversion of Auden from humanism to religion, and (b) by the fact that Auden has tried to rewrite much of his early humanistic verse to make it conform with his later views. The question of rewriting one's early poems to make them sound ideologically like the later ones is such a curious question of literary morals that we had better not try to deal with it at all. This "police" question has been dealt with in J. W. Beach's book, *The Making of the Auden Canon.* The question of Auden's religious conversion from a youthful revolutionary fervor, on the other hand, is a common literary question, one we meet in poets who live through more than one phase of history. I do not find this question very important, however; a poet's politics and his religion are pretty much his own affair, unless they actually do run afoul of the law, as Pound's did. Auden, as far as this reader knows, has never broken any laws and is not likely to; he is thoroughly law-abiding and is in fact a great respecter of the law, in poetry and elsewhere. A poet's religious and political attitudes are of no concern to the reader unless they become part of the poetry.

From the beginning Auden adopted a position about religion and about history; and this meant a personal encounter with Eliot. Auden was too much the scholar and the gentleman ever to be other than respectful to Eliot, but he presented himself as the chief member of the loyal opposition. By the time Auden began to publish, in the early thirties, Eliot was so deeply entrenched in his self-styled Classical revetment that it had become heroic for the young to adopt the pose of the Romantic poet. One could not be a simple Romantic like Rupert Brooke or Shelley (whom Auden always goes out of his way to tell how much he detests); one must be a Romantic and an intellectual to boot. The construction of a Romantic program was a simple matter of drawing a diagram of the Eliot-Pound-Hulme platform and then writing in the opposite terms. Instead of Classicist there would be Romantic; instead of Monarchist there would be Socialist; instead of Anglican there would be Agnostic. Not that Auden was ever so unsophisticated as to write a manifesto, but he saw the literary opportunity quite clearly. And he had organizational ability. Social revolution was thick in the air when he began; clinical psychology and "depth" psychologies were all over the place; and textbooks of every description were as much "experience" to Auden as fields of daffodils to Wordsworth. While Eliot is a learned poet, one who adjusts his poetry to his education, Auden adjusts all knowledge to the poem. It is interesting to note about Auden that he never espouses an extreme cause; his opinions are extensive in range and thorough in their digestion of the material, but never radical. In this he differs from his early associates like Spender and Day Lewis, both of whom were willing to take Causes literally. Auden has always been too detached from people, one gathers from his poetry, and too excited by theories about people (psychology) to ever become more than a paper Romantic. A more horrendous way of putting it would be to term him a Cultural Romantic. Even his religious poems give the impression that he is concerned with the idea of religion, rather than with the religious experience.

Auden's disinterest in unseating Eliot and the things which Eliot symbolizes is one of the chief factors in the continued pre-eminence of Eliot as a critic. Either Auden failed to see the profoundly reactionary quality of Eliot's poetics, or he was content to compromise with them. The latter is probably the case. In the long run, as we all know, Auden became completely magnetized to the Eliot position and is today only a satellite spinning around him. The fact is that Auden never did develop a poetics of his own, as one would expect the author of so much criticism to do. Auden's poetics are inclusive: they comprise the sum total of poetry in the English tongue, from *Beowulf* through the young poets he chose to appear in the Yale Younger Poets series. This is quite a different thing from Eliot's "Tradition" which excludes practically everybody in English poetry—and includes almost no living poets. Auden's rejections are dislikes rather than principles. When Eliot points his finger at John Milton and says, "Go!" Milton must be gone. When Auden, on the other hand, tells us that Shelley is loathsome, we feel that this is more of a personal than a literary matter. Auden is the editor of the best general anthology in English poetry, among his other numerous anthologies, and he knows the tradition in a true sense, and loves it. He is part of it; he is heir to it. In fact, one can understand Auden best by seeing him in the role of curator of the tradition of English poetry. One of the reasons Auden fled England must have been his fear of being recognized as a traditional English poet to the manner born. He has Poet Laureate written all over him.

But the career of Auden is curiously without center; it is uninteresting. It consists of a series of reports on the goodness and the badness of English poets and their ideas. These reports are sometimes in prose, just as frequently in verse. He arranges and classifies, he is meticulously neat, tireless, painstaking, accurate, patient, polite (except on rare occasions of schoolroom outburst), thoughtful, intelligent, sensitive, and more knowledgeable "in his field" than any other poet of the time. For all of this the world is immeasurably in his debt. Eliot once made the remark, which was quite far from the truth, that Pound's poetry is a kind of textbook of modern versification. But such a remark would be true of Auden; Auden is the teacher of prosody.

There is a consistent ambiguity about Auden's position at whatever point we observe it. We must give him the benefit of the doubt and hope that his uncertainties are not fatal. While Auden has a somewhat ferocious capacity for belief, we can never be sure whether it is belief or love of argument that moves him. Auden is a highly argumentative poet and he is always trying to convince the reader of something; one begins to wonder if he isn't trying to convince himself as well. From the standpoint of poetry this constant debating is foreboding; a poet's beliefs, after all, should be taken for granted in his poetry. A tremendous quantity of Auden's poetry fades quickly; very seldom does it rise above the argument, whatever the argument happens to be at the moment. In Auden one is constantly thrown back on the "content" because the content is never purely taken for granted. He is forever washing his intellectual linen in public. His most interesting poems are those in which he generalizes the troubled "I" into "we"; Auden's preoccupation with pronouns is famous.

In his work we see an enormous mass of unrelated poems and verses covering every possible category of the poem, as the textbook and anthology classify the English poem. The poet's hallmark is always evident; the turn of phrase, the vocabulary, the rhythms themselves are always distinctively his, so characteristic that one can spot them in a second. And these forms run from the smallest to the largest, from the minutest epigram to the oratorio, libretto, verse play, prose-poem; everything, in fact, except the modern "epic" like the *Cantos* or the straight narrative, like "Roan Stallion." Yet we cannot find a particular form which we identify as Auden's, one he has invented.

As a guide in this essay I will use Auden's *Collected Poetry*, published over a decade ago, with mention of his later works at random. This is not a study of Auden's totality of production but only of his significant books, the most significant being the *Collected Poetry* published in 1945. The book is the first great landmark in his career, his first plateau of achievement. It is in many respects a peculiar book, not so much a collection as a final rewriting of all the nonrejected poetry—an attempt, in other words, at a unity which Auden covets and seems unable to accomplish.

The book, close on to five hundred pages, has as an epigraph a tellingly ambiguous quatrain. It reads:

Whether conditioned by God, or their neural structure, still
All men have this common creed, account for it as you
   will:—
The Truth is one and incapable of contradiction;
All knowledge that conflicts with itself is Poetic Fiction.

In this dedication, as in so many of Auden's poems, it is hard to tell where he stands. There is an antithesis as follows: The Truth (with a capital T) is one. But all knowledge that conflicts with itself (that is, which is not *one*) is Poetic Fiction. What the reader has to dope out is whether Auden is being serious about the

meaning of Truth and serious about Poetic Fiction
(also capitalized). Or whether he is being serious
about one and not the other. Or finally, whether he
is being serious at all. Even his initial statement is
open to question—that all men have this common
creed. It is Auden's typical way of saying that what
he believes at the moment, all men believe. The
epigram is therefore a subjective statement around
a typical dualism. It is at once a justification for his
poetry and a kind of poetics. It gives him an aim
(Truth) and it rationalizes "conflicting knowledge"
as poetry. In what sense of irony Auden uses Poetic
Fiction is hard to tell. Evidently he both accepts and
rejects the idea of Poetic Fiction. In one of his recent poems Auden writes about wanting to live in a
cave "with two exits." The epigram I have cited has
more than two exits. Notice that Auden does not
say that all knowledge that conflicts with itself is
Poetry, as Yeats would have it, but Poetic Fiction.
Perhaps Poetry is Truth and near-poetry is poetic
fiction; it is hard to tell. We rather expect Auden to
say something startling like Truth is Beauty, but in
a more Modern manner, more subtly. This poem is
not important except that it is the frontispiece to
the *Collected Poetry* and is a web of dualisms.

The poems themselves are arranged in a manner
which every critic has noticed and been annoyed at.
Many of the poems did not have titles originally, but
are given offhand titles and put in a sequence depending on the spelling of the first word of the first
line. The purpose here, aside from the obvious one
of scrambling the chronology, is to suggest a unity
and spontaneity which lie beyond any preconceived
plan. There is a kind of waggery and even tom-
foolery about the arrangement which is supposed
to bear out the poet's notion of poetry as "play." The
notion that it is play is paired with the somewhat des-

perate hope that this play, this Poetic Fiction, will somehow lead to the Truth.

But a chronological view of Auden's poems will not yield much insight anyway; at any one time Auden can be found practicing a goodly number of "forms." In every case they are retrospective and can be related to a model from the past or the present. He makes no effort to invent in the sense that, say, Hopkins invents or Pound strives to invent; there is a different "prosody" operating in Auden and it is the prosody in the old-fashioned sense of line, stanza, and rhyme. Auden's great achievement, on the other hand, is the modernization of diction, the enlarging of dictional language to permit a more contemporary-sounding speech. In this endeavor he has created a revolution in English poetic speech for our time *which is in effect part of the counterrevolution of T. S. Eliot.* In Auden's case this was an honest and perhaps inevitable development, not a scheme to rule the poetic roost. The Eliot-Pound "form" is, as we know, barren, and nothing new has grown out of it. Its failure permitted Auden to return to the standard forms. English poetry, as I mentioned, has been singularly weak in the aspect of invention for a hundred years in comparison to French or American poetry of the same period. The fact that an inventive poet like Gerard Manley Hopkins went unnoticed in his lifetime is evidence of this. Even Yeats, a basically conventional writer, thought Hopkins a bit queer. While Auden has no part in the polemics of the American Moderns about schools of poetry, his work in bulk represents a slowing-up of the formal process, through a broadening of the diction for the sake of inclusiveness. The Auden poem is intelligible, with the logic of beginning, middle, and end, and intelligible within the semantics of the dictionary.

Diction is that aspect of style which refers back

to wording; its final authority is the dictionary. The inventive poet uses the dictionary, if at all, as a point of departure, not as a resting place. The orthodox poet, or classical poet, or academic poet, or intellectual poet, however you call him, always gravitates toward language in its accepted state. It is his authority. In this respect Auden is a dictionary poet, one who refers to the authority of the lexicon and the authority of the anthology. He is himself a scholar and superb editor, with a tremendous grasp of his material. Even his theorizing is handsomely documented.

But Auden has no poetic direction; his theory as well as his practice of poetry reverts to play; he develops a kind of self-defeating technique which prevents even his followers from making him the center of a poetic cult. He would like to be as dogmatic as Blake, for instance, but cannot; as flamboyant as Byron (or Dylan Thomas); or as desperate as Rimbaud. But he is in fact too much a poet of debts and obligations, too happy with books, and too civilized a man to kick over the card catalogue and run howling to his Muse.

"About suffering they were never wrong, /The Old Masters:" begins his *Collected Poetry*. It is one of his best-known poems and a poem that has become the prototype for younger writers throughout the English-using world. Everything about it makes it a model poem, a poem for the album. The title is "Musée des Beaux Arts," signifying that the poem is and is not a museum piece. It suggests the poet magnetized to the museum, whose experience is limited to the big city where the masterpieces settle down after their hard careers in the outside world. The poet is not really looking at the picture of Brueghel's *Icarus* but thinking about it as he walks away. The poem is

something like a twenty-one line sonnet. It has the
grace and structure and smugness of the sonnet. But
of course it is not a sonnet, any more than it is a poem
about a picture. The theme of the poem is Icarus in
relation to the landscape of man as seen in a famous
painting and put into a poem. The whole tone of the
poem is that of the man walking down the street
after having been to the museum, explaining the
significance of a certain famous work of art to a young
friend. This is the peculiar intimacy of Auden and it
is never without its charm. It is serious, accurate, and
urbane with the authoritative urbanity of the city-
cultivated man. The example of the work of art is
indispensable to Auden as a center of value; for he
can provide none without the examples of art. Thus
Auden has led us back to the art-gallery poem, the
poem suffused with the golden light of the museum
and the library. It is Browning without the narration.
It is what young people mean by "academic."

Auden regards his own book as an anthology, a
museum, not out of conceit but because of a confidence that his poetry is part of the great flux of the
past, as it is. His earliest poems are the most exciting
as experiment, with their play on the rhythms of
Skelton and Old English, the primitive movements
of a great literature. In these poems the meaning is
more approximate than precise and it appears that
Auden will try for a breakthrough into new forms,
like Williams. But it transpires quickly that Auden is
not thinking of poetry in this aspect but of poetry as
it has always been; he reverts to the forms, loosening
them, making them generally available and comfortable to use. And meanwhile he uses the poem as a
blackboard to chalk out his views. Voltaire, Freud,
Yeats, places he has been, wars he has lived through,
Utopias he has dreamed and which have or have not

failed him, psychological types, the great artifacts like the Sphinx, and Oxford. At the same time there is never the poem bound wholly to a subject; the subject in Auden's poetry is always moving away from the subject, toward the psychological monologue. This monologue develops naturally from discussion of societal man to spiritual man, from social science to spiritual science, theology.

One finds it impossible to do more than to praise Auden for his extraordinary competence, and after that to talk about the significance of this competence. Each work of his achieves its own perfection; and there is probably no poet in English who has written so much whose successes are so many. In this excellence Auden is like a superb athlete, unaware of his own agility, and spectacularly lucky. I leave to others the discussion and analysis of Auden's scholasticism, his observations about society and about man's spiritual place in the modern world. The pageantry of Auden's poetry is the pageantry of ideologies; to the degree that Auden makes his poetry serve the ends of argument his poetry is in mortal danger of dying with the century. While *The Waste Land* and the *Cantos* may always be retained in the museum of literary knickknacks, Auden's poetry suggests the fate of period literature. It appears that Auden has already lost touch with a contemporary audience and that even his enormous influence over the diction has been assimilated and forgotten. But it is Auden more than any other poet who has stamped the modern poem with a style. To Auden belongs the honor of having brought to perfection what everyone nowadays calls the Academic Poem.

The academic poem is discursive poetry; it is versified thinking. I am not speaking of Auden now but of Audenesque. Eliot and Pound returned poetry, as William Carlos Williams never tires of saying, to the university by making literary data the center of the poem. Auden followed the cue and made all printed data of every description the center of the poem. This was the revolution in diction that I mentioned earlier. <u>If Pound quotes a saying by an American soldier it is to demonstrate the degeneration of Americans in language.</u> When Auden studies <u>and adopts American journalism, he is not trying to demean it but to see its possibilities as poetic usage.</u> Auden uses all the jargons, from social science to advertising, accepting them as current languages of communication, allowing for just enough irony of tone to save himself from being identified with these jargons. The dictions border on the comic, sometimes even imitating Ogden Nash or Edward Lear. They open the door to the old rhetorical devices like the capitalized abstraction of allegory, which with Auden is an unserious way of being serious. By doing this with such apparent ease, he has made the discursive poem casual and universal.

What distinguishes Auden from, say, the "Georgian" poets is the intellectualizing of emotions. Yeats admired greatly a villanelle of Ernest Dowson's with the refrain "Wine and women and song, /Three things lighten our way." Auden writes "I sit in one of the dives /On Fifty-second Street" and shortly begins to talk about the "low dishonest decade." Dowson mourned in the bar about his fellow artists and his own emotional griefs; Auden in the bar mourns about politics, society, and war. This fusion of personal emotion with intellectual debate was something quite new. Eliot and Pound had rid the poem of emotion completely and talked about "felt" ideas. Eliot advised poets to "feel their thought" like Dr. Donne. Auden reversed the process and showed the poet how to "think his emotions" in poetry. Eliot and Pound failed to create a following because poets

are enormously emotional animals, and do not want
to use thought as an experience, as Eliot advises.
Poets would much rather feel sorry for themselves
(if that is the only emotion available, as it seems
to have been for Ernest Dowson) or generalize
their emotion into "universals," like Keats in his somber odes. They do not want to "feel their thoughts"
like the Wits and the Metaphysicals Eliot is so fond
of. But in a pinch they are quite willing to "think"
their feelings, like Auden.

The Auden poem is intellectualized emotion. The
academic poem is intellectualized emotion, when
there is any emotion to intellectualize. Most often
there is only a pretense of emotion and this pretended emotion is intellectualized and versified.
Auden's emotion is usually vital and warm, even
though he chews it over in the poem. The truly
academic poem is cold and clammy; whatever feeling it had to begin with is filtered through the screen
of wit until it is unrecognizable as feeling. In the
academic poem the reader does not know what the
emotional direction is; to this charge the academic
critic replies that that is not important: if you want
your emotions directed, go to the movies.

I suppose I should give an example of an academic
poem, one in which the original feeling is lost through
talk about it. For this purpose I might use almost any
poem chosen at random from the big literary quarterlies or the small reviews, as this is the type of poem
most in favor with editors today. But I do not feel
that I should make fun of some other poet's work and
I will use a poem of my own. The only thing I want
to say in defense of the poem is that I rather like
my version of the academic poem. Notice that there
is a double meaning of some kind in almost every
line of the poem, that some words are used simul-

taneously as nouns and verbs or adjectives and that
there are so many instances of this kind of play in
the poem that I find new ones every time I look at
the poem. Such a remark would elicit a chuckle
from the modern critic to the effect that "I told you
so; there is even more to your poem than *you* think."

The poem is titled "A Calder," the title being a
play on words for: Alexander Calder, the inventor of
mobile art; the article "a," signifying a particular
Calder mobile; and also his initial. Here is the
poem:

> To raise an iron tree
> Is a wooden irony,
> But to cause it to sail
> In a clean perpetual way
> Is to play
> Upon the spaces of the scale.
> Climbing the stairs we say,
> Is it work or is it play?
>
> Alexander Calder made it
> Work and play:
> Leaves that will never burn
> But were fired to be born,
> Twigs that are stiff with life
> And bend as to the magnet's breath,
> Each segment back to back,
> The whole a hanging burst of flak.
>
> Still the base metals,
> Touched by autumnal paint
> Fall through no autumn
> But, turning, feint
> In a fall beyond trees,
> Where forests are not wooded,
> There is no killing breeze,
> And iron is blooded.

No one, I think, could tell from this poem that I am a fervent admirer of Calder. I am. The feeling is almost entirely obscured by paradoxes: an iron tree, a wooden irony, the use of work and play as both nouns and verbs, and so on. I call this an Audenesque poem, a poem in which the emotion is thought to pieces. Auden himself would never be this obvious in a poem; he would think the poem a good deal further along the line than I have. Or he might write one stanza with the mobile in it and then take off into a rarer atmosphere of speculation, as Yeats does in his schoolroom-visiting poem, another model of the age in which the human element is all but snuffed out by Yeats' talk about metaphysics.

To recapitulate what I have said: Eliot and Pound destroyed all emotion for poetry except emotion arising from ideas. (The formula is theirs, not mine, and I take no responsibility for the obscurity of it.) Observing their stigma against emotion, Auden used emotion in the poem as a subject for intellectual speculation. Auden's use of emotion-as-conversation was the model for what we call the academic poem. It was not only Auden's great skill in making this kind of poem readable that turned it into a genre; it was also the fact that people in the twentieth century tend to intellectualize emotion anyway. The curse laid upon emotion by the Moderns was inherited by Auden, who apologizes for his emotions by talking about them in the poem. To use the critical jargon, the academic poem can be recognized by its Objective Form, objective form being anything from jamming the text, the use of concealed metaphor, involved stanzaic form, "personae," to anything else that prevents direct expression of feeling. The modern critic considers the expression of personal or subjective emotion a "fallacy."

Auden is essentially a lyric poet but lyricism also was frowned on by the inventors of Modernism. Pound had expressed some interest in Robert Burns and Villon, it appears mostly for the dialect quality of their poems; but what he called in his terminology "Melopoeia" was not at the top of the poetic heap. At the top of the heap was the "poetry of ideas." People used to speak of Dylan Thomas as a great "lyric" poet, meaning that they liked his work but didn't think it would produce much intellectual aftermath. It didn't; but it produced the first spontaneous audience for good poetry since the moderns ruled out audiences as immaterial. Auden's own lyric talent has been subsumed under his own intellectual talent. Auden, in fact, has created a genre, the intellectual lyric: he says:

> O who can ever praise enough
> The world of his belief?

Every Auden lyric or ballad has an intellectual point to make—there is no story for the story's sake, no song for the song's sake.

The lyricism of Auden is almost always spoiled by self-conscious siftings and ruminations. Many of them are little parables, some are leftovers from plays, but very few are lyrics. Generally Auden treats the lyric too gingerly, like an archeological find which he has just dusted off. Here is an example, using the recently discovered American folk-song idiom, which our poet is a little uncertain about.

> "Gold in the North," came the blizzard to say,
> I left my sweetheart at the break of day,
> The gold ran out and my love turned grey.
> *You don't know all, sir, you don't know all.*

"The West," said the sun, "for enterprise,"
A bullet in Frisco put me wise,
My last words were "God damn your eyes."
You don't know all, sir, you don't know all.

In the streets of New York I was young and swell,
I rode the market, the market fell,
One morning I woke and found myself in hell,
You don't know all, sir, you don't know all.

In Alabama my heart was full,
Down by the river bank I stole,
The waters of grief went over my soul,
You don't know all, ma'am, you don't know all.

In the saloons I heaved a sigh,
Lost in deserts of alkali I lay down to die;
There's always a sorrow can get you down,
All the world's whiskey won't ever drown.

Some think they're strong, some think they're smart,
Like butterflies they're pulled apart,
America can break your heart.
You don't know all, sir, you don't know all.

Many of Auden's lyrics are all that endure of some
of his plays. This may be as good a place as any to
add a note about the use of drama among modern
poets. What do we find is the state of the drama in
the hands of modern poets whom we have been
talking about?

In the first place, Pound puts a virtual ban on
drama. To him the theatre is too public and all sorts
of illiterate and noisy folk crowd into the playhouse.
Pound turns his back on the Greek dramatists and on
Shakespeare, and all other drama except perhaps the
Japanese Noh. What Pound understood about the Noh
was its subtlety as a spirit-play and dance-play; and

it was this element that he recommended to Yeats. Pound's insight was excellent here. But Pound also recommended the "aristocratic" quality of the Noh, a typical Pound misinterpretation. The Noh had been killed off by the Western opening of Japan in the nineteenth century, but it was not aristocratic; it began in fact as a public and even mystical art connected with the sect of Zen Buddhism. Yeats followed up the Noh as best he could and wrote dance plays and closet drama and other "aristocratic" forms, some of them quite beautiful, all of them far out of reach of a living stage. Even the quality of the poetry in the Yeats play is thinned out, and there are no characters in the sense that Synge knew and used character. Yeats' dramatic defect was that of the Modern Poet who does not really recognize the existence of people at all, but only voices and masks.

Eliot's place as dramatist is more interesting. In the absence of any poetic drama in our language for centuries, Eliot approached the problem cautiously and intelligently, experimenting with such simple and traditional forms as the church pageant: *Murder in the Cathedral* is not only his best play; it is one of the best "miracle" plays of the literature. Eliot uses only pre-Shakespearian dramatic forms and post-Shakespearian dramatic forms. The high period of English drama he does not try to duplicate. *Family Reunion* is an attempt to reproduce tragedy in the old sense. The later drawing-room plays are evidently modeled on Oscar Wilde. (Eliot's understanding of character is Wildean and requires a static social atmosphere in which the characters can make epigrams.) The success of some of Eliot's drawing-room plays is based not on any use of character or plot or poetry, for the poetry grows less and less and finally disappears, but on the use of the quasi-supernatural

man, in reality a *deus ex machina.* Eliot's inability to
deal with true character is similar to that of Yeats,
neither poet evidently having had sufficient knowledge of, or sympathy for, people to know what to do
with them. The chief virtue of Eliot's plays is that for
a moment they reversed the tendency of realism in
the theatre.

Auden is more attuned with dramatic literature
than any of the foregoing poets and from the very beginning of his career has stayed close to the uses of
dramatic poetry and theatre poetry. It is interesting
to note that Auden has never had a stage success like
Eliot or even Yeats, while his use of dramatic forms
not intended for the stage is better than that of
any other contemporary. He is a librettist, not a
dramatist; Auden's use of character is even weaker
than Eliot's. There are no characters proper in his
plays, only literary voices, or rather radio voices, for
Auden prefers not even to delineate the face and form
of a character. By far the most brilliant of these voice-
poems is *For the Time Being,* which is to date the
best work of Auden's and one that promises to survive much of his other poetry. This oratorio, as Auden
calls it, uses all the lyric forms in a burlesque mode,
saucily and with all the voices of wit. Considering the
subject, which is the "Christmas story," the whole
poem is light and pleasant and enlivened by a great
deal of sophisticated talk about society and community. There is no particular unity to the poem; Auden
prefers the lyric plus recitative form which allows full
use of the intellectual choric voice. *The Age of Anxiety*
makes even less pretense of being playable; like *The
Sea and the Mirror* and *New Year Letter,* it is discursive poetry in voices. Auden's inventiveness in this
realm is another of his contributions to literary form;
the basis of the form is again diction and the action is

all verbal and psychological. One is reminded of the masque of Jonson or Milton.

Auden has moved drama even further from the stage than Yeats. Eliot has moved it closer to the stage than any other poet since the Jacobeans, but only in a technical sense. The Eliot play is a *tour de force* tending toward the kind of brittle stylization we get in Christopher Fry. A true poetic drama must begin from the theatre as it exists today, not from the poem as it exists today. We have the seeds of this drama in a playwright like Tennessee Williams, really a poet, not in Eliot or in Auden or Yeats. Williams' exaggeration of character and situation is poetic exaggeration; the characters are rooted in reality but are not realistic; Eliot's and Auden's are not rooted in reality but in "ideas." Tennessee Williams represents a beginning of a poetic view of character and circumstance. The lurid and baroque atmosphere of his plays should not distract us from the fact that Williams is dealing with recognizable realities. The popularity of his plays attests to the fact that his audiences see beneath the surface distortions, violences, and perversions of their situations. And in general, what is called "Southern" literature in America is more vital than any other literature, not because of its dark and catastrophic surface but because certain effects of American life are best seen through characters who live closer to the real nature of American violence and passion. This is where the poet comes in. It is not a question of setting a play in New Orleans or Oxford, Mississippi, but of dealing with characters whose daily emotions are forced into overt behavior by the spirit of place. Synge could do this with the Aran islanders; Yeats could not do it because he could not see emotion on the streets; he could see it only in dreams. Some of Eliot's characters are convincing in

scenes of domestic altercation but in nothing else.
Eliot has to get rid of characters by pushing them off
boats or sending them into the tropics to be eaten by
ants. Auden's characters, on the other hand, have a
kind of Gilbert and Sullivan charm, "real" enough,
but only for *opéra bouffe*.

The career of Auden thus far has demonstrated one
fact over all others, that he has advanced the "Classicism" of Eliot and Pound. With more than half the
twentieth century gone it is now possible to see the
pattern of poetry as it was established by the founders of Modern Classicism and to see the meaning of
the discipleship of Auden.

In the face of the enormous productivity of Auden
and the relative success of all his work, it is difficult
at first to see his connection with Eliot. Where Eliot
and Pound failed to effect a revolution in poetry they
succeeded in providing cultural sanctions for poets
and critics of the next generation. There is no indication that Pound approves of Auden; he would consider him one of the second category of poets, those
who consolidate the "inventions" of their masters.
Eliot, of course, would take a much more sympathetic
view of Auden. Eliot abandoned the pretense of free
verse after it had served his purpose; actually he
never used it at all except in a few early "imagistic"
poems. Eliot used modified French forms which he
admittedly copied; by the time of the *Quartets* he no
longer pretends any loyalty to new forms but relapses
into a gauche lyricism, alternating with a slack line of
prose. Pound has, on the other hand, stuck to his conception of a new form of verse, enough to impress
William Carlos Williams, among others. Auden evidently saw through the "experimentation" of his elders
to their real purpose, which lay beyond poetry. It may
be that Auden took literally the Classicists' talk about

Tradition, as later he seems to have taken seriously their talk about religion. In any case, Auden's service to Modernism, Classicism, or whatever you want to call it, is the determinant of the common style of poetry in English today.

All of Auden's talk about Romanticism, the romantic voyage, the quest, loneliness, the romantic artist as *poète maudit,* and so on—is all talk. It is well documented, handsome talk, but it comes from books and nothing but books. The sectarian battles between Romantic and Classic one would have thought had died ages ago, but we find them revived by Eliot and his friends, with Auden providing a little fencing practice for the Romantic team. The great "Romantics"—Nietzsche, Whitman, Rimbaud, Lawrence—do not enter into the game, having been polished off by Eliot long since. The whole point of Auden's "Romanticism" seems to have been to accommodate that persuasion to the tenets of the Classicists. In any case, this most academic of struggles has simmered down in Auden to textbook discussion and no longer plays any serious role in poetry as a living art.

Ironically, Auden brings to our attention the fact that "modern" poetry still has not come into existence. What has passed for Modern Poetry is in no wise comparable to the painting and music of our time, but a weak imitation of those arts. The new poetry which Eliot and Pound bragged they were bringing into existence has its fruits in the stanzas, sestinas, oratorios, and libretti of Auden, the typical New-Classical and academic literature of our time. Nor has Auden profited from the true modern poetry outside of the English language. Except for one translation of Cavafy, which had already been done quite well, Auden shows little sign of interest in the poetry of modern Spain, Italy, Greece, France, Germany, or

South America. Stephen Spender has done far more
to introduce the European poets into English than
Auden.

It is an astonishing fact about the twentieth century that it is without its poet. Auden set out to be
the Poet of the Age: at least he was always inventing
slogans which the literary journalists readily picked
up. He had the air and authority of a Spokesman, but
for whom did he speak? We remember that Auden
began as the voice of English revolutionary youth and
that the enemy was the entrenched bourgeoisie with
its country-club ethics, its smug clericalism, and its
imperialist bank account. This was the intellectual
fashion in England until after the Spanish Civil War
and the famous Moscow trials; Auden was the first of
the Marxist poets to slip quietly out of the meeting.
By the time he was missed he was already ruminating
in New York over the failure of Collective Love and
the sad truth of the need for personal love. An extraordinary amount of Auden's poetry of this time is an
anguished repetition of the cry that self-love is the
only possible love. The recoil from the class-war morality was very severe for Auden; in exile he became
an American citizen and a parishioner of the Church
of England. Auden has always had to have his papers
in order; an intellectual decision to him means sign-
ing on the dotted line. He shuffles his papers, or re-
shuffles them and is ready to begin again. But for
whom is he the Spokesman this time? It becomes
harder and harder to tell. The tone of conviction is as
firm as ever; the generalizations as sweeping as before,
but now they are couched in theology. As far as
Auden's instinct for the public sensibility goes, he is
probably right to switch from the language of anthropology and depth psychology to the language of
Angst, Eros and Agape, for there is no question that

the Dismal Science, Theology, is in the ascendency in the mid-century. And I have no doubt that Auden can hold his own among the best of the doctors of religion. But my interest in him stops there.

Auden's achievement is thus far that of the great stylist, not that of the primary poet, the actual creator of poetry like Hopkins or Rimbaud or, among his own contemporaries, Dylan Thomas. Auden is more than a literary movement: he is practically a period of literature all to himself. But his is a period of re-examination—of forms, of vocabularies, of ideologies. He is the great amateur of our time; he has taught us all how to improvise. But one would be hard put to find the small handful of poems which are the core of Auden, the man himself, the poet himself. Auden is already forgotten by the present generation, the poets who have begun to write since about 1940; he has been absorbed completely. This is sad for a poet of such rich talents and a man of such good will; but the reason is at hand: he calls his own integrity into question. I began with Auden's quatrain about Truth and Poetic Fiction and I must end with an example of his Poetic Fiction (or is it his Truth?) contradicting itself.

This is part of the passage from his play *The Dog Beneath the Skin*, which, among other things, is a bitter anticlerical diatribe. A hypocritical vicar is delivering a sermon and Auden is pulling out all the stops to show how revolting are the vicar and his message. The sermon is, in fact, a violent satire on religion at its worst. But note this: when Auden publishes his *Collected Poetry*, ten years after the play itself, he makes a separate place for this very sermon and calls it "Depravity," introducing it with a strange bit of Pecksniffiana:

I can only hope that this piece will seem meaningless to those who are not professing Christians, and that those who are, and consequently know that it is precisely in their religious life that the worst effects of the Fall are manifested, will not misinterpret it as simple anticlericalism which always implies a flattery to the laity.

It is concerned with two temptations: the constant tendency of the spiritual life to degenerate into an aesthetic performance; and the fatal ease with which Conscience, i.e., the voice of God, is replaced by "my conscience," i.e., the Super-Ego which . . . holds one variant or another of the Dualist heresy.

In this passage the vicar is attacking the idea of freedom and social revolution which Auden (at least when he wrote the play) was defending. (The stage directions have the vicar in an hysterical frenzy, crying and with saliva flowing from his mouth.)

And so, today, we are here for a very good reason. His enemies have launched another offensive, on the grandest scale, perhaps, that this poor planet of ours has ever witnessed. As on the first awful occasion in Eden, so now; under the same deluding banner of Freedom. For their technique of propaganda has never varied . . . that three-syllable whisper: "You are God," has been, is, and alas, will be sufficient to convert the chapped-handed but loyal ploughboy, the patient sufferer from incurable disease, the tired economical student or the beautiful juvenile mama into a very spiteful maniac indeed . . . [The vicar then draws a picture of what it would be like to live under the slave state in the name of Freedom. Then he exhorts his congregation:]

But mind, God first! To God the glory and let Him reward! God is no summer tourist. We're more than scenery to Him. . . . Oh delight higher than Everest and deeper than the Challenger Gulf! His commodores come into His council and His lieutenants know His love. Lord, I confess! I confess! I am all too weak and utterly unworthy. There is no other want. . . .

Oh Father, I am praising Thee, I have always praised Thee, I shall always praise Thee! Listen to the wooden sabots of Thy eager children running to Thy arms! Admit him to the fairs of that blessed country where Thy saints move happily about their neat, clean houses under the blue sky! O windmills, O cocks, O clouds and ponds! Mother is waving from the tiny door! The quilt is turned down in my beautiful blue and gold room! Father, I thank Thee in advance! Everything has been grand! I am coming home!

Here is Auden in a nutshell. A passage condemning an idea is used ten years later to defend the idea that the passage originally condemned. What was a burlesque of ecclesiastical rhetoric is now presented as a sober sermon. Which is the Truth, which the Poetic Fiction? You will have to decide for yourselves. For as Auden says in one of his poems:

> This might happen any day;
> So be careful what you say
>   And do:
> Be clean, be tidy, oil the lock,
> Weed the garden, wind the clock;
>   Remember the Two.

Thus the master of the Middle Style, the poet who will probably give his name to our age of moral expediency and intellectual retreat—the age of Auden.

WILLIAM CARLOS WILLIAMS:
The True Contemporary

W<small>HEN</small> I <small>WAS</small> twenty years old I published a little book of poems privately. It was a confused book, a mixture of Elizabethan and Modern. This volume I sent to several famous poets, only one of whom took the trouble to reply. He was William Carlos Williams. Williams did not praise my book, but his letter, the first I had ever received from a real writer, was full of sympathy and kindliness for a young man who wanted to be a poet. While he had nothing encouraging to say about my poems, he had a good deal to say about the month of March and his anger at T. S. Eliot. The month of March figures a great deal in Williams' poetry, a violent and beautiful season in Williams' New Jersey, as it was in Maryland, where I lived. The diatribe against Eliot disturbed me deeply. I was a worshiper of Eliot then and a devout reader of the *Partisan Review*, which, although a highbrow left-wing magazine, took Eliot to be the sovereign poet and critic of the twentieth century. I could not understand how any modern poet, especially Williams, who seemed of an extraordinary freshness and originality, could say unkind things about Eliot. If I had ever developed the habit of reading literary criticism I would have known what he meant. But my natural antipathy for criticism kept me away from it for many years. It was not until I began to teach in universities that I was forced to examine criticism; and it was not until I examined it carefully that I began to appreciate Williams' opinion of Eliot, the true significance of Eliot and everything he has promulgated under the name of criticism.

The radical difference between Williams and, say, Eliot, is that Williams divorces poetry from "culture," or tries to. Williams is fighting for the existence of poetry (while Eliot and Pound fought for the "uses" of poetry). Williams' entire literary career has been dedicated to the struggle to preserve spontaneity and immediacy of experience. His explanations of these aims are certainly not as impressive as Eliot's and in fact lead to such confusing theories as Objectivism. In defense of Williams one can say that his theorizing is innocent, while in the case of the Pounds and Eliots it is calculated and tricky. Williams does not stand or fall on theory; he is willing to void it at a moment's notice. But it is unfortunate for him that he must engage in theory at all. At bottom Williams is not an intellectual, and he is too human, too sympathetic, too natural to become a symbol of the anti-intellectual. Besides, as he says in his published letters, he is illogical. He would never be able to impress the quarterly reviews or the highbrows who consider him a kind of intellectual slob. The literary quarterly follows a party line of Culture, any Culture, but Culture is a *sine qua non* for the poet, according to them.

Williams is a guinea pig of modern poetry. He lends himself to the literature of the laboratory and a thousand trials and errors of criticism. He even writes a

"mythic epic" like Pound and Eliot which all the culture critics seize on as proof that Williams is not a
literary imbecile but one you can practically write
books about. *Paterson* is a typical culture poem, the
only full-dressed one Williams ever wrote but, according to the critics, the real thing, a kind of New
Jersey *The Waste Land.* Williams is so innocent that
he would even do that. In writing his large bad poem
Williams was perhaps trying to test the validity of
works like the *Cantos* and *The Waste Land,* even to
compete with them. While he carried on a lifelong
fight against Eliotism—a one-sided fight, for Eliot
hardly deigned to notice this gadfly—he maintained
a lifelong relationship with Pound. Williams' relationship to Pound is very much like Yeats': an antimag-
netic relationship. Pound leaned on Williams in the
same way that Eliot and Pound leaned on each other.
And Williams remained loyal to Pound because Pound
seems to remain American rather than English. Williams is faithful to Pound through thick and thin,
always annoyed with him, and always attempting to
understand his position. Williams can see the demagoguery of Eliot but not of Pound. Somehow he iden-
tifies himself with Pound. Williams a few years ago
was unseated from the poetry consultantship of the
Library of Congress, with no organized protest from
writers and scarcely any mention of it in the press.
Pound was awarded a prize from the Library of Congress which was backed up by all the self-styled Great
Poets of the English-speaking countries. Pound got
his prize, was feted in the editorials of the national
magazines, and was eventually freed without a trial.
Williams went home and had a series of strokes. My
point is that because Williams abhors fixed positions in
politics as in poetics he cannot impress officialdom.

Williams is the American poet who tries to fight off

Europeanism. He fights it off, singlehanded, but he cannot impress the European with his cause. Neither can he impress the American. Lacking the arrogance of an Eliot or a Pound, lacking philosophy or religion or logic, he is battered back and forth by the literati, who are always armed to the teeth with Positions and who can make anything out of him they want, except a bad poet. Eliot tried to polish him off by remarking that he had a kind of "local interest." To Eliot anything that is not of world cultural interest is "local."

Williams belongs to the generation of Modern Poetry, those poets who suddenly organized literature in 1920 or thereabouts. He was not a high-powered Modern because he lacked the political instinct, but he was aggressive and fought the distortions of Modernism throughout his life. His letters and essays and even his poems are all "local" in the sense that they are contemporary. He wanted poetry to belong to the present, not the past. This is the clue to his involvements with Ezra Pound and his hatred of Eliot.

Williams has written a good deal of literary criticism himself, but he is not a critic in any accepted sense of that word. He is a poet even in his criticism; he refuses to use terminology and everything terminology stands for. He builds up no system; he abjures "style" in his prose, except when he is not sure of his ground. (In such cases he writes a jaunty, affected lingo reminiscent of Pound or Hemingway.) A good many of his judgments seem to be affected by personal loyalty mixed with an overpowering desire to be fair. One time, because of a letter from Robert Lowell, he seemed about to revise his opinion of Eliot. In Williams' world there are no hard and fast rules; the entire literary process is fluid; the governing principle is contemporaneity—immediacy.

There are basic contradictions of judgment in Williams' appraisals. For instance, he praises Marianne Moore excessively while he sees nothing of importance in Eliot. Williams also places Gertrude Stein with Pound as an important innovator. Pound he is inclined to favor from the start, even to a slight imitation of Pound's ideas of American history and banking. But the treatment of Pound is always anguished. One is inclined to feel that Williams does not look up to Pound but is pleased by Pound's interest in *him!* Williams has little use for Stevens, but this is consistent with Williams' objections to prettified language. At the bottom of Williams' specific poetic judgments lies a theory of language, which is practically a *mystique.* Usually it is referred to as a *prosody,* and in the widest meaning of that term it is.

Compared with Pound's prose, which has the tone of the Public Address System, Williams' critical style is weak and plaintive. At times it contains a note of hysteria, frequently its shrillness gets in the way of the clarity, but on the whole there is the pervading innocence and warmth of personality, heightened by genuine excitement. But when he intellectualizes he follows in the footsteps of the Eliot-Pound faction. He praises Joyce for his clarity and his great interest in form but his basic liking for Joyce has to do with Joyce's humanity. This is not a virtue that the Joyceans usually single out. And of course Williams is attracted by the banality of subject in *Ulysses.*

His allegiances are unstable and extreme. Williams reacts sharply to the immediate political or literary event. He is as prone to follow the Right (where the politics are not too obviously putrescent) as he is to follow the Left. Extremism seems to him worth a diagnosis. His detestation of Eliot seems to be a hatred for compromise; Williams does not compromise but

he veers crazily from side to side. He writes about
Lorca with a political passion while clinging with one
hand to the coattails of Pound. He follows Pound's
admiration of Jefferson while taking a "leftist" position
on Jefferson. "Let's have a revolution every ten years,"
is Williams' view of Jefferson. Whereas Pound would
say: a solid aristocracy without hereditary rights. At
the end of a stirring, almost scholarly essay on Lorca
he works in a little stab at Whitman, saying that
Whitman was a romantic "in a bad sense." Williams is
always looking over his shoulder at Pound; in himself
he feels no critical authority. Here he mimics the
Modern Classical view of Whitman.

Frequently he takes off into the realm of esthetic
speculation, always with a certain desperate gaiety
that characterizes his criticism. "The poem alone
focuses the world," he says. This pleases the Pound
side of Williams. Or in an essay about E. E. Cummings: "We are inclined to forget that cummings has
come *from* english to another province having escaped across a well defended border . . ." This is
about the difference between English and American,
which Williams makes the center of his criticism. But
he knows he is on the side of the Romantics, on the
side of anyone who is opposed to "lapidary work,"
anyone who opposes a literary poem. Williams is always more or less on the right track, but he never
comes to the point in his criticism. He does in the
poems. Again he will buckle down to a first-rate piece
of criticism in his bitter essay about the failure of
Sandburg to continue as a poet. Here he is on safe
ground. Williams is as close to Sandburg as twins but
he can tell the difference between himself and the
professional Americanism of Sandburg. He understands Sandburg because he has been through the
same process of handling Americana. But Sandburg's

soft-pedaling is to Williams the worst sort of propaganda verse. Sandburg follows the identical course Williams does in his own "formless" poetry; but Sandburg settles for a "form" and Williams still continues the search. When Williams talks about Auden he can say something as mixed-up and as *true* (reading Williams' criticism one begins to write like him, on both sides of the fence) as: "I wish I could enlist Auden in . . . a basic attack upon the whole realm of structure in the poem. . . . I am sure the attack must be concentrated on the *rigidity of the poetic foot*." When Williams begins to underline something like the "rigidity of the poetic foot" he sounds even more sophomoric than his friend Ezra. It is as though Williams had reduced all the cultural viciousness of modernism to prosody—which in fact he has done. Marianne Moore seems to him to have taken recourse "to the mathematics of art." He adores her persnickety syllable snipping but he cannot abide Auden's much more fluid and graceful "feet." The point of argument seems to be British versus American. Puzzling over Dylan Thomas' poems after his death, Williams said that they smacked of the divine. But having fallen between the two stools of the "divine" Thomas and the agnostic Pound, one is not sure what *divine* is, except, as Williams says, "drunken." Clinging desperately to the only poetic he knows he cries at last: "Without measure we are lost." *Measure* is used prosodically and abstractly, as the rule, the law—one is not sure how it is used.

As a critic Williams has no credit whatever. Eliot puts up a full-scale esthetic which anticipates every question and answer. Pound bludgeons his opinions across to a few listeners. Yeats weaves over the crystal ball in a trance of culture sensibility. And poor Williams is haunted by the two specters of Whitman and

Pound, the genius and the crank. All of which ends up as an unresolved internal monologue on *Prosody!* The prosody *mystique* in Williams is the center of all his prose and must be understood if the nature of Williams' poetry is to be vindicated. As my own opinion of Williams as a poet puts him over and above Pound and Eliot and Cummings and Marianne Moore, all the theorists and purveyors of sociological opinion, I will attempt to examine Williams' "prosody."

Williams has no critical reputation but he has somehow maintained the respect of the official literati. Simultaneously, he has maintained the loyalty of the literary "underground." (It was Williams who introduced Allen Ginsberg's *Howl,* and dozens of similar works which only poets have ever heard of.) He is the only modern poet who searches everywhere for new poetry.

Imagine any of the official critics, new critics, or editors of the highbrow quarterlies taking notice of a poem like Siegel's *Hot Afternoons*—which Williams alone had the courage and honesty to reintroduce as one of the best twentieth-century poems. *Hot Afternoons* was one of the last authentically American poems, save Williams' own, before the final triumph of Eliot's culture poetry.

The new schools of criticism have always tried to give Williams the benefit of the doubt as a poet of their persuasion. Especially the poem *Paterson* appeals to them as a work comparable to *The Waste Land* and the *Cantos* or the *Anabase* of St. John Perse. *Paterson* to these critics seems an epic in modern style, a "mythic" poem. Controversy over *Paterson* has been considerable; but at least it is recognized by these critics that Williams is as culturally ambitious as his contemporaries in such an undertaking.

It is a waste of time to discuss this kind of criticism, but it is necessary to set it aside if one is to get at a fair judgment of Williams' poetry. There is at least one full-scale intellectual probe of Williams. It is a quibbling book, laden with minor points of pedantry and with a dark knowledge of "structures." It is apparent in this work that the author is not able to read poetry except as "comparative ideology." For instance, in speaking of a character in Williams' *Paterson* named Elsie, the critic says: "Elsie is a kind of Yeatsian 'Crazy Jane' presented without Yeats' idealization of the desecrated woman as the authentic guarantor of some superior wholeness, an authenticity with which Yeats also endowed his fools and lunatics." This gibberish rises from the critic's intense interest in "mythic" character rather than poetry. But one of the funniest examples of this kind of criticism is as follows. A critic takes a delightful little poetic quip by Williams and treats it to the following exposition. Here is the poem, "This Is Just to Say":

> I have eaten
> the plums
> that were in
> the icebox
>
> and which
> you were probably
> saving
> for breakfast
>
> Forgive me
> they were delicious
> so sweet
> and so cold

The irony of this poem, the critic says, "was that precisely that which preserved them (the plums) and increased the deliciousness of their perfection (the refrigeration) contained in its essence the sensuous quality most closely associated with death; coldness. So the plums' death (or formal disappearance and disintegration) was symbolically anticipated in the charm of their living flesh. This is, I believe, the exact pathos of this brief poem. . . ."

Whenever I quote something like this I feel constrained to add that this is a true quotation and not a parody I have made up. Most criticism about Williams is written in this patois: in a discussion of the poem "The Yachts" we are told that "suddenly the physical referents are expanded into universals more overtly than had been Williams' earlier custom when the reader had been given the responsibility for making the concrete particulars yield the universals . . ." etc. What the critic is trying to say is that in this poem Williams is using symbols; she cannot say anything so obvious; and she invents a way of saying the obvious to make it look profound.

A similar "explication" is published by the poetry editor of *The Nation* about the little wheelbarrow poem. This is the poem, "The Red Wheelbarrow":

> so much depends
> upon
>
> a red wheel
> barrow
>
> glazed with rain
> water
>
> beside the white
> chickens

Says the critic: "The poem's design is a striving for value, for significant realization, against the resistant drag of the merely habitual." This kind of highbrow marginalia is, funnily enough, *sanctioned* by Williams, who is always looking for someone to bestow critical respectability upon him.

Williams' poetry is bounded by *Kora in Hell* (1917) at the beginning of Williams' literary life and the epical *Paterson* at the other end. Pound wrote him about *Kora in Hell* and said, "The thing that saves your work is *opacity*, and don't forget it. Opacity is NOT an American quality." The opaque was something Pound might praise; and there is no telling how deeply influenced Williams might have been by this great literary law of Pound's. There are two books preceding *Kora* but the original preface to *Kora* is a mightily opaque and gossipy monologue in the Pound style. More important, Williams announces that the plan of *Kora* is "somewhat after the A.B.A. formula, that one may support the other, clarifying or enforcing perhaps the other's intention." This is the "form" of the *Cantos, The Waste Land,* and other "mythic structures" of the twenties. The real precedents for the book, however, are the so-called prose-poem, the *Illuminations* of Rimbaud, the poetic notes of Baudelaire, the abortive prose experiments of Eliot, etc. Probably the model of the poem was the pretty little French poem, for children perhaps, called *Aucassin et Nicolete.* Williams was charmed by this piece and evidently kept it in his mind as a form using both verse and prose. But the official precedent for *Kora,* we are told, is a book called *Varie Poesie* dell'Abate Pietro Metastasio, Venice, 1795, designedly dropped on Williams' desk by Pound.

Kora in Hell is a series of observations about poetry and the stance of the poet, full of little psychological asides about our civilization, not in the Poundian political way but in the Surrealist associational manner. Williams is concerned, like all the *avant-garde*

writers of his time, with the feasibility of "associations"—the random use of intellectual and personal
experience. Williams simply made it his business to
jot down something every night, however nonsensical,
and then make a comment on it. The chief and it may
be the only fact of interest about *Kora* is that *Paterson*, coming at the apex of Williams' poetry, uses the
identical method. The method consists of a free use
of poetic languages in various states of excitement,
alternating with a free use of prose languages. Eliot,
Pound, and Joyce all attempted the same technique,
with varying success.

But in between *Kora* and *Paterson* we have close to
a thousand pages of some of the best or most interesting American poetry in our history. Almost all of this
poetry is in a style which is immediately recognizable
as Williams' own; further, it is a workable style, one
which permits him to write a poem almost at random.
At its best, which is a good bit of the time, it is not
"experimental" poetry or crank technique. Naïve it
certainly is, even what some writers call primitive; it
is precisely Williams' innocence of forms that frees
him to respond to daily experience as a poet. Williams
went on writing, day after day, year after year, losing
manuscripts, not finishing them, giving them away,
but never letting up. Poetry to him was a daily function of life, a means of seeing. In a sense, he is our
first American poet since Whitman. It hardly matters
that his counselors poisoned his mind against Whitman; Whitman is his mentor after all.

Critics and journalists tend to heroize Williams for
writing poems late at night after a hard day's work at
the hospital. Williams has never felt heroic about
being a physician. It is pointless to try to imagine
Williams ensconced in some village on the Italian
Riviera brooding over the effects of the 1905 nickel

on the souls of little children. Williams was a New Jersey doctor and that is that. His poetry is the poetry of a very busy man, as busy, say, as Sir Walter Raleigh or Gerard Manley Hopkins. Not that one can generalize about busy poets and poets of leisure. Williams wanted to be a doctor, have a family, live near New York City, and write poetry. As far as anyone knows, he did all these things very admirably.

But the seeming offhandedness of Williams' poems *is* a condition of his life. Obviously the poems would be different had Williams not been a doctor. New Jersey, New York City, Ezra Pound, the delivery room, the back alleys of charity patients, home, the little magazine, the month of March, these are all the elements in which his poetry moves. Williams accommodates himself to the brutal round of modern professional life. It does not embitter him; it sweetens him. And the poems are "scrappy," as the critics note, but there is a method to their scrappiness. And they are not astrology or economics or theology. The element of speed in composing the poem is part of the technique of his poetry, just as speed is a factor in certain kinds of painting. There is, in fact, a definite "Oriental" tendency in his work, not cultural Orientalism like Pound's but an instinct for the work that is as natural as nature herself. And the daily life has a lot to do with it. He survives as a poet even better than his contemporaries, a consequence, perhaps, of his roots in a pedestrian world. Williams never became an "exile;" how can an obstetrician be an exile?

The earliest poems are marked by the ornate imprint of Pound (the use of foreign exclamations and translation-sounding rhetoric and even the "Browning" dramatics which Pound quickly switched away from when he discovered that he could be opaque with impunity). The character of this style is that of a half-biblical, half-Victorian tone which is the quality of all of Pound's early adaptations. In Williams it sounds like:

> Eight days went by, eight days
> Comforted by no nights, until finally:
> "Would you behold yourself old, beloved?"

Actually Pound never rose above this style, either in the *Pisan Cantos* or in the latest additions to his epic. Williams saw through it more quickly. It goes on intermittently through "So art thou broken in upon me, Apollo" and many such imitations of Style, but soon it stops abruptly. One can see the sudden transition in:

> Your thighs are apple trees
> whose blossoms touch the sky.

which is more or less phony Pound, but is followed by:

> Which sky? . . .
> Which shore? . . .
> what/sort of man was Fragonard?

This is the beginning. Williams sheds figurative language as a snake sheds its skin; henceforth he is naked, a poet without decoration, without metaphor.

> March,
>   you remind me of
> the pyramids, our pyramids—

There is still a lot of mincing Italian, Spanish, Latin quotation, but this falls away also.

> a green truck
> dragging a concrete mixer
> passes
> in the street—
> the clatter and true sound
> of verse—
>
>   • • •

```
Moral
        it looses me
Moral
        it supports me
Moral
        it has never ceased
        to flow
```

(through various series of data, menus, signs on walls
and labels on bottles). Then a descent into pure
spoken idiom, the rejection of all the devices of poetry
for speech, always a sign of the poet's sincerity. Where
Eliot ends up snipping philosophy from textbooks,
Pound cutting whole chapters from history documents
and statistics, Williams dives back into the spoken
tongue.

It can never be said of Williams that he writes a
well-rounded poem like "Ode on a Grecian Urn" or
"The Love Song of J. Alfred Prufrock" or even "my
father moved through dooms of love." He loathes the
fait accompli in poetry or in painting. On the other
hand, he does not worship the "fragment" for the fragment's sake. He tries to find the center of his experience in relation to the art of poetry; and he finds it
over and over again. His "discoveries" are many more
than "The Red Wheelbarrow" or "The Botticellian
Trees"—good poems but two of many hundreds which
are not repeated in the anthologies.

Williams puts his poetry in a direct relationship with
daily experience. With Eliot there is no daily experience: there are "symbols" of the quotidian (empty
lots, carbuncular young men, sandwich papers along
the Thames, the silence in the subway) and with
Pound there are stock-market reports, the struggles of
artists and war communiqués. Williams tries to accommodate his poetry to what the day brings to a
poet in a place like New Jersey, where there is no

dazzle of the past or of the cultural present. Williams writes about an apple rotting on the porch rail.

He does not exploit his knowledge. It does not occur to him that what he happens to know as an expert might be turned to the uses of poetry. Yet he himself is the organizing center of the poem, bringing together around him the untold *disjecta membra* of the day. *Without metaphor*. This is the challenge. Hence the directness of all his poems and their somewhat shocking physical quality. Williams is like Catullus in his outspokenness and unthinking sensuality and amorality—for there is no bragging or sexual athleticism (or asceticism either) in the poems. Pound is sexless, Eliot ascetic, Yeats roaring with libidinal anguish and frustration. Williams includes the physical in the day's work; he meets it at every turn, being a doctor, and is not obsessed.

> The young doctor is dancing with happiness
> in the sparkling wind, alone
> at the prow of the ferry! He notices
> the curly barnacles and broken ice crusts . . .

or

> I bought a dishmop—
> having no daughter—

There is very little twentieth-century poetry like this except outside the English language. But Williams does not "translate" or "adapt" except infrequently. He refuses to improve upon the language—this is the whole secret of his flatness of style and the inconclusiveness of the forms. He writes in his speaking voice.

In his autobiography, Williams refers to the publication of *The Waste Land* as "the great catastrophe." Looked at from Williams' point of view and from that

of all the *avant-garde* of his time, it was indeed the
great catastrophe. "It wiped out our world," says Williams, "as if an atom bomb had been dropped upon
it . . . I felt at once that it had set me back twenty
years . . . Critically Eliot returned us to the classroom
just at the moment when I felt that we were on the
point of an escape . . . I knew at once that in certain
ways I was most defeated." Williams' recognition of
the true nature of *The Waste Land* marks him as
first-rate prophet in criticism. And the effects of Eliot's
poem were even more far-reaching than Williams said;
not only was it the poem the academy needed as a
pseudomodern example; it was a poem that made
poetry and criticism one and the same thing, and that
provided a justification for a new critical philosophy.
Williams was also right in seeing that he was more
damaged by this poem than anyone else. He was left
high and dry: Pound, who was virtually the co-author
of Eliot's poem, and Marianne Moore were now polarized to Eliot. Williams felt all this and would feel it
for another twenty years. His own poetry would have
to progress against the growing orthodoxy of Eliot
criticism.

At first glance, Williams' remarks about poetic form
seem superficial and even inane. One thinks, well, here
is a nice man who is sick and tired of effeminate
poeticizing and who would like American poets to
display some gusto and originality. On second glance,
one thinks, the old boy is becoming a bore with his
din about prosody and "the line." All that shrieking
about the "language" in *Paterson* is as bad as "the precise definition" in the *Cantos* or the "way of saying it"
in the *Four Quartets*. And because Williams refuses to
use the standard terminology of criticism, because he
has a sincere interest in an American poetry, and because he is so suggestible, at least in his early years,

to the literary politics of his fellow writers, he generally sounds half unintelligible. But there is a lot more to his "prosody" than that, much more, in fact, than exists in the new criticism.

Prosody is the science of verse. In English there is not and there has never been such a science. English scholars have long since given up prosody studies as a hopeless task. Because prosody and versification have such a justifiably bad name in English literature, no reader is apt to prick up his ears when William Carlos Williams or anyone else introduces the subject. Prosody is a mare's nest. Eliot and Pound took care not to identify themselves as prosodists, even while they were quietly laying down laws for it. In public they always guffawed at the mention of the word.

By prosody Williams does not mean versification. If you examine his own poems or his own remarks about what he calls mysteriously "the line," you will see the following things: He neither preaches nor practices "foot" prosody; he does not preach or practice meters; nor syllabic versification, such as Marianne Moore adopted; nor is his prosody accentual; nor is it "typographical" or what one critic calls grandly "spatial" form; nor does he base versification on rhyme nor on the internal figurations which rhyme may produce. The prosody of Pound is based on cadence which runs close to foot prosody—an imitation of Homeric and English trisyllabic. Eliot's prosody is extremely conservative, either a copy of Laforgue, at its most daring, or of Milton's *Samson Agonistes* (though I have never examined this closely) and it degenerates easily into modified "iambic." Williams' prosody is more advanced than any of these: it consciously departs from every intonation of the past. This is also its danger, as it is its advantage.

The thing to remember about Williams' "line" is that

it is not a prosodic line at all. The word "prosody" for him is a metaphor for the whole meaning of the poem. Iambics to him mean cottages all in a row: sameness, standardization of things and of lives. His refusal to write iambic is therefore the same thing as Whitman's. It means that the iambic is not a language for the American poet. Pound and Eliot maintained the same doctrine, each in a less convincing way.

A good start for understanding the significance of Williams' belief about prosody and language (they are the same thing) is to consider his contempt for the modern sonnet. The virtue of the sonnet (which is the only "set" form in the English language) is that it prescribes a kind of syllogism. A sonnet in its simplest form makes a statement, develops or contradicts it, then resolves it. It is a game; hence its popularity with lovers. Eliot began by rejecting the sonnet; Pound rejected it after a few acrobatic flops. On the other hand, a poet like Cummings has advanced the sonnet to a new fame. With him it becomes the most ironical sonnet in English literature. What Williams resents about the sonnet form, even in the hands of Cummings, is the neatness of it. That is what the sonnet is for. The sonnet "line" can lead to nothing but a trick poem or exercise. A poem, according to Williams, should not be that closed, should not click like a box (which was Yeats' way of describing his own metrical poetry). The "closed" poem—the poem that clicks like a box—is the type of poem which has lately become a standard in the twentieth century; the most recent models were made by W. H. Auden.

All the appurtenances of the closed poem, especially the stanza, become anathema to Williams from the beginning. Rhyme itself seems to him meretricious; when he uses it (and he uses it as well as anybody), it is with a slur. The poem must not be governed by meters—any meters—nor by periods and paragraphs (stanzas), nor by the figures of speech. What is left? Nothing. The raw material of the poem is all. It is the same process that Whitman went through: a rebirth.

But Williams had even rejected Whitman's line. (We must try to remember that Williams uses the word "line" in the metrical sense, and in the linguistic sense at once.) The turning away from Whitman is all but fatal in Williams, but he manages to do pretty well in his own way. Williams grew up in the day when Whitman seemed incorrigibly nineteenth century and Emersonian. How Williams could have missed the lesson of Whitman is beyond me. But Williams started over, too. No ideas, no meters, no forms, no decorations; only the search for the raw poetry of experience.

"No ideas but in things," Williams said over and over, for a time. He became an "Objectivist," a man on the search for objects instead of thoughts. But this was just a variation of Pound's Imagism; for there could be no object-poetry that would lead anywhere; any more than Imagism could stand on its own legs. Williams dropped the Objectivist idea, just as he dropped the "antipoetic." These were harmful simplifications. Williams' larger conception of poetry is based on the understanding that a thing is neither poetic nor antipoetic, neither prose nor poetry: there is something else which cannot be so bound. To write a poem about a rotten apple is not "antipoetic"; people laugh at such a poem and love it precisely because it is the poetry of the thing. The poetry of the rotten apple lies outside prosody, outside what is proper for apple-poetry, and outside what is called Symbolism (if you say *apple* to a modern critic you will be pelted with religion, mythology, and Freud before you can duck— but to Williams an apple is an apple).

As for Williams' versification, it goes entirely by ear, and luckily for him he has a good ear most of the time. It is not cadenced, not accentualized, not syllabified, not metered. It may or may not have a "typographical" form: sometimes it has, sometimes it hasn't. For certain periods Williams will print in "couplets"; at other times in tercets; he is not averse to the single word per line nor the long line. Generally (and this is the significant thing) he accommodates the "line" —that is, the typographic or verse line—to the sense of the whole poem. Thus he is doing approximately what Hopkins did in sprung rhythm, creating a total form rather than a unit form. It was a horror to Williams to see *The Waste Land*, partly because of Eliot's use of the old "unit" forms: an iambic passage here; a trochaic passage there; an image poem here; a long rhetorical build-up there and so on, with no organic principle anywhere.

But Williams himself in his desperate moments does the same thing. *Paterson* is just as artificial as *The Waste Land* when it comes to the "line."

Williams and his contemporaries had been schooled to despise "narrative poetry." To tell a tale in verse seemed to the early modern poets of our century the weakest excuse for writing a poem. They tried to get rid of tale-telling altogether and switch to Ideas, which are much more "masculine" than narratives. There is a large residue of narration in Williams' collected poetry which for years he did not know what to do with. The wonderful episode 17 in *Paterson,* one of the most powerful passages Williams ever wrote, was without a context until he stuck it in *Paterson.* But true to his Modernist upbringing, he could not even then *narrate* it, any more than he could narrate *Paterson.* Williams' "epic" poem is thus just another example of *The Waste Land* technique. He is better when he writes about Sacco and Vanzetti (a theme which could not move the great culture poets to even a single word) or about the death of D. H. Lawrence (which the culture poets also avoided like the plague). An interesting thing about Williams' poems is that they move from one to the next easily. The "secret of that form," as Williams calls it somewhere, is to make poetry natural, not literary. This is, in fact, the secret of his "prosody," the secret of his "antipoetic" line, the secret of his concentration upon objects as ideas. *The "secret of that form" is the eradication of the line between poetry and prose, between life and art.* Eliot speaks of an art emotion, an emotion reserved for the moments when one turns on the esthetic faucet. And it is precisely this attitude toward poetry that Williams condemns.

At the present, at the end of his long struggle with prosody, Williams turns to something very like a "form" but so loose that one can hardly call it a form. Perhaps it began with an admiration of a little quatrain by Byron Vazakas which resembled typographically a toy pistol or the State of Oklahoma. Vazakas managed this thing for speaking in his own voice. Williams hit upon a step-down kind of typography which he has used constantly in recent years. But it is not a be-all and end-all; he may drop it any time he likes. It is not a syllogistic sonnet or sestina at any rate. This style differs from Williams' earlier style only in that it appears to conform to a certain regularity. But there is none, except the regularity of thought as it progresses in the poem.

Had Williams been as good a theoretician as he was a poet he would probably be the most famous American poet today. But Williams cannot explain, fortunately for him, or he explains badly when he does. It is the poem he is after. His kind of poem may be the chief development of the American poem since *Leaves of Grass*. When it is successful, as it is an amazing number of times, it abolishes the dualism of form-content, expression-artistry, and all those other dualisms which get in the way of art. Williams' almost mystical repetitions about "the line" (and somewhat wildly in *Paterson* about the *Language*) are a decree against critical speculation about forms. He knows that forms are not predetermined, not inherited, not traditional. He knows, too, that forms do not matter for the honest artist, whether he uses them or not. It is when form becomes a fetish that he draws back and howls.

Speaking of howling, Williams has been the sole example in twentieth-century poetry, along with Lawrence, for hundreds upon hundreds of poets, the majority of whom are Americans who oppose the Eliot "line." Williams knows too much about poetry to set up a critical shop or lay out a curriculum like Pound. He is the godfather, all the same, of nearly all the existent *avant-garde* poetry, all the free poetry that exists in the English world today. This is recognized by the young poets who long ago branched away from the cultural highway and took to the backstreets and bohemias of the land. Williams is no bohemian; he is a serious man of letters (as the stuffy expression goes) but he is closer to the life of the poet than any of his contemporaries. By the life of the poet I mean the man to whom the daily life is the poetry itself, whatever his occupation. Williams may have been trying to do the impossible in taking for granted the unity of expression and artistry in the early years of the century, but he was one of the few who accepted this high premise of the poet. When the "great catastrophe" (the publication of *The Waste Land*) occurred, most of Williams' friends dropped by the wayside or split into little groups or went over to the enemy, as Williams put it. It is curious that through all the ensuing years Williams remained loyal to Pound and could not perceive that it was Pound who was the lever for the catastrophe and would continue to be.

A newly published book by Williams serves better than anything I have ever read about him to clarify and sum up his poetry and his poetics. It is a strange and charming work called *I Wanted to Write a Poem*. The book is an informal bibliography which is also a kind of autobiography. The editor (Edith Heal) lists the books chronologically, fifty of them, and gets the poet to discuss their inception. Mrs. Williams, the poet's editor throughout his career, makes additional comments. Throughout this running commentary one can follow the fifty-year search for form which has been Williams' lifelong preoccupation. I would like to conclude by condensing and commenting upon his own findings, after which I will give my evaluation of his achievement.

His earliest influences, he says, are Keats and Whitman. He would rather be a painter than a poet (his mother is an artist) but cannot because of the medical profession. He finds his contemporaries quickly: Wallace Stevens, Marianne Moore, Hilda Doolittle, Ezra Pound. Pound is the only one of these to whom he feels literary loyalty. Stevens tags him with the label "anti-poetic," which Williams resents ever after. (Mrs. Williams, curiously enough, does not understand the poet's rage over this designation.) He abandons rhyme and meter in his second book (1913). While he is writing *Kora*, "Prufrock" appears; Williams says: "I had a violent feeling that Eliot had betrayed what I believed in. He was looking backward; I was looking forward. He was a conformist, with wit, learning which I did not possess . . . But I felt he had rejected America and I refused to be rejected . . . I realized the responsibility I must accept. I knew he would influence all subsequent American poets and take them out of my sphere. I had envisioned a new form of poetic composition, a form for the future. It was a shock to me that he was so tremendously successful; my contemporaries flocked to him—away from what I wanted. It forced me to be successful . . ." He consciously rejects free verse, simultaneously rejecting metered verse. "The greatest problem [he says] was that I didn't know how to divide a poem into what perhaps my lyrical sense wanted." *Paterson* seems to him the answer: he personifies a city and follows its river (the Passaic) and the river-of-history from Paterson down to the sea. Documentary prose breaks the flow of the poetry. Evidently it is the formless form that he has been searching for. In *Paterson, II* he hits upon the step-down form in which all his subsequent poems are written. The line he now refers to as the "variable foot."

What then is the "prosody" of the Williams poem? If we can believe that every good poem ever written in form is good despite the form, and that every formless (free verse) poem that succeeded has succeeded despite its formlessness, then we will be getting close to the idea of Williams' form. It is the purest theory of poetry I have ever heard of and I take it to be the ideal of all poets, formalists or *vers librists*. For meter has nothing to do with it; meter is an aftereffect. Metaphor and simile have nothing to do with it. "The coining of similes is a pastime of very low order, depending as it does upon a merely vegetable coincidence . . ." Structure has nothing to do with it: you cannot remove the parts from the whole; or rather you cannot find the structure. Beautiful language has nothing to do with it any more than the antipoetic. And finally, poetry is a secular art "free from the smears of mystery."

I am not sure I understand all this (assuming I've got it down accurately) but I know in my bones it is right. It is not theory; it is the laborious explanation of an artist stammering out the reasons why his poem came out the way it did. Each poem is its own form, as it must be. The poem is unique and unrepeatable; it is when you repeat that form arises, for form is imitation, as in Eliot, precedent heaped upon precedent. With Williams the poem is raw, quivering, natural, an *objet trouvé*, something you look at twice before you pick it up. It is the extreme of the original, the condition of poetry which frightens off most poets, a complete breakthrough to his own language. It is the kind of poetry which it may take years to see but once seen remakes all other poetry and conceptions of poetry.

But I do not mean that Williams' works are perfection or even that he has written a score or two of poems which will set him beside Milton or Catullus or Marlowe. It is hard to judge such work comparatively; it is too new, too unlike anything else. But there is one sure sign of its value; it has already penetrated the poetry of a whole generation of American poets, not the ones we read month after month in the apple-pie-order journals of letters or the fat anthologies, but in the less-known, less-official magazines and pamphlets strewn over the countryside, which Williams has always lent his hand to. With D. H. Lawrence, Williams is the leader of what authentic American poetry is being written today. Little enough of it is up to his mark, yet the tendency is the right one. The example is there in Williams' poems, not in his criticism. And it is being followed. When I read his poems

I feel I am reading a foreign language, my language. After all, there is practically no American poetry to speak of, and nearly all of it has come in the twentieth century, and a good portion of that has been written by William Carlos Williams.

I call him the true contemporary because he saw the challenge from the beginning and saw it whole: to create American poetry out of nothing, out of that which had never lent itself to poetry before. To do this without betraying the present to the past (like Eliot) and without exploiting the present (like Sandburg) and without trying to force the future (like Pound). I call him the true contemporary also because he could not resist trying to write the Great American Epic. But in Williams' case this can be overlooked: he has written enough true poetry to show the twentieth century that *American* and *poet* are not contradictions in terms.

Dylan Thomas

THE DEATH of Dylan Thomas in 1953 was the cause
of the most singular demonstration of suffering in
modern literary history. One searches his memory in
vain for any parallel to it. At thirty-nine Thomas had
endeared himself to the literary youth of England
and America, to most of the poets who were his contemporaries, and to many who were his elders; he was
the master of a public which he himself had brought
out of nothingness; he was the idol of writers of every
description and the darling of the press. (The Press
scented him early and nosed him to the grave.)
Critics had already told how Thomas became the
first poet who was both popular and obscure. In an
age when poets are supposed to be born old, everyone
looked upon Thomas as the last of the young poets.
When he died, it was as if there would never be any
more youth in the world. Or so it seemed in the
frenzy of his year-long funeral, a funeral which, like
one of Thomas' own poems, turned slowly into a
satanic celebration and a literary institution.

When Yeats and Valéry died, old and wise and

untouchable, there were held, so to speak, the grand state funerals. It was Civilization itself that mourned. When Thomas died, a poet wrote wildly how, to get him up in the morning, he plugged Thomas' mouth with a bottle of beer—"this wonderful baby." All the naughty stories were on everybody's lips; all the wrong things began to be said, and the right things in the wrong way. Someone quoted bitterly: Kill him, he's a poet! and this childishness was the signal for a verbal massacre of the bourgeoisie, reminiscent of the early decades of our century.

The death of a young poet inflicts a psychic wound upon the world and is the cause among poets themselves of frightening babbling and soothsaying. Such doings may be likened to a witches' Sabbath, and some have seen in these morbid celebrations the very coming-to-life of Thomas' poems. It is his death as an occasion for literary and psychological insurrection that must interest us today, if we are to understand the meaning of Thomas' poetry and the significance his contemporaries have given it. It is one thing to analyze and interpret poetry and keep it all in a book; it is another to watch that poetry enter an audience and melt it to a single mind. I want to speak about the second thing, the live thing, the thing that touched the raw nerve of the world and that keeps us singing with pain. The poetry of Thomas is full of the deepest pain; there are few moments of relief. What is the secret of his pain-filled audience? How are we to place Thomas among the famous impersonal poets of our time, when this one is so personal, so intimate and so profoundly grieved? Thomas was the first modern romantic you could put your finger on, the first whose journeys and itineraries became part of his own mythology, the first who offered himself up as

a public, not a private, sacrifice. Hence the piercing
sacrificial note in his poetry, the uncontainable voice,
the drifting, almost ectoplasmic character of the man,
the desperate clinging to a few drifting spars of
literary convention. Hence, too, the universal acclaim
for his lyricism, and the mistaken desire to make him
an heir to Bohemia or to the high Symbolist tradition.

Writers said of Thomas that he was the greatest
lyricist of our time. The saying became a platitude.
It was unquestionably true, but what did the word
mean? It meant that, in contrast to the epic pre-
tensions of many of the leading modern poets, he
was the only one who could be called a singer. To call
him the best lyric poet of our time was to pay him
the highest, the only compliment. Nearly everyone
paid him this splendid compliment and everyone
knew its implications. Few realized, however, that
this compliment marked a turning point in poetry.

During his life there were also the armed camps
who made him honorary revolutionary general; and
we cannot be sure Thomas refused the homemade ep-
aulets of these border patrols. I rather think he was
proud to be taken in. Who were these people? First
there was the remnant of Bohemia. These are people
who exist in the belief that everyone is dead except
themselves. I saw one of these poets lately; he had
just come from England and he informed me casually
that everyone in England is dead. To change the
subject I asked him if he was glad to be home; but
it turned out that everyone in America is also dead.
Among these poets there is a sincere belief in the
death of our world, and it is curious to speculate upon
their adoption of Thomas as a leader and a patron
saint. In the same way nearly all of Thomas' followers
have spoken of him as a Symbolist. The Symbolists

praise the love of death as the highest order of poetic knowledge. "Bohemian" and Symbolist are never far apart.

All the same, this theory of posthumous vitality seems to make sense when we speak of Thomas. How much did Thomas subscribe to official Symbolism? Just enough to provide ammunition for those people. How much did he love death as his major symbol? As much as any poet in the English language. These factions have a claim on Thomas which we cannot contradict.

Thomas is in somewhat the relation to modern poetry that Hopkins was to the Victorians—a lone wolf. Thomas resisted the literary traditionalism of the Eliot school; he wanted no part of it. Poetry to him was not a civilizing maneuver, a replanting of the gardens; it was a holocaust, a sowing of the wind. And we cannot compare Thomas, say, with Auden, because they are different in kind. Thomas' antithesis to Auden, as to Eliot, is significant. Thomas grew up in a generation which had lost every kind of cultural leadership. The poets who began to write during the Depression, which was worse in Wales than in America, were deprived of every traditional ideal. The favorite poem of this generation was Yeats' "The Second Coming." Yeats' poems gave to a generation of prematurely wise young poets an apocalypse, a vision of Antichrist and a vision of the downfall of civilization. The theatricality of the Yeats poem was a great convenience to a poet like Thomas who, having nothing of true philosophical or religious substance to fall back upon, could grasp this straw. The acknowledged precedence of Yeats in modern English literature—in world literature perhaps—has been a makeshift consolation to all modern poets. Yeats, with his cruel forcing of the imagination, his jimmying of the spirit, is a heroic figure in modern poetry. Yet he belongs to the past, with all its claptrap of history and myth. Thomas' poetry was born out of the bankruptcy of the Yeats-Pound-Eliot "tradition" and all it stood for. It was born out of the revulsion against the book-poetry of Auden and the system-mongering of the social revolutionaries. Thomas' poetry was orphaned from the start.

Thomas suffers from the waifishness imposed upon his generation. The so-called Apocalyptic poets, which he was supposed to be a member of, never existed. Nor is he one of the Metaphysical school. One can see that he plays around with copying the superficies of Vaughan and Herbert and Traherne and maybe David ap Gwilym (who in English is not much better than James Whitcomb Riley) and Yeats and Hopkins. But Thomas was outside the orbit of the English poets and maybe the Welsh. He was antitradition by nature, by place, by inclination. Certainly Thomas' grisly love for America can also be seen in this light; America is the untraditional place, the Romantic country *par excellence*.

Thomas' technique is deceptive. When you look at it casually you think it is nothing. The meter is banal. It is no better and no worse than that of dozens of other poets his age. There is no invention and a great deal of imitation. There is no theory. But despite his lack of originality, the impress of Thomas' idiom on present-day English poetry is incalculable. One critic said not many years ago that Thomas had visited a major affliction on English poetry. This was an unfriendly way of saying that Thomas had captured the young poets, which he certainly had. How did he do this? He did it through the force of emotion, with the personal idiom, a twist of the language, bending the iron of English. Once he had bent this iron his way everybody else tried it. Thomas has more imitators today than any other poet in the literature. Whether this excitement will last a year or a hundred years, no one can tell. But it is a real excitement.

Yet even when we examine the texture of his language we fail to find anything original, although we find something completely distinctive. It is hard to locate the distinctiveness of Thomas' idiom. There are a few tricks of word order, a way of using a sentence, a characteristic vocabulary, an obsessive repetition of phrase, and so on—things common to many lesser poets. Again, if we scrutinize his images and metaphors, which are much more impressive than the things I have mentioned, we frequently find overdevelopment, blowziness, and euphemism, on the one hand, and brilliant crystallization on the other. But no system, no poetic, no practice that adds up to anything you can hold on to. The more you examine him as a stylist the less you find.

What does this mean? It means that Thomas is a quite derivative, unoriginal, *unintellectual* poet, the entire force of whose personality and vitality is jammed into his few difficult half-intelligible poems. To talk about Thomas as a Symbolist is dishonest. Not long ago in Hollywood Aldous Huxley introduced a Stravinsky composition based on a poem of Thomas'. Huxley quoted that line of Mallarmé's which says that poets purify the dialect of the tribe. This, said Huxley, was what Thomas did. Now anybody who has read Thomas knows that he did the exact opposite: Thomas did everything in his power to obscure the dialect of the tribe—whatever that high-and-mighty expression may mean. Thomas sometimes attempted to keep people from understanding his poems (which are frequently simple, once you know the dodges). He had a horror of simplicity—or what I consider to be a fear of it. He knew little except what a man knows who has lived about forty years, and there was little he wanted to know. There is a fatal pessimism in most of his poems, offset by a few bursts of joy and exuberance. The main symbol is masculine love, driven as hard as Freud drove it. In the background is God, hard to identify but always there, a kind of God who belongs to one's parents rather than to the children, who do not quite accept Him.

I went through the *Collected Poems* recently to decide which poems I would keep if I were editing the best poems of Dylan Thomas. Out of about ninety poems I chose more than thirty which I think stand with the best poems of our time. If this seems a small number, we should remember that there are not many more poems upon which the fame of Hopkins rests; of Rimbaud; or, for that matter, of John Donne. And yet we expect a greater volume of work from such an exuberant man. Thomas' sixty poems that I would exclude are short of his mark, but they are not failures. I would like to name by name those poems which I think belong to the permanent body of our poetry— or most of them anyway: "I see the boys of summer"; "A process in the weather of the heart"; "The force that through the green fuse drives the flower"; "Especially when the October wind"; "When, like a running grave"; "Light breaks where no sun shines"; "Do you not father me"; "A grief ago"; "And death shall have no dominion"; "Then was my neophyte"; "When all my five and country senses see"; "We lying by sea-sand"; "It is the sinners' dust-tongued bell"; "After the funeral"; "Not from this anger"; "How shall my animal"; "Twenty-four years"; "A Refusal to Mourn"; "Poem in October"; "The Hunchback in the Park"; "Into her Lying Down Head"; "Do not go gentle"; "A Winter's Tale"; "On the Marriage of a Virgin"; "When

I woke"; "Among those Killed in the Dawn Raid"; "Fern Hill"; "In country sleep"; "Over Sir John's hill"; and "Poem on his birthday." I leave out the sonnets, which I think are forced, and the "Ballad of the Long-legged Bait," and the "Prologue," and many others. My list is probably off here and there, but I think it is the substantial list of works by which Thomas will be remembered.

The "major" poems, that is, the more pretentious poems, such as the ten sonnets (called "Altarwise by owl-light"), reveal most of what we know of Thomas' convictions and what we can call his philosophy. He believed in God and Christ; the Fall and death, the end of all things and the day of eternity. This is very conventional religion and Thomas was uncritical about it. Add to this the puritanism which runs through his whole work, and, finally, the forced optimism in the last poems such as "In country sleep," in which, although the whole sequence is unfinished, there is a recognizable affirmation of faith in life. But one feels that these matters are not of paramount importance in the poetry of Thomas. Thomas was not interested in philosophical answers. Religion, such as he knew it, was direct and natural; the symbolism of religion, as he uses it, is poetry, direct knowledge. Religion is not to be used: it is simply part of life, part of himself; it is like a tree; take it or leave it, it is there. In this sense, one might say that Thomas is more "religious" than Eliot, because Thomas has a natural religious approach to nature and to himself. The language of Thomas, not the style, is very close to that of Hopkins, not only in obvious ways, but in its very method. Hopkins, however, arrived at his method philosophically, abstractly, as well as through temperament and neurosis. Thomas, with no equipment for theorizing about the forms of nature, sought the "forms" that

Hopkins did. The chief difference between the two poets in terms of their symbols is that Hopkins draws his symbology almost entirely from the God-symbol. God, in various attributes, is the chief process in Hopkins' view of the world. Sex is the chief process in Thomas' view of the world.

Thomas' idea of process is important. The term itself is rather mechanistic, as he uses it. He always takes the machine of energy rather than some abstraction, such as spirit or essence. Hence the concreteness of his words and images; obscurity occurs also because of the "process" of mixing the imagery of the subconscious with biological imagery, as in Hopkins. But there is also a deliberate attempt to involve the subconscious as the main process: Thomas' imagination, which is sometimes fantastic, works hard to dredge up the images of fantasy and dreams. Very often the process fails and we are left with heaps of grotesque images that add up to nothing. I would equate the process in Thomas' poetics with his rather startling views of the sexual process. Aside from those poems in which sex is simply sung, much as poets used to write what are called love poems, there are those poems in which sex is used as the instrument of belief and knowledge. Using the cliché of modern literature that everyone is sick and the whole world is a hospital, Thomas wants to imply that sex will make us (or usually just him) healthy and whole again. And there are suggestions of Druidism (perhaps) and primitive fertility rites, apparently still extant in Wales, all mixed up with Henry Miller, Freud, and American street slang. But sex kills also, as Thomas says a thousand times, and he is not sure of the patient's recovery. In place of love, about which Thomas is almost always profoundly bitter, there is sex, the instrument and the physical process of love. The activ-

ity of sex, Thomas hopes in his poems, will somehow
lead to love in life and in the cosmos. As he grows
older, love recedes and sex becomes a nightmare, a
Black Mass.

Thomas moves between sexual revulsion and sexual
ecstasy, between puritanism and mysticism, between
formalistic ritual (this accounts for his lack of invention) and vagueness. In his book one comes, on
one page, upon a poem of comparative peace and
lucidity, and on the next page upon a poem of absolute density and darkness. His dissatisfaction with his
own lack of stability is reflected in his devices which
tend to obscure even the simple poems; he leaves out
all indications of explanation—quotation marks, punctuation, titles, connectives, whether logical or grammatical. In addition he uses every extreme device of
ambiguity one can think of, from reversing the terms
of a figure of speech to ellipsis to overelaboration of
images. There is no poetic behind these practices—
only catch-as-catch-can technique. One is always confused in Thomas by not knowing whether he is using
the microscope or the telescope; he switches from one
to the other with ease and without warning. It is significant that his joyous poems, which are few, though
among his best, are nearly always his simplest. Where
the dominant theme of despair obtrudes, the language
dives down into the depths; some of these complex
poems are among the most rewarding, the richest in
feeling, and the most difficult to hold to. But, beyond
question, there are two minds working in Thomas, the
joyous, naturally religious mind, and the disturbed,
almost pathological mind of the cultural fugitive or
clown. On every level of Thomas' work one notices the
lack of sophistication and the split in temperament.
This is his strength as well as his weakness. But it is
a grave weakness because it leaves him without de-

fense, without a bridge between himself and the world.

Thomas begins in a blind alley with the obsessive statement that birth is the beginning of death, the basic poetic statement, but one which is meaningless unless the poet can build a world between. Thomas never really departs from this statement, and his obsession with sex is only the clinical restatement of the same theme. The idealization of love, the traditional solution with most poets, good and bad, is never arrived at in Thomas. He skips into the foreign land of love and skips out again. And he is too good a poet to fake love. He doesn't feel it; he distrusts it; he doesn't believe it. He falls back on the love-process, the assault, the defeat, the shame, the despair. Over and over again he repeats the ritualistic formulas for love, always doubting its success. The process is despised because it doesn't really work. The brief introduction to the *Collected Poems* sounds a note of bravado which asserts that his poems "are written for the love of Man and in praise of God." One wishes they were; one is grateful for, and slightly surprised by, the acknowledgment to God and Man, for in the poems we find neither faith nor humanism. What we find is something that fits Thomas into the age: the satanism, the vomitous horror, the self-elected crucifixion of the artist.

In the last few years of his life Thomas was beginning to find an audience. No one, I think, was more taken aback than he at this phenomenon, because most of the poems which the audience liked had been in books for five or ten years already. Thomas was the one modern poet who by his *presence* created an audience. His audience was the impossible one: a general audience for a barely understandable poet. His way of meeting this audience, at the end, was no solution for Thomas as a poet. He became a dramatist, a writer of scenarios, a producer. What he wrote in this phase was not negligible by any means; but it was probably not what he wanted and not what his audience wanted. His audience wanted the poetry; they wanted the agony of the process.

The frenzy that attended Dylan Thomas' death was a frenzy of frustration. Many times, in his stories and letters and his talk, Thomas tried to leap over this frustration into a Rabelaisian faith; but it never rang true enough. After the gaiety came the hangover, the horrible fundamentalist remorse. Yet through the obscurity of the poetry everyone could feel the scream of desperation: not a cry of desire; on the contrary, it was the opposite; it was the cry of the trapped animal; the thing wanting to be man; the man wanting to be spirit.

He is a self-limiting poet and an exasperating one. He runs beyond your reach after he has beckoned you to follow; he arouses you and then slumps into a heap. He knows, more than his readers, that he has no bridge between life and death, between self and the world. His poetry is absolutely literal (as he himself insisted all the time). But its literalness is the challenge to literature which is always significant. He is too honest to rhapsodize or to intone over the great symbols; rather he growls or rages or more often hypnotizes himself by the minute object, which he is likely to crush in his anger. Unlike Hopkins, he has no vision of nature and cannot break open the forms of nature; he cannot break open words. He focuses madly on the object, but it will not yield. He calls a weathercock a bow-and-arrow bird. Metaphor won't come and he resorts to riddle, the opposite of metaphor. A good half of his poetry is the poetry of rage; not rage at the world of society or politics or art or anything except self. He is impatient for a method and the impatience early turns into desperation, the desperation into clowning. He is another naïf, like Rimbaud, a countryman, who having left the country wanders over the face of the earth seeking a vision. He is running away from his fame, which he does not feel equal to. He is running away from the vision of self, or keeping the integrity of self by fleeing from the foci of tradition. I interpret the life and work of Thomas this way: the young poet of natural genius and expansive personality who recoils from the ritual of literary tradition and who feels himself drawn into it as into a den of iniquity. This is both the puritanism and the wisdom of Thomas. Such a man can never acquire the polish of the world which is called worldliness, and he turns to the only form of behavior, literary and otherwise, permissible both to society and to self. That is buffoonery. All the literary world loves a buffoon: the French make a saint of the clown. But folklore has it that the clown dies in the dressing room.

It is the most certain mark of Thomas' genius that he did not give way to any vision but his own, the one authentic source of knowledge he had—himself. And it is the most certain mark of his weakness that he could not shield himself from the various literary preceptors who buzzed around him. He became immobile, I think, out of pure fright. He wrote personal letters (which are now being published) apparently meant for publication, in which he adopted the modern clichés about modern life. He pretended to be horrified by the electric toaster, or maybe he really was.

The doctrinaire impersonality of our poetry demands allegiance to a Tradition, any tradition, even one you rig up for yourself. Thomas represents the extreme narrowness of the individual genius, the basic animal (one of his favorite symbols) in man. The animal to Thomas is everything and we listen because he calls it animal, not spirit or essence or potentiality or something else. It is the authentic symbol for a poet who believes in the greatness of the individual and the sacredness of the masses. It is Whitman's symbol when he says he thinks he could turn and live with animals, because they are natural and belong to nature and do not try to turn nature out of its course. They do not try to believe anything contrary to their condition.

But Thomas is drawn away from his animal; he becomes brute. And this he knows. In the brute phase of his poetry (which is the phase loved by the modernists who picked up his scent) the poetry is a relentless cutting down to the quick—surgery, butchery, and worse. And as Thomas is the one and only subject of his poems, we know what is being destroyed.

It is some of the saddest poetry we have. It leaves us finally with grief. The pathos of Thomas is that he is not diabolical, not mystical, not possessed; he has not the expansive imagination of Blake nor even the fanatical self-control of Yeats. He is the poet of genius unable to face life. Like D. H. Lawrence he is always hurling himself back into childhood and the childhood of the world. Everyone speaks of Thomas as a child. He became a child.

It is easy to dismiss him but he will not be dismissed. He was a tremendous talent who stung himself into insensibility because he could not face the obligations of intellectual life, which he mistakenly felt he must. He could not take the consequences of his own natural beliefs; and he could not temporize; there was no transition, no growth, only the two states of natural joy and intellectual despair, love of trees and fascination of the brute process. He said everything he had to say: it had little to do with wars and cities and art galleries. What he said was that man is a child thrust into the power of self, an animal becoming an angel. But becoming an angel he becomes more a beast. There is no peace, no rest, and death itself is only another kind of disgusting sex.

But something happened to his poems. Somehow the spark escaped; it leapt out of the hands of literature and set a fire. Thomas, I think, did the impossible in modern poetry. He made a jump to an audience which, we have been taught to believe, does not exist. It is an audience that understands him even when they cannot understand his poetry. It is probably the first nonfunereal poetry audience in fifty years, an audience that had been deprived of poetry by fiat. Thomas' audience bears certain characteristics of the mob—but that, under the circumstances, is also understandable. The audience understands Thomas instinctively. They know he is reaching out to them but cannot quite effect the meeting. The reaching ends in a tantalizing excitement, a frenzy. It is not a literary frenzy, the kind that ends in a riot with the police defending Edith Sitwell after a reading of *Façade*. On the contrary, it is the muttering of awakening, a slow realization about poetry, a totally unexpected apocalypse. This audience sees Thomas as a male Edna St. Vincent Millay, or perhaps a Charlie Chaplin; they hear the extraordinary vibrato, a voice of elation and anguish singing over their heads. They know it is acting. They know this is poetry and they know it is for them.

He is like the old cliché of vaudeville in which a tragicomic figure engaged in some private act (such as keeping his pants from falling down) wanders onto a stage where a highly formal cultural something is in progress. Naturally the embarrassed clown steals the show. One must remember Thomas' own story about himself in which he gets his finger stuck in a beer bottle. He goes from place to place, beer bottle and all, meeting new people. The beer bottle becomes Thomas' symbol of his natural self: it is his passport from the common people to the literary life, and back again. It is both his symbol of self and his symbol of other-self. But to Thomas it is mainly a horror symbol. It is the key to No Man's Land. Because Thomas is an uncivilizable Puritan and a hard-shell fundamentalist of some undefinable kind, the puritanism sets up the tension in his poetry—a tension based upon love and fear of love: the basic sexual tension, the basic theological tension. The greatness of Thomas is that he recognizes the equation; and the weakness of Thomas is that he takes to his heels when he has to grapple with it.

Everything I have said can be said better in the little poem by Thomas that takes nine lines. The last line of the poem is so much like a line of Whitman's that I have searched through Whitman's poems to find it. I am sure it is there and yet I know it isn't. The line reads "I advance for as long as forever is."

> Twenty-four years remind the tears of my eyes.
> (Bury the dead for fear that they walk to the grave
>   in labor)
> In the groin of the natural doorway I crouched like
>   a tailor
> Sewing a shroud for a journey
> By the light of the meat-eating sun.
> Dressed to die, the sensual strut begun,
> With my red veins full of money,
> In the final direction of the elementary town
> I advance for as long as forever is.

The First White Aboriginal

D. H. LAWRENCE has more in common with Walt Whitman than any other man has, and it was Lawrence who called Whitman the first white aboriginal. Coming from Lawrence, the epithet was the highest praise. Lawrence's quest was for the aboriginal, the pure energy of the soul. Being an Englishman, he fled from the white man and his white religions and the terrible whiteness of consciousness (which he called mentality) and raced with all his strength to the dark races and beyond, to the blood religions, the spirit of the serpent, and all that. Lawrence made a magnificent leap across civilization into the aboriginal darkness. He is one of the supreme heretics of white, modern civilization. And so for him to bless Walt with the title of the first white aboriginal is a matter of tremendous import. Lawrence is one of the great spirits of our age, as Whitman is, although from Lawrence stems a good deal of the negativity of modern creative life. From Whitman stems much of what there is of the opposite. Lawrence sprang from a modern industrial hell which he never forgave and was never far enough away from to understand. Whitman did not have to spring; he sprouted, he vegetated, he loafed out of nowhere into the role of prophet and seer. At a single stroke, apparently without preparation, he became the one poet of America and Democracy. He is the one mystical writer of any consequence America has produced; the most original religious thinker we have; the poet of the greatest achievement; the first profound innovator; the most accomplished artist as well (but nobody says this nowadays). Yet in the twentieth century Walt Whitman is almost completely shunned by his fellows. He has no audience, neither a general audience nor a literary clique. Official criticism ignores him completely; modern Classicism, as it calls itself, acknowledges him with embarrassment. (Ezra Pound "forgives" Whitman because he "broke the new wood," meaning he broke iambic pentameter). And modern scholars, happily confused by the scholarly complexities of contemporary poets, look upon Walt as a grand failure and an anachronism or a bit of Americana, the prow of a clipper ship, perhaps.

Lawrence, in his search around the world for a pure well of human energy, acknowledged Whitman with love. It is a rare thing for Lawrence. He says:

Whitman, the great poet, has meant so much to me. Whitman the one man breaking the way ahead. Whitman, the one pioneer. And only Whitman. No English pioneers [says Lawrence], no French. No European pioneer-poets. In Europe the would-be pioneers are mere innovators. The same in America. Ahead of Whitman, nothing. Ahead of all poets, pioneering into the wilderness of unopened life, Whitman. Beyond him, none. His wide, strange camp at the end of the high-road. And lots of new little poets camping on Whitman's camping ground now. But none going really beyond. . . .

But at this point Lawrence changes his tune and explains how Whitman failed. He says that Whitman fell into the old fallacy of Christian love, confusing his great doctrine of Sympathy with Love and Merging. Nothing was more loathsome to the puritanical Lawrence than Merging, and when Whitman merged Lawrence disgorged. How Lawrence longed to merge! And how the mere shake of the hand horrified him! Lawrence in thousands of passages obsessively records his taboo against touching. *Noli me tangere!* It is the opposite of Whitman's obsession *for* touching:

Is this then a touch? quivering me to a new identity,
Flames and ether making a rush for my veins,
Treacherous tip of me reaching and crowding to help
    them,
My flesh and blood playing out lightning to strike
    what is hardly different from myself,
On all sides prurient provokers stiffening my limbs,
Straining the udder of my heart for its withheld drip,
Behaving licentious toward me, taking no denial,
Depriving me of my best as for a purpose,
Unbuttoning my clothes, holding me by the bare
    waist. . . .

(This is the passage in "Song of Myself" which, after a parenthesis, "What is less or more than a touch?" leads into "I think I could turn and live with animals, they are so placid and self-contained, I stand and look at them long and long. . ."—one of the greatest moments of poetry.)

Lawrence, with his deep love of animals and his irritable suspicion of mankind, was the inferior of Whitman. Whitman had the natural love of man which Lawrence, rightly, called American. Lawrence was fascinated, hypnotized, and slightly sick in the stomach. Lawrence says if Walt had known about Charlie Chaplin he would have assumed one identity with him too. What a pity, Lawrence sneers. He'd have done poems, paeans and what not, Chants, Songs of

Cinematernity. "Oh, Charlie, my Charlie, another film is done—"

But in the end Lawrence gives in; he knows a kindred spirit when he sees one. He looks down his nose at Whitman's paeans upon Death—Lawrence, who is one of the true poets of Death—and then adds:

> But the exultance of the message remains. Purified of merging, purified of Myself, the exultant message of American Democracy, of souls in the Open Road, full of glad recognition, full of fierce readiness, full of joy of worship, when one soul sees a greater soul.—The only riches, the great souls.

That is the last line of Lawrence's book called *Studies in Classic American Literature*, and I submit that it is a fine concession to be wrung from Lawrence, the archetype of tortured modern man, the man without heroes. Lawrence and Whitman are two modern poets with the deepest concern for mankind, the furthest insight, the widest sympathy, the simplest and best expression. They are scriptural writers in the long run, despising professionalism and literary fashion. But Lawrence fails to do more than pose the problem of modern civilization versus the individual intelligence. He has no answer. He half invents fascism; he is torn between the image of the free natural male (the father who is always leaving home to become a Gypsy) and the image of the leader, the aristocrat. He had it both ways: he remains unresolved. But he also had the vision. He became, in effect, an American, an American among Red Indians and rattlesnakes, close to that darker America betrayed by the white religions, Mexico, which he also loved. But it was Whitman's America that he held out for, "the true democracy [as Lawrence said] where soul meets soul, in the open road. Democracy. American Democracy where all journey down the open

road. And where a soul is known at once in its going."
Strange words coming from the author of *Kangaroo*
and *The Plumed Serpent*.

Lawrence suffers somewhat the fate of Whitman
today. He is declassed. He enjoys a kind of underground popularity among writers, but he is outside
the pale of the Tradition. He is too violent, too special,
too original. And he is too outspoken. But Lawrence
could never survive within a tradition, any more than
Whitman. And he has, at his best, a style so lean, it
matches the burnt-away clean language of prophets.
Most of Lawrence's disciples, it seems to me, misun-
derstand him; but at least he has disciples. Whitman
has no disciples and practically no living literary reputation. He is only a name.

What has happened to Whitman in the century
since *Leaves of Grass* was published? There were the
usual false praises and the usual false deprecations,
and enough of the true acclaim to give us a little faith
in criticism. There has never been anything we could
call popularity for Whitman. Publishers are inclined
to prepare elaborate editions of *Leaves of Grass*, in
the same way that they release erotic editions of The
Song of Songs: in a wrong-headed way it is a compliment to Whitman. But the best minds of the present
century have not closed with Whitman, in my opinion.
And the leading poets of the twentieth century have
coolly and with relentless deliberation suppressed
Whitman and kept him from exerting his force. Any
Whitman advocate of great talent, for example Hart
Crane, is forced to apologize for this allegiance before
he is admitted to the company of Moderns. There is no
question that an Act of Exclusion has been in perpetual operation against Whitman since 1855 and is
carried on today by the leading "Classicists" of English and American poetry. Walt just won't do. He is
vulgar; he is a humbug; he copies the names of rivers

out of the sixth-grade geography book; he is an optimist; he is unlettered; he is a theosophist; he abhors institutions; he is auto-erotic; he loves everybody; he is a Rotarian; he goes to the opera; he can't distinguish between good and evil; he has no sense of humor; he cannot solve his own paradox about the greatness of the individual and the greatness of the En-Masse; he has no style—etc., etc.

All such accusations are true, and one could multiply them for pages and pages. Yet in the last analysis, they do not matter. Emerson saw a little humor in Whitman, though he called it wit. But Whitman thought he was writing a kind of bible! And it is the biblical quality of Whitman (as with Lawrence) that is so offensive to lovers of Literature. What insolence! they say, and they are right. For neither Whitman nor Lawrence were "writers"; they were prophets. Literature makes it its business to stone prophets.

Whitman is indeed full of humbug, as when he talks about his experiences as a wound dresser:

> One night in the gloomiest period of the War, in the Patent Office Hospital in Washington city, as I stood by the bedside of a Pennsylvania soldier, who lay, conscious of quick approaching death, yet perfectly calm, and with noble, spiritual manner, the veteran surgeon, turning aside, said to me, that though he had witnessed many, many deaths of soldiers, and had been a worker at Bull Run, Antietam, Fredericksburg, etc., he had not seen yet the first case of a man or boy that met the approach of dissolution with cowardly qualms or terror. . . . Grand common stock! to me the accomplished and convincing growth, prophetic of the future; proof . . . of perfect beauty, tenderness and pluck, that never feudal lord, nor Greek, nor Roman breed, yet rivalled. Let no tongue ever speak disparagement of the American races, north or south. . . .

This sounds like Winston Churchill at his worst.

Whitman is not a complicated case of poor manners, confusions and paradoxes; of philosophical muddle and literary naïveté; of good intentions, high passages and bad dreary bogs. He is the one and only poet of America who has ever attempted to adumbrate the meaning of America. The twentieth-century American poet avoids this commitment, by and large: he considers it fitting and proper to take refuge in History against the horrors of progress; or in pure dialectic; or in the catacombs of established faith; or, failing that, in what is called the Language. Whitman's vision has degenerated into a thing called the Language; that is, the American Language, the natural nonhieratic language out of which a mythos might germinate. But Whitman contended that the mythos was at hand. He defined it; he sang it; he argued it; he poured it out. To no avail.

Twentieth-century poetry is a poetry of perfections. It is the least spontaneous poetry since—whatever date for the birth of artificiality you call to mind. It is the pride of twentieth-century poetry that even Yeats was brought to heel by critics who called for a "hard brittle technique." It is the pride of twentieth-century poetry that one publishes a poem once a decade. It is the boast of our poetry that it is impersonal, and that it can mean more or less what you think it means, and be right in the bargain. All of which is "traditional." Whitman and Lawrence were death to Tradition. Yet Whitman did not repudiate the past; nor did he look with any unctuousness upon the present, the America of a hundred years ago.

Never was there . . . more hollowness at heart than at present, and here in the United States. Genuine belief seems to have left us. The underlying principles of the States are not honestly believed in . . . The spectacle is

appalling. We live in an atmosphere of hypocrisy throughout. The men believe not in the women nor the women in
the men. A scornful superciliousness rules in literature.
The aim of all the literateurs is to find something to make
fun of. A lot of churches, sects, etc., the most dismal phan-
tasms I know, usurp the name of religion . . . The depravity of the business classes of our country is not less
than has been supposed, but infinitely greater. The official
services of America, national, state, and municipal, in
all their branches and departments, except the judiciary are saturated in corruption, bribery, falsehood, mal-
administration; and the judiciary is tainted. . . . In
business, (this all-devouring modern word, business), the
one sole object is, by any means, pecuniary gain. . . . I
say that our New World democracy . . . is, so far, an almost complete failure in its social aspects, and in really
grand religious, moral, literary, and esthetic results. . .

Whitman sees the corruption and persists in his
faith that the principle of democracy will overrule the
corrupt. Let us call it the romantic position. But Whitman (like Jefferson) does not feel that the written
word of democratic principle is sacrosanct. He goes
to the heart of the matter. Man must do good, he says,
because that is his ultimate nature. The man who falls
a prey to corruption, dandyism, superficiality, selfish-
ness, is a fallen man. Whitman despises him. He believes it natural to be pure: nature purifies. He has a
kind of worship of chemistry, shared by his country-
men, an animal faith in the god of the sun, and the
god of water. It is precisely his contempt for ideas of
sin and evil which places him among the great teachers of mankind.

What chemistry!
That the winds are really not infectious,
That this is no cheat, this transparent green-wash of
the sea which is so amorous after me,

That it is safe to allow it to lick my naked body all
    over with its tongues,
That it will not endanger me with the fevers that
    have deposited themselves in it,
That it is all clean forever and ever,
That the cool drink from the well tastes so good,
That blackberries are so flavorous and juicy. . . .
That when I recline on the grass I do not catch any
    disease . . .

He did not have a simple faith in the frontiers of
"science"; on the contrary, he held a limited belief in
physical achievements.

Not to you alone, proud truths of the world,
Nor to you alone, ye facts of modern science,
But myths and fables of eld, Asia's, Africa's
    fables,
The far-darting beams of the spirit, the unloosed
    dreams,
The deep diving bibles and legends
. . . You too with joy I sing.

America to Whitman was not a laboratory, but a place
in the journey of mankind where the best in man
might flower. America was not the goal; it was a
bridge to the goal. In "Passage to India" he says of
Columbus:

Ah Genoese thy dream! thy dream!
Centuries after thou art laid in thy grave,
The shore thou foundest verifies thy dream.

But the dream is not satisfying enough. We must steer
for the deepest waters and take passage to the skies
themselves. We must go where mariner has not yet
dared to go, risking the ship, ourselves and all. It is
not a geographical poem or a historical poem, much
less a "war poem," although when Whitman talks
about the Atlantic cable and its eloquent gentle wires,

he sounds silly enough. But the physical achievement is his symbol of, not progress but goodness! It is axiomatic to Whitman that we shall lay cables, build the Union Pacific Railroad, and fly airships to Jupiter. That is the childlike and wonderful faith of the ordinary modern man who is not thrown into reverse by the terror of it all. Whitman is not even talking about that. It is the twentieth-century "classical" poet who is materialistic and who writes scathing books of poems against the electric toaster. For Whitman says in the same poem that the seas are already crossed, weathered the capes, the voyage done. Everything is already known. The advancement of man physically seems to him good but only a trifle. What really concerns him is that man shall explore the soul.

Passage indeed O soul to primal thought, . . .
Back, back to wisdom's birth, to innocent intuitions,
Again with fair creation.

Whitman is a mystic and he admits it. This is one more reason for his unpopularity. The best modern poets are allowed to admire the mystic but aren't allowed to be one. Whitman is too close for comfort. Furthermore, he has no theology worth sorting out, except a kind of Quakerism, and religion isn't his concern. Man is his concern. And not American man. Whitman is not only the first white aboriginal; he is the first American; or that may be the same thing. When I read Whitman, good or bad, I always feel that here is first and foremost an American. The fundamental religiosity of Whitman plus the contempt for religion is American.

Whitman dissociated himself from mere poets and other writers. Who touches his book touches a man and men of all faiths.

I do not despise you priests, all time, the world over,
My faith is the greatest of faiths and the least of
faiths,
Enclosing worship ancient and modern and all between ancient and modern,
Believing I shall come again upon the earth after five
thousand years,
Waiting responses from oracles, honoring the gods,
saluting the sun,
. . . Helping the lama or brahmin as he trims the
lamps of the idols,
Dancing yet through the streets in a phallic proces-
sion, rapt and austere . . .

and so on, down to the Mississippi Baptists with the
jerks and spasms.

Whitman is too faithful in his belief in man to lay
down the rules for a creed. It is unnecessary. If man
is of Nature, and Nature is good, good will triumph.
Evil is the failure of man to be as good as he can. For
man to become all that is utterly possible is divine.
And as every man is divine, inside and out, even the
lowest are divinities. What is commonly looked down
on nowadays in Whitman's talk about the divine
average, is the average. Whitman emphasized the
divine, rather than the average. Each person to him
possessed divinity, and to repudiate that divinity was
criminal. It is the god in each man and woman (which
Lawrence called the Holy Ghost) that we can communicate with. I have *rapport* with you (Whitman's
hieratic terminology is always couched in some kind
of American French)—I have rapport with you because my divinity has a mouth to speak with. My
lower self cannot speak; it can only commit acts of
instinct. Yet there is a hierarchy of acts. Each thing
to its nature:

The moth eggs are in their place.
The bright suns I see and the dark suns I cannot
see are in their place,
The palpable is in its place and the impalpable is in
its place.

And Whitman says he is not stuck up and is in his place. Being "in place," of course, is not humility; nor is it a sign of any known orthodoxy.

Whitman asserts his divinity and he cannot evade it, despite a passing show of humility. He has the vision of himself as well in the scale of things. But he acknowledges the god in oneself—and here he makes a break with conventional poetry and conventional thought which is the core of his philosophy.

Divine am I inside and out, and I make holy whatever
I touch or am touched from.

It is Whitman's creed of the equality of the body and the soul. The body is not cursed; it is the miraculous materialization of the soul. The origin of this body-soul Whitman does not explain; he merely states that it is holy and the holy of holies. If he can find an object of worship more worthy than another it shall be his body or a part of his body. And while he is doting on himself he slips without warning into sun worship, nature worship, love worship, and then back to himself.

If I worship one thing more than another it shall be
the spread of my own body, or any part of it,
Translucent mould of me it shall be you!
Shaded ledges and rests it shall be you!
Firm masculine colter it shall be you!
Whatever goes to the tilth of me it shall be you!
You my rich blood! your milky stream pale strippings
of my life!

Breast that presses against other breasts it shall be
    you!
My brain it shall be your occult convolutions!
Root of washed sweet-flag!
Timorous pond-snipe! nest of guarded duplicate eggs!
    it shall be you!
Mixed tusseled hay of head, beard, brawn, it shall be
    you! Trickling sap of maple, fibre of manly wheat,
    it shall be you!
Sun so generous it shall be you
Vapors lighting and shading my face, it shall be you!
You sweaty brooks and dews it shall be you!
Winds whose soft-tickling genitals rub against me it
    shall be you!
Broad muscular fields branches of live oak, loving
    lounger in my winding paths, it shall be you,
Hands I have taken, face I have kissed, mortal I have
    ever touched, it shall be you.
I dote on myself, there is that lot of me and all so
    luscious. . . .

He begins with his own corpus, which he finds so
luscious; he forgets himself and begins looking around
the park, then he recalls the amorous uses of parks;
and after a breath, he comes back to himself and "the
lot of him." If you read on and on you see that Whitman is not talking about himself at all and acting like
a baby discovering its toes—but that is the superficial
trick of it; he is talking about the primal discovery of
self. He is talking about consciousness in the only way
it can be talked about: physically. I do not think for
a second that Whitman was either narcissistic or ego-
maniac; he was trying to obliterate the fatal dualism
of body and soul. All his monotony about keeping as
clean around the bowels ("delicate" was the word he
used) as around the heart and head is not a swipe at
Victorian convention; it was his way of acknowledging
the physicality of the soul, or the spirituality of the

body. Lawrence shied away; and most American writers in more or less the same Puritan tub get the backwash of revulsion from this physical "obsession" of Whitman's.

But this is only the beginning. Whitman wanted to create the full individual *in order to put this free man into the world*. The dialectical conflict in Whitman, as in everyone else I suppose, is the free individual versus the crowd of mankind. The twentieth-century poet slinks into his study and says, No crowds for me. But Whitman took it on. He is the only modern poet who has the courage to meet the crowd. And falling back into his demotic French he delivers the abstraction En-Masse. "Endless unfolding of words of ages! And mine a word of the modern, the word En-Masse." This becomes one of the most ridiculed passages in Whitman, in which he drunkenly chants: "Hurrah for positive science! long live exact demonstration!" and "Gentlemen, to you the first honors always!" But these funny passages of Whitman are there, not because he is a fool, but because he has the courage of his convictions. For just after this idiotic hurrahing for exact demonstration comes another of the great bursts of poetry, the one beginning "Walt Whitman am I, a kosmos, of mighty Manhattan the son, /Turbulent, fleshy, sensual, eating, drinking, and breeding. . . ." (Whitman is always aware of the comic possibilities of his position, like many prophets.) The balanced man, the free man, the man who meets his potentiality is a fit man for the new world, the democracy he envisions. "The purpose of democracy," says Whitman in prose, "is, through many transmigrations, and amid endless ridicules, arguments, and ostensible failures, to illustrate, at all hazards, this doctrine or theory that man, properly trained in sanest highest freedom, may and must become a law, and series of laws, unto himself, surrounding and providing for, not only his own personal control, but all his relations to other individuals, and to the State; and this as matters now stand in the civilized world, is the only scheme worth working from, as warranting results like those of Nature's laws, reliable . . . to carry on themselves."

The concept of En-Masse is not absurd and not laughable, as other expressions of his certainly are, such as Democracy, Ma Femme. But even Whitman's tendency to view Democracy as feminine is penetrating. Whitman was the first great American feminist.

A great poet is not merely a poet of his nation but a poet of all peoples. Whitman, who had little enough reward for his book, and has little enough today, looked beyond literature and beyond the greatness of art. His true personality went out beyond America, beyond religions and even beyond mankind. His poems about the self and the mass of America were written before the Civil War, but the war between the North and South brought everything home to Whitman. His vision might well have been destroyed, but with his natural passion for unity he embarked on a new discovery, not of the body and soul, or rapport, or the En-Masse, but of the exploration of Death. Whitman had always believed in Death as the purposeful continuity of existence, but he had had no significant experience of it. One can barely imagine what the Civil War was to Whitman, this fanatically intense American, this New World man, the first white aboriginal, with his lusty physical joy of life, his love of comrades, his genius for poetry, and his natural mysticism. Whitman was stricken by the war but he was recreated by it. Columbus had been a rather nebulous hero; Lincoln was the reincarnation of the American god to him. Half of Whitman's great poetry is war poetry and poetry on Lincoln and his death, and death

poetry, though it cannot all be dated from the war.
Whitman accepted death as he did sex and otherness,
self and not-self. The war returned to him the partic-
ularity of death, and it produced in him not bitterness
but love. He triumphed over it. He saw beyond history and beyond America. But what he saw was with
the American vision. In Whitman's dialectic, you do
not give up the past for the vision: the past is of the
vision as much as the future. In the open air "a great
personal deed has room" and it is such a deed that
seizes upon the hearts of the whole race of man. And
this deed is not discovery or triumph or a formula of
belief: it is the giving oneself—the Whitman in oneself—to the other, the comrade. Whitman knew that
giving in the past had always been a form of taxation
and protection. This new kind of giving is reckless and
mystical, differing from the old giving because Whitman gives body and soul without sacrificing one to the
other. Whitman is no "humanist" and no ordinary
libertarian but a seer who dreams of free individuality
in a world of free souls. The open road may be a commonplace symbol, but it is a deliberate symbol, and it
stands for an actuality. That actuality is America as
Whitman sees America in himself. The anti-Whitman
party of our time attempts, of course, to deny the
vision of the New World with its physical materialism,
experimentalism, and the whole concept of man for
the world of the present. It turns out that Whitman is
not for the "people" and not for the impressively
learned poets of our time. He is for man who begins
at the beginning—all over again. There is more to
poetry than books, he says.

> I think heroic deeds were all conceived in the open
> air, and all free poems also,
> I think I could stop here myself and do miracles. . .

Here a great personal deed has room. . .
Here is realization . . . here is adhesiveness. . .
Do you know what it is as you pass to be loved by
strangers? . . .
These are the days that must happen to you:
You shall not heap up what is called riches. . .
What beckonings of love you receive you shall only
answer with passionate kisses of parting,
You shall not allow the hold of those who spread
their reach'd hands toward you. . .
Allons! after the great companions, and to belong to
them!
They too are on the road—they are the swift and
majestic men
They are the greatest women. . .
They go, they go! I know that they go, but I know
not where they go,
But I know that they go toward the best—toward
something great. . ."

It is all there: the greatness of the body and the greatness of the soul; the touching of the world and the
heroism of departure; the magnificent motion of death;
the expanding cycle of consciousness; the essential
holiness of all things. And always at the center, the
self, the moment of incarnation, the Walt Whitman of
oneself. The aboriginal or, if you like, the American.

The power of Whitman in the world is incalculable.
In literature it has long been calculated as nothing. It
is because of poets like Whitman that literature exists
but it is always Literature that determines to extermi-
nate its Whitmans, its Blakes, its Lawrences, its Henry
Millers. The probability is that Whitman will never be
"accepted" as one of the great writers of mankind; acceptance is always a function of the writers who assume the power of literature, for whatever reasons,
and who make literature one of the arms of the law.
Because Whitman is beyond the law of literature he

is condemned to extinction from generation to generation. Like Lawrence, who rescued him in our century, Whitman is beyond the reach of Criticism, beyond the library and the curriculum, beyond Congress and and Church, and yet there, right under your nose, as you step out of doors.

The Jewish Writer
in America

In the course of writing these chapters and delivering them as public lectures I made the awful discovery that I must define my Jewishness to the reader.
What has being a Jew got to do with literary criticism? Quite a bit, evidently. The mere act of defending oneself against the shallow Jew-baiting of Pound
or the profound racism of Eliot constitutes a "position." And insofar as I have a position, it is bound to
be something of a "Jewish position." Even while I was
delivering these notes as lectures I was accused of
criticizing modern poetry on "Jewish" grounds. A
philosophy professor conspicuously stalked out of
the crowded hall where I was speaking unfavorably
of Eliot; he gave it out later that my remarks about
Eliot's Anglo-Catholicism offended him personally.
The unphilosophical departure of this gentleman
paved the way for the criticism which I heard frequently later on—my quarrel with the Pound-Eliot
school was a *Jewish* quarrel. Against this accusation
I must defend my book. And for the sake of my "re-

ligious" readers I must spell out my Jewishness, such as it is.

One of the chief strategic triumphs of the new Classicism has been its ability to quash the opposition, whether literary, sociological, or religious. Eliot carefully flattered the conservative mind in government, in philosophy, and in religion. Pound flattered the sense of culture aristocracy and the political authoritarianism which goes hand in hand with the religion of culture. The anti-Americanism of both writers is of that variety which connects commercialism with "mass taste" and "freethinking." What Eliot calls the freethinking Jew, Pound calls the international Jewish banker. Indeed, it is the medieval image of the Jew as Shylock and Christ-killer which the Classicists perpetuate in the twentieth century. And, miraculous to report, the intellectual Jewish writers do not resist this image but tend to accept it guiltily! I refer particularly to the Jewish editors of cultural journals who purvey Marxist-Freudian anti-Semitism (in the belief that a Jewish identity is an historical anachronism) and I refer to the many Jewish professors of literature who are "new critics" and who thereby deprive themselves of any humanitarian standard of judgment. A book of verse I published last year called *Poems of a Jew* was most bitterly assailed by Jewish New Critics, while the nonintellectual Jewish press tended to accept the poems as an awkward but serious expression of modern Jewishness.

The intellectual faction among Jewish professors, critics, and editors has been led quietly by the nose into the Pound-Eliot preserve. They were content to accept the Culture religion which in Eliot's criticism apparently subsumed any actual religion. They were content to accept Eliot's second-hand ideas of "pluralistic culture" which apparently subsumed mere nationalisms. Thus it was precisely the "freethinkers" whom Eliot despised who became his staunchest defenders. And those intellectuals who were not captivated by Eliot's version of the Tradition were taken in by his esthetic of the "objectivity" of the work of art. Even a critic as political in his thinking as F. O. Matthiessen convinced himself that it was somehow indecent to expose Eliot's beliefs to view. So holy was Eliot's reputation as poet, thinker, and man that criticism of his work became the chief taboo in twentieth-century literature. William Carlos Williams alone dared attack the master. And for a Jew to raise his voice against Pound, Eliot, or Hulme was considered an act of savagery by the New Criticism and the New Pedagogy. It is extraordinary how much the defense of Pound has been placed on a hypocritical "Christian" footing. With what relief the intellectuals seized on the trashy and meretricious canto about humility to prove old Ezra's purity of heart. Pound on the throne of humility evidently cancels out Pound as the Great Dictator.

As a twentieth-century American writer I grew up to respect the British literary tradition above all others and to share in the famous American "guilt" about our own heritage. As a Jew I was misled by Jewish intellectuals, ex-Marxists and Freudians, to minimize and even accept the fashionable anti-Americanism and anti-Semitism of the Moderns. In all probability I would never have been led to examine the ideas of these Moderns had I not been driven to do so—by participating in the Pound affair over the Bollingen Prize, and by having to teach modern poetry. Whatever Jewish consciousness I possess today I can trace to the writings of the American Classicists who made it their business to equate "American" and "Jew" as twin evils. This consciousness of myself as American

Jew restricted and narrowed my writing for many
years, erecting a private ghetto in my mind. To break
out of this ghetto is one of the reasons for writing this
book.

There is no Jewish writer *per se* in America. But the
American writer, generally speaking, does not mention his ancestry, even if he happens to know what
it is. The American writer tends to cut himself off
from his past and even to deride it. There are exceptions, of course—the Henry Jameses and the Eliots—
but most American writers favor the approach of
Mark Twain: that dukes, kings, and ancestors are
flotsam and jetsam one would do better to steer clear
of. A poet from an old New England family wrote me
when he saw my book *Poems of a Jew* and said, "You
go back so much farther than I do!" He said this almost with a kind of envy, I thought. Then he added
cryptically: "You write like an Arab," one of the
strangest compliments I have ever had. At least, I
think it was a compliment.

It is only in the last generation or two that an
American Jew could write Jewishly and still be
thought of as an American. Twenty years ago, when
I was beginning to write for publication, I wrote an
American poet whom I knew to be Jewish and asked
him what obstacles one had to overcome to publish
poems under a Jewish name. His reply was so ambiguous that I decided his own name wasn't very Jewish
after all. I was not imagining things: many years later
a non-Jewish poet said to me: "When I first saw your
poems I thought you had an impossible name for a
poet." This remark did not indicate anti-Semitism or
anything of the sort, but it suggests the persistence of
the British tradition in American letters until a very
late date. In this respect I feel I have done a little
pioneer work for American writers: changing of

names has always shocked me deeply, even though it
has always been a common practice among writers.
But in poetry or any other art, the question of race
or religion is of the highest significance. Nowadays
the Jewish writer in America meets with no obstacles
qua Jew in publication or in other forms of recognition, but this happy circumstance only brings us closer
to the question: What *is* an American Jewish writer?

To me the answer is—an American Jewish writer
is a Jew who is an American who is a writer. Everybody knows what an American is; everyone knows
what a writer is; but very few people seem to know
what a Jew is, including Jews, and including American Jewish writers.

A few years ago I participated in a symposium
called "The Jewish Writer and the English Literary
Tradition." It was published in *Commentary*—itself a
kind of literary phenomenon: an upper-middle-class
magazine sponsored by an American Jewish organization and the highbrow editorship of the *Partisan
Review*. The question for the symposium was this:
"As a Jew and a writer in the Anglo-American literary
tradition, how do you confront the presence in that
tradition of the mythical . . . figure of the Jew as
found in the (anti-Semitic) writings of Chaucer, Marlowe, Shakespeare, Scott, T. S. Eliot, Evelyn Waugh,
Thomas Wolfe, Henry Adams, etc. In what way do
you find this a problem to you? etc."

Reading between the lines, I took the question to
mean: Do you think the Jew will be able to break
into high literary society? That is, we were given a
sociological question, one in which any element of
a Jewish *mystique* was distinctly absent. And the
replies also struck me as sociological, or, as we say
more often, rationalistic. The replies ran along these
lines:

(*a*) The Jew defends a pluralistic culture; therefore he is attacked as "international." (The term "pluralistic" has been popularized by T. S. Eliot, whom most of the symposium felt it necessary to bow to in passing.) (*b*) Anti-Semitism is pathological, a disease like the black plague, and just as medieval. Get a well-doctored society and it will disappear. (*c*) Jews are also secretly anti-Semitic, parochial, and self-pitying. Let the Jewish writer be *more* cosmopolitan. (*d*) Writers like Eliot really love the Jews, but you must learn how to take insults. (*e*) Is anti-Semitism really real? (Stephen Spender answered this way.) If a Jew didn't know he was a Jew he wouldn't think he was a Jew.

The summation of the other approaches was by Philip Rahv, an honest and ruthless logician. What we must do, said Rahv, is to "conduct a struggle against the new religiosity, along with those non-Jewish intellectuals who refuse to abandon the progressive and secular outlook. This . . . religiosity tends to divide rather than unite humanity; it is historically vacuous and metaphysically permeated with nostalgia . . ."

The best statement made in this list of responses was by Harold Rosenberg, who put his finger on the weakness of the question itself. Rosenberg noted that to move from a personification like Shylock to the sociological cliché is a serious mistake. For instance, some German critic sees *The Merchant of Venice* with the repulsive Shylock and writes a review that says in effect: Down with the Jews. Thus Shylock becomes the Jew-with-the-knife and an instrument for political propaganda. As a result the Jew tends to blame Shakespeare for anti-Semitism.

To me the symposium was meaningless because it took for granted that religion is obsolescent, and racism the product of religion. The writers who took

part in it seemed to be saying that religion is evil but
Culture is good (whatever Culture is). Let's save
Culture and get rid of religion.

My own answer was this: We are Jews by popular
consent of the Jewish-Christian community and not
by choice or ambition. We accept our Jewishness because to reject it would be a betrayal not of our
electors but of ourselves. In the same way I felt when
I was conscripted that to avoid military duty would
have been a betrayal of my identity as an American.
If this is negative Americanism then I can also call
myself a negative Jew. But my election to America
and to Israel gives me my total identity, the kind of
identity which has never been permitted to survive
in all of Europe's history.

The most curious aspect of this affair is that the
Jews who are recognized writers of one kind or
another shrink back from Judaism but defend, however half-heartedly, their right to be Jews. In a sense
they would welcome the extinction of the Jewish religion as long as they could maintain their identity as
Jews. How this can be done in actuality is beyond me.
And what sense it would make is also beyond me.
I read somewhere that a Christian writer asked a
Jew what it was to be a Jew. The Jew answered: We
are a religion. This is a beautiful answer and a true
one, but perhaps not true enough. We are even more
than a religion.

Our symposium people seemed to interpret the expression "American Jewish writer" to mean one who
infused into the American idiom something of the
Jewish idiom or of Jewish psychology. To me this is
trivial; and in any case the American idiom is a vast
complex of such idioms, all of which are tending
toward the making of a great national (American)
literature. A brilliant novel like Saul Bellow's *The*

Adventures of Augie March is saturated with Jewish witticisms and sentiments; the very language seems almost a transliteration of—what? I can't read Yiddish but I recognize the idiom. And the American reader need not know of the presence of this element in Bellow's writing, for by now it is as much American as it is Jewish. What is really Jewish in Bellow lies much deeper: it is the poetry of the Jew that makes his hero what he is, in Chicago, in Mexico, wherever Augie happens to be. Bellow has translated Singer's story "Gimpel the Fool" from Yiddish. It is one of the most side-splitting and yet painful tales I have ever read, but it might have been written in New York instead of Poland, or wherever it came from. This is Jewishness far beyond culture, social problems, history, and the rest. It is even beyond religion, as far as I can see.

Sociological Judaism seems to me completely pointless; and the preservation of national memory for its own sake, mere narcissism. The business of the Jewish writer is not to complain about society but to rise above such complaints. Nearly all social protest literature is superficial anyhow; the greater realities of difference lie below the bickerings of ideologists. I would say there are two kinds of Jewish American literature, the kind recommended by our symposium —a psychologically Judaistic literature—and the real kind, which I would recommend: a God-centered literature. That is a poor way of putting it but I will try to explain what I mean.

A merely Judaistic literature is only a kind of "regional" literature, even though this "region" takes in most of the world and all of history. In such literature the Jew may be good or bad, Shylock or the Wandering Jew or Leopold Bloom, but he is simply a man of memory, an anachronism. He is not the Jew who "lives life," as Martin Buber puts it. He is the Jew of the past, the Jew of the Wailing Wall. Recently I read a new *Oxford Book of Irish Verse* and was struck by the centuries-old struggle of the Irish poets to regain their Irishness, to throw off the cosmopolitanism of the world-writer and to renew that particular consciousness which is not a "cultural heritage" but an identity. In the case of the Irish I can sense only dimly what that identity is. But in the case of the Jew I know what it is. The Jewish writer everywhere in the modern world has the problem of regaining the Jewish consciousness, which in our case is God-consciousness. I am not talking about religion; religion is only a by-product of this consciousness. For the Jewish writer who wants to turn his back on this consciousness we can only give him our blessing and let him go. But for the consciously Jewish writer in America or anywhere else we must recognize his obligation to establish this consciousness centrally in his work, the right, so to speak, of the existence of God. If this encourages religious progress that may be to the good; but I am not talking about religion. I am opposed to all organized religion, including Judaism.

Jewish creative intelligence has been driven into by-paths for centuries. We are just beginning to return to the era of Jewish philosophy, but our abstract thinking generally still belongs to the Middle Ages. We produce an Einstein, who from the religious or even political viewpoint is a baby. We produce a Freud who foists upon the world a surrogate religion while striving mightily to destroy both Christianity and Judaism in one breath. The fantastic intellectual powers of the Jews of our time go into everything under the sun except Jewish consciousness, or to use a really lofty word, holiness.

The Jews have written one of the greatest holy books. And that book is the beginning and the end of our literature. Jewish literature is not great. Jewish philosophy is not great. Jewish scholarship—perhaps. Our contributions to science, government, law and the humane knowledges, even the arts of music, and in our lifetime, painting, have been advanced by Jews. But the great arts of the written word have not been advanced by the people of the book. Not to any significant degree.

Our friends of the symposium on the Jewish writer in the United States were more interested in setting up fresh literary symbols than they were in understanding a religion or in seeking the *mystique* back of it. Consequently I think of them as literary social climbers and not poets.

As far as one can tell these things, there are only two countries in the world where the Jewish writer is free to create his own consciousness: Israel and the United States. Everywhere else the Jew seems to live on the past. Even Proust's re-creation of consciousness is a kind of Jewish nostalgia. In Europe it is either nostalgia or nightmare: Proust or Kafka. The European Jew was always a visitor and knew it. But in America everybody is a visitor. In this land of permanent visitors the Jew is in a rare position to "live the life" of a full Jewish consciousness. The Jews live a fantastic historical paradox: we are the spiritual aborigines of the modern world, and we are the ethical and sometimes intellectual conscience of the modern world. History has hated us so deeply because every Jew is regarded as a living witness of the Christian and Muslim revelations—which he is. The Jewish assumption of holiness and his rather *laissez faire* attitude toward religion make him a natural target in almost any historical situation. Only in America (as the expression goes) can the Jew be a natural Jew. There are fewer religious tensions in America than any place else in history—the national tendency to vulgarize religion and to experiment with new sects has allowed the American Jew to relax—to emerge from the historical consciousness to a contemporary Jewish consciousness.

I was speaking of the creative man and by that I mean not only the poet or novelist, painter or composer but the mystic and saint. Our rational modern upbringing prevents us from even thinking of God. In our time we say or think that God is for women and children. We go to houses of worship possibly, but only because it is too troublesome not to. Now, the true writer and mystic does not ransack the storehouse of religion for literary plunder; rather he adds to the spiritual storehouse. He does not take; he gives. He may never even go near a synagogue or church, and in many cases in the past he has been forbidden to enter the official house of prayer. Poets and mystics are always having the door slammed in their faces; especially the church door.

This full Jewish consciousness which is today possible in America as in Israel is a way of life, so to speak. And it does not necessarily involve ritual or anything of the sort, though it may in some cases. It does not involve piety and may in fact involve the exact opposite. I am paraphrasing the modern Jewish philosopher, Martin Buber—I hope I am not corrupting what he means. He says: "The true hallowing of man is the hallowing of the human in him . . . In life, as Hasidism [Jewish mysticism] understands and proclaims it, there is no essential distinction between sacred and profane spaces, between sacred and profane times, between sacred and profane actions, between sacred and profane conversations." I am not sure how many Jews accept this kind of belief, but I suppose very few. All the same, in my ignorance of my own religion, it seems to me the very core of Jewish consciousness. It is antiascetic and joyous— the Hasidim dance wildly with the Torah. "Man," says Buber, "cannot approach the divine by reaching beyond the human; but he can approach Him through becoming human." In the last century, when rationalism touched everything, a doctrine like this was thought of as the wildest superstition. To me it is like a breath of fresh air. It is the highest form of Humanism.

What does this have to do with the problem of the American Jewish writer? Nothing, probably. And yet I see a striking similarity between this mystical humanism and American secular humanism. It matters very little whether the American Jewish poet or novelist writes *about* the American Jew (the good artist is seldom that self-conscious anyway); it even matters little whether he lives as a Jew in the conventional sense of "living as"; what does matter is that he accept the consequences of Jewishness. He cannot escape them in any event, and I do not think he should *suffer* these consequences but revel in them.

The Jewish writer is presented with a kind of freedom which is almost inconceivable. The Jewish plus American combination only doubles this freedom.

Modern literature attempts to perpetuate the Jew as imaged in Christian theology and story. But this Jew is as dead as the Negro of the minstrel show. Both images come from the age of slavery. The Jew today is free in his mythological homeland Israel and free in America, the mythological homeland of freedom. Creatively he has begun to flourish as never before, nor can the medievalism of the New Classicists prevent this flowering, as much as they fear it.

Freedom in any form is anathema to modern Classicism. Even "free verse" is not really free, says the poor fettered Eliot. And the "freethinking Jew" is, of course, a grave danger to whatever is the opposite of freedom.

Poets and Psychologists

O<small>NCE UPON A TIME</small> I received an invitation from a psychologist who wanted to examine my imagination. He was a young man who came well recommended from his university. The young psychologist invited me to his hotel room, where he wished to record my responses to his questions, or rather my reactions to his stimuli. For what he produced from his paraphernalia was a set of testing cards, which I shall describe in a moment, and a recording machine—a kind of lie detector. The whole procedure seemed to me doubtfully scientific at the outset. I am not a scientist but I suppose like most laymen that the environment of a scientific operation is crucial, to say the least. Here was a trained scientist trying to find out something about my innermost psychological processes: I had never met him; we were sitting in a typically depressing hotel room where he had set up a machine to capture my most involuntary stammers and stutters. Then there was the examination itself. It is known in the trade as the T. A. T. It consisted of a pack of cards about eight by twelve inches on which were drawn montages, prepared (I was told on asking) by a Senior psychologist. The poet was to look at each picture for a specified time and let his imagination dilate upon the subject expressed in the montage. I am sure I failed the examination miserably. My immediate reaction to the pictures was that they were very poor *pictures,* and whatever testing value they might have had was entirely obscured for me by this fact. I wasted part of the psychologist's time arguing about the uselessness of the test. Far from running away with the show, my imagination was affronted by these artificially surrealist things. They made me giggle. My giggles, expostulations, and objections were faithfully recorded, and I received a check for a hundred dollars for my pains!

Money is even more distracting to poets than hotel rooms. It is rare for a poet to get a hundred dollars for a poem he writes, even if it is one of the best poems in the world. Yet a psychologist from a great university travels around America giving away who knows how much money to people who are known as poets. The psychologist is not interested in my poetry but *in the fact that* I am a poet. And to establish this fact and to try to ascertain some meaning from it, his mysterious and benevolent sponsors have put aside a large sum of money. We must therefore swallow our pride as poets when the scientist comes by to examine us. We are not poets to him. We are something that has gone wrong perhaps, something that doesn't quite fit into his scheme of things. At the same time he respects us for our peculiar usefulness.

Six months after the examination I received a letter with a long questionnaire from the same man. We had now become friends of a sort, or at least collaborators. We agreed (in the interest of science) to publish some of the questions and answers to provoke discussion, among I am not sure whom. My answers, he said, were so bold and to the point that they might well improve the Laboratory Environment. On the other hand, I could not be sure of the honesty of my own intentions.

Do poets tend to scoff at science? Certainly their poetry betrays a powerful aversion to it, however they construe the term. And they know that this antipathy for "pure inquiry" is a form of ignorance, although the revulsion against the more intrusive by-products of this science is widely applauded by all men of good will. Most literary people share this repugnance for Science with a capital S and for the artifacts which this Science produces, but what poets probably dislike about Science is its absolute monopoly of the Truth. Also, the artist tends to regard scientific method as a kindergarten. The ordinary person does not become suspicious of scientific method until the scientist enters the world of people or the world of literature; then he is suddenly appalled by the failures of science—in economics, statistics, history, psychology. The poet, with a deeper distrust of Science, would rather read a work on palmistry or physiognomy than he would a textbook of any description. What good is astronomy without astrology? It is interesting to see in our own lifetime the reactions of positive scientists against techniques of pure measurement—even in medicine, where it is now recognized that illnesses may be self-induced, without bugs. And the realm of Psychology today is filled with renegade scientists who provide much of the most fascinating— the most imaginative—data. These rebel scientists (and science mystics) stand between the artist and the positivist. Paracelsus is being reprinted in our time and there is a widespread revival of alchemy and the sciences relating to the study of the soul.

The attempts of some contemporary poets to bring themselves into sympathy with modern science are mostly abortive. The poet sees clearly that the technological age flowers only where there is a total surrender of the imagination to something totally without intrinsic interest to man. Pure scientific interest in poetry is bound to raise prejudices in the poet's mind —especially when that interest is manifested by the branch of science called Psychology, which is a borderline science in any case. The psychologist was bound to enter the field of poetry (everything being a Field). He has more tests up his sleeve than you can count; his statistics are probably foolproof, and his objectivity is perfect. But he won't find a thing. We shall tell him everything we know but it will do no good. He will be more in the dark than ever. He is like a child looking into a phonograph to see the little men who make the music. He (child or psychologist) *knows* there is a minuscule band of musicians hidden somewhere in the depths of the mechanism. You can give up telling him there isn't. For in the last analysis he will say that A, B, and C are at work: this turns that, and there you have it. Scientists once thought electricity was a fluid: now they call it an agency, but secretly they still think it is a fluid. If electricity, why not poetry?

Now I am going to recite the psychologist's questions and my answers, and I feel that I must add humorlessly that these are true questions. I did not make them up.

Question: What is the role (function as poet, plus the expected social behavior) of the contemporary American poet?

Answer: I don't know who expects any sort of recognizable behavior from poets. The people who know most about poets probably expect anything.

Revised question: Is the role of the American poet different from the role of the poet in other societies, other ages?

Answer: The role of the poet is always the same, I think. He makes poems. But it is true that the *psychology* (using the word in its vulgar sense to mean mental states)—the psychology of the poet changes from time to time and place to place. My poetic psychology is different from that of a poet laureate. I would not, I hope, make a good poet laureate. The difference of psychology would depend upon whether the poet is going with or against the grain of his time, i.e., official opinion. Tennyson went with the grain, sometimes rather reluctantly, like a fractious boy. Hopkins went against the times and was considered a harmless eccentric. At any time there are poets going in opposite directions and at cross-purposes. But a later generation may catch up with a poet like Hopkins and make him a touchstone. What are we to infer from this—that Hopkins had no role as a poet during his lifetime? Perhaps the contrary is true: his was the purest role—that of making poems which only he could fully appreciate. The poet who thinks of his role as a national figure or spokesman is usually a prig.

Question: What *should* be (ideally) the role of the poet?

Answer: The poet has more than a vocation, which is a call from without. He has an imperative to write poems, a call from himself. For whom is this demand?

For himself. It is his means of life. Others may call him and he may not answer. In writing poetry he answers the deepest need of his nature. The craving to write a good poem becomes as deep a hunger as any physical desideratum. And such a hunger can become habitual. Or at least the poet may reach that point of no return at which he is condemned like most people to his vocation, whether he likes it or not.

Revised question: What does the ideal American reader expect of the poet?

Answer: Being trained in positive science, a psychologist can formulate the idea of an ideal American reader. I cannot. Anyway, the two questions don't match, and I don't know what the ideal reader is supposed to be. The ideal reader presupposes someone who appreciates the poet best. Perhaps this ideal is some critic or another poet. I have a few actual readers in mind when I write a poem, or usually after I've written one, but no ideals. And these readers are usually certain poets or critics whose talent or judgment I admire, and who may be dead. Few poets write *to* an audience however, but they may write to a standard. Would Rilke like this poem, I sometimes ask myself. Would Catullus? Other poets may have a different audience. I would never ask if Dr. Johnson would like a poem of mine. This puts the living audience in a strange perspective. Sometimes a reader will say to me that he likes a certain poem of mine, and I then reread the poem in the light of my knowledge of this *person*. For frequently one is puzzled, or just curious, at such a response.

Question: What qualities of personality are essential to the writing of poetry (creativity)?

Answer: My guess, based on random observation, would be something on this order. The poet is egoistic to the point of narcissism. He sees himself as a fixed point around which the motion of life circulates. He is compacted of imagination, to quote Shakespeare. He is obsessed by language. In fact he is a man of frequent and diverse obsessions. Often he shows a paranoid character, with some reason. He suspects that he has numerous enemies who are really trying to put him in jail or the lunatic asylum. Frequently he really lands in such places. He has a supremely guilty conscience, born from his ego and his passionate desire to know more than his senses tell. He experiences frequent pure states of mind, pure love, pure rage, pure knowledge. He is a man of infinite discipline (something which only other artists know about him). He is capable of great cruelty and something akin to saintliness. He is in love with heresies and regards the forbidden as his rightful province. He is nevertheless the most pious of men. He is both the most infantile and the most sage of creatures. He exploits his defects. He is full of practical jokes and self-pity. He has a kind of contempt for possessions. He is very witty and very verbose. He is at once excitable and profoundly indifferent to what excites him. He has an uncanny faculty for organizing the unorganizable. He is accurate. He thinks incessantly of the nature of things, a habit he has in common with philosophers and adolescents. He is dogmatic and deliberately immerses himself in the occult. He is effeminate and, as the public thinks, often worse. Sometimes he is physically and, as I think, deliberately, dirty. He tends to speak with authority, as if he were a kind of god. He is a hypochondriac who is not yet averse to ruining his health for some whim. He is, as history shows, frequently suicidal, frequently alcoholic, frequently a victim of one of the known types of sexual aberration. Yet these are characteristics of other men as well. We can only say: the chief characteristic of the poet is that above all he is obsessed by a desire to write poems.

Question: What qualities of personality are a handicap to the writing of poetry?

Answer: Everything is against the possibility of good poetry, and unpleasant traits of personality seem to be no handicap. I think there *is* such a thing as a poetic type but the type is fairly common compared with the number among this type that develop into poets. No mother or father in his right mind would ever set out to encourage a child to be a poet, that mass of handicaps, as the world sees him. Yet I believe in such a thing as a poetic type, sometimes even a somatic poetic type. I remember a South American I met at a party once who grabbed me by both shoulders and bent me backwards and stared into my eyes—to *see* if I was a poet. I don't know what he was looking for specifically, but I think he was on the right track. It is not easy in the twentieth century to spot a poet: almost all of them go in disguise of one sort or another. He dare not express himself by his appearance in this age or even admit to a stranger that he is a poet. Most poets nowadays disguise themselves as college professors.

Question: What is the pattern of the poet's life style?
  (*a*) Working day (scheduled hours).
  (*b*) Nature and significance of other-than-writing activities (reading, recreation, etc.).
  (*c*) Type of dwelling place and location of home.
  (*d*) Interaction with friends on an informal social plane.

Answer: Of course, it would be nice to say like a California poet: I live in a house on a deserted cliff. I built the house of boulders which I tore from the bed of the Pacific with my bare hands.

I don't see what difference it makes.

Revised question: Is there a discernible pattern of life style among poets? On this question, which was phrased in a general form, I was also interested in your personal answers.

Answer: (a) Working day. Poets work at different schedules, different hours of the day and seasons of the year. Who knows? They work when they get time and when the time they get seems conducive for writing. Almost no poet gets the time he needs; this is a consequence of the almost total absence of remuneration for his work. There may be one or two living poets who actually earn enough money by their books of poetry to gain something like a full working-day for writing; but mostly they must write other things in order to get this leisure. (We call it leisure, although we never say a businessman has *leisure* to go about *his* business). Now and then a poet gets a fellowship for writing for a year or two, but frequently the artificiality of the circumstances and the novelty of freedom are too much for him. I had such a fellowship once and couldn't get over the feeling that I was out on time. I got very little done. The fact is that the poet steals time whenever he can get it.

(b) Nature and significance of other-than-writing activities. This subtle thief of time has enough to do without inventing hobbies and vacations. Yet there *is* always a nonpoetic form of creation in which the poet indulges, and it may be criticism or fiction writing or painting. Perhaps the poet needs this larger and more constant field of work in order to feed on it for his

poems—or in order to *find* his poems. Reading consumes much of a poet's time; and his reading also
drives him to overexcitement and the desire to write.

(*c*) Type of dwelling place, etc. Supposing anyone
to have a choice, we still couldn't generalize. Poets of
my generation would prefer living in slums to living
in suburbs, but that may be a pose of a kind. On the
whole, one must ignore his surroundings. Good writing can be done anywhere. Perhaps one writes where
one feels secret and enclosed in oneself.

(*d*) Interaction with friends. I have never thought
of friendship as an interaction before, but we may as
well be scientific. I prefer writers to other people, or
artists of any kind. But a room with too many poets
is very like a tiger pit. (I am not sure whether the
psychologist and I would agree on what a friend is.)

Question: Economic bases of the poet's life.
   (*a*) Origin of income?
   (*b*) Importance of a comfortable monetary re-
        ward?
   (*c*) What occupations mesh best with the poetic
        role (i.e., teaching, business)?

Answer: We have touched on this already but there
are other things to say. As the public suspects, many
poets have an honest contempt for what is called security. They like rewards, more for the noise than for
the money; they are genuinely surprised when people
give them money and always resentful when they
don't. Most occupations are unsuitable for them, not
because of the occupations but because writing poetry
is their occupation. Poets are the only people who
recognize that writing poetry is a full-time job. But
the generalizations break down here also. There are
impecunious poets and those who are pedantically

acquisitive. The only certainty in the matter is that poets cannot live by writing poetry, not even the best of them, nor the most famous. They must become teachers or historians or lecturers, critics or novelists or journalists. Some are even businessmen. The question *how* a poet is to earn his living is a profound bore; how he can get time to write is more interesting. As I say, he steals time from his job and from his family. No one can say what occupation is suitable for a poet. I suspect that none is, really. He may be capable of doing any kind of job quite well, only because he is intelligent and sympathetic, but he may pull up stakes at any minute and go off. The poet is not quite at home in the academic climate, nor in any climate. He kicks against the pricks: it is his nature. Speaking of the poet's livelihood, I would also add that personal patronage seems to me the most honorable and successful method for the support of the poet. I am inclined to distrust government patronage. The poet should be answerable to nobody for his work—least of all taxpayers. The main problem here —if there is one—is something tangential to the psychologist's questions, that is, whether the poet worries about his livelihood as much as other people or even other writers. I don't think he does.

Question: Choice of a career in poetry.
  (*a*) At what period of life did you feel you would become a practicing poet?
  (*b*) What renunciations were or are necessary to the performance of the poetic role?
  (*c*) What are the criteria of success or failure as a poet?
  (*d*) What specific training might be required for the aspirant of poetry writing?

Answer: Does anyone *choose* poetry as a career? I suppose so. The use of the word *career* in this context makes me think I don't know what it means. But to go on. (*a*) At what period of life I felt I would become a practicing poet. There is much badinage over this term *practicing*. It has the connotation of law or medicine about it: after a certain specified time one is given a license to practice poetry. This question, which I would never have asked myself, nevertheless reminded me of something I had totally forgotten: I was writing verse in the sixth grade and was apparently a kind of class poet. But I don't remember why, nor do I attach any importance to this memory. Now I was *practicing* poetry (or whatever it was) at the age of eleven or twelve, but that is not the answer. At a more responsible age I spent all my time writing sonnets. That is still not the answer. Still later I published a book of poems privately, but no one outside a radius of a mile from where I lived ever heard of it. That too is not the answer. It was when I began to publish poems in literary magazines that I began to take myself seriously.

(*b*) What renunciations were or are necessary to the performance of the poetic role. To answer in kind: the renunciation of quotidian responsibilities. But they are not renunciations in the ordinary sense. It is easy (sociologically speaking) to be a poet. You can get away with a great deal and keep people at bay. The poet is free; he is specially privileged; he is detested and admired. We can say also that the poet is hardly ever a model member of the community, family, or nation. Many poets, aware of their unfitness for "normal" responsibilities, avoid these duties from the beginning. The chief difference between the poet and any other man is that the poet *acts* like a free man—but he may elect responsibility like William Shakespeare, Esquire, or not, and no psychologist will ever find the pattern.

(*c*) The criteria of success and failure as a poet. They are his own. Recognition from the poets and critics he admires is the only acclaim that matters. All the public acclaim in the world is nothing to the praise of one's peers. Happy is the poet who achieves both!

(*d*) Specific training required for the neophyte poet. There is none. It is notable that a mere adolescent may be a great poet, even if there is only the one example of Arthur Rimbaud. Poetry, like higher mathematics, seems as much a gift as an acquired skill. The great poetry of youth is romantic, on the whole, and brief in its brilliance. The poetry of maturity may be another thing entirely. But for the first kind there is no time for training in anything: the poet wakes up, he sees everything in a flash; he consumes himself setting it down. For the rest, it is presumed that the poet has a mastery of poetry and a mastery of his own tongue. The poet should read deeply in mythology, esoteric writings, scriptures, and symbolic writings. He will anyway. The subject furthest from his interests and sympathy will probably be history. The positivism of modern historians is almost the perfect foil for the poet. And philosophy will chill his blood.

There is a sense in which the poet knows everything: in another sense he is the most ignorant of men. The poet learns, but learning in his mind changes into beautiful and ugly, good and evil, true and not true.

Question:
   (*a*) Of whom must the poet be independent?
   (*b*) With whom should he interact most frequently?

(*c*) What support is most essential to the poet (popular success, critical acclaim, family or friends)?

Revised question: For *interact* read *communicate*. (One Latinism for another).

Answer: The question probably means morally and psychologically independent. A poet who had never behaved too well told me sententiously: We are all responsible. That may well be, but the poet is a neutral gear in the machine of society; he is not engaged. He may be passionately interested in politics but never vote. The poet makes moral choices all the time: *and he makes them for others.* In effect, the poet secretly agrees with Shelley's doctrine of the power behind the throne.

Question:

(*a*) Is American society congenial to a career in poetry?

(*b*) What contemporary nation would be most congenial?

(*c*) What kind of society would be the ideal context for a poet?

Answer: I once had a letter from a lady who was trying to institute a National Poetry Day. She wanted my support (which I refused) and that of other poets. Even in the most enlightened world we could imagine, the idea would be a horror. Periclean Greece, Renaissance Florence, Victorian England may have been ages when great numbers of people were congenial to poetry. But the poet survives just as well in an "antipoetic" climate. He may even flourish in a world like ours where everything is against the existence of poetry. We get poetry everywhere. So when we are asked what contemporary nation would be most congenial to the encouragement of poetry, we cannot answer. Sometimes it appears that a national revival, like the founding of the Irish state, gives life to a national literature. But the Irish revival in letters was largely William Butler Yeats and, if anything, he helped the Irish revolution more than it helped him. I cannot think of a single condition of history which would totally obviate poetry. Even Soviet Russia has a great poet (in disfavor of course—but so are most of ours here). What kind of society would be the ideal context for a poet? There is none. If there were an ideal society the poets would probably be the first ones to revolt against it. If the *poet* were empowered to set up his own version of a perfect society, it would probably be a mixture of the worst features of the worst autocracies—plus Boys Town.

Question: What is the importance of the "received tradition" esthetically, socially?

Answer: Sometimes very great. But the poet believes in the princess and the pea and the tales told by his blood. He may not be traditional in Eliot's sense at all.

Question: Why does the poet continue to write?
  (*a*) Intrinsic value in creative work?
  (*b*) Desire to provide others with valuable experience?

Answer: I don't think the desire to provide others with valuable experience has anything to do with it. "Intrinsic values" is one way of putting it; but the real answer is that his *raison d'être* is writing poems, if he is really a poet; it is inconceivable to him that he can stop writing. It is not a giving-out experience as much as it is a form of self-nourishment and self-experience for the writer. For the poet, his writing is akin to spiritual and psychic exercises which ready him for his final work. In any case, whether he reaches that final stage or not, the poet becomes his poems in the process.

Question: What is the importance in the creative process of
   (*a*) Inspiration?
   (*b*) Craftsmanship?
   (*c*) Memory?
        What is the "normal"
   (*a*) Speed of work, progress toward a completed poem?
   (*b*) Postcreative feeling?

Answer: This is a jumble of questions, some sounding like a laboratory chart, others like a questionnaire from the employment office. "Inspiration" is really a term of measurement; it refers to the speed of a conjunction of all the bits of broken glass that fall into patterns in the field of light—the poet's mind. The poet need not know all the things that happen to him while he is writing a poem: the rise of memories, images, sounds and associations, all more or less immediate and below the threshold of consciousness. Undoubtedly most "inspirations" are eventually rejected. But let us say at least that inspiration describes an interior not an exterior action. The psychologist probably wants us to say that the process of composition of a poem like "Kubla Khan"—the dream poem—creates the *essential* kind of poem. The answer is it does not matter whether Coleridge wrote the poem in twenty minutes or twenty years—it is just as miraculous either way—or whether he dreamed it, thought he dreamed it, or just cooked up the whole story. People in the nineteenth century thought that God could not have created the world *because it took too long!* And we feel that a poem that takes too long can't be the real thing. Romantic poetry, to be sure, is more "inspired" than another kind. This is because of its poetics: one of the aims of such poetry is to present states of feeling in their immediacy. Romantic poets try to induce the mood which will influence (color) the thing they are writing about. We do not think of a Classical poet taking opium.

What is called craftsmanship is the work done on the verses after the poet has decided he has a start on a poem. But this may be the first as well as the last stage of composition. Yeats supposedly would begin with a sound pattern and not a subject, much less an inspiration of the emotional kind. There is also Poe's famous account of how he wrote "The Raven" in cold blood: it is such a bad poem that one is inclined to believe his story. On the other hand, most of Poe's best "poetry" is in his criticism.

Sensory memory is probably more important than factual memory to the poet.

What is the normal speed of work toward a completed poem? The speed of composition is completely irrelevant to any consideration of art.

Postcreative feeling: this inquiry seems another irrelevancy. One wonders what Milton felt like when he finished *Paradise Lost.* Maybe he wanted to tear it up or begin a new version. More likely he wanted to hurry down to the printers. Still more likely he said to himself, now I can begin *Paradise Regained.*

Question: What is your attitude toward the scientific study of poets and poetry?

(*a*) Can the attempts succeed in discovering anything new?

(*b*) Should the attempt be made at all? If not, what might be some undesirable consequences of such efforts?

Answer: Poetry can only puzzle people who go at it scientifically. The scientific study of poetry will only make poets laugh at science and the public laugh at poets.

Revised question: Do you believe that psychoanalysis has been more harmful than beneficial to a true understanding of the poet's life and work?

Answer: Psychoanalytical criticism offers two criticisms of poetry: it says that the poet (or artist) makes good out of bad. And it says that art is not what it is, but something else. It places art in the realm of dream, thus making it essentially automatic, personally symbolic, and counterfeit. Its value becomes incidental to its etiology. It is a kind of beautiful symptom of a mortal disease. As for a true understanding— whatever that is—of poets and poetry, psychoanalysis has probably done more harm than good by running the understanding of literature into a cul-de-sac. We may be wryly amused to see poetry re-enter the general curriculum of schools by way of Freud and Jung: nowadays one knows doctors who are beginning to read poetry for the first time, but what this interest comes to is just as annoying to the writer as the nineteenth-century attitude that the writer was a geological specimen. The twentieth-century doctor confers an honorary medical degree on the poet. Let me reproduce a letter I once received from a doctor in a county mental hygiene division.

Dear Mr. Shapiro:

Thank you very much for your letter regarding some poetry I have obtained from a patient while in hypnosis. I can readily see your point regarding the evaluation of the material on its literary merits alone. It is in this connection that your critical appraisal would be most valuable since I feel one of the vital factors involved in creative efforts of the type I described would be the role of hypnosis and hypnotic productivity rather than psychotherapeutic projectivity per se. The problem of simulation both therapeutically and hypnotically may well be involved in this material and an opinion as to the level of productivity involved would be most meaningful.

I am enclosing several examples of hypnotic poetry from one patient. . . .

Perhaps I should translate this document into my own words:

Dear Mr. Shapiro:

Thank you for your letter regarding some verse which I obtained from a patient while under hypnosis. You may be right in thinking that literary work must be judged by literary standards alone, but my interest is something else. Are the patient's poems any good? If they are, we may be able to shed some light on the creativeness of the unconscious mind, and perhaps even decide what the relationship is between conscious and unconscious writing. For the time being, we are not interested in curing this patient. . . .

The doctor's letter is funny and also a little frightening. (I considered it a possible hoax, but it is too expectable for that.) I started to reply: "Dear Dr. Blank: It is an unspoken law among poets that we will not help anybody write poetry in his sleep." But the implications of the doctor's letter are disturbing: that he is going to pump poetry out of a sick person; that poetry *can* be unconscious; that there is a direct con-

nection between poetry and the poet's unhappiness—
i.e., that poetry is a fusty nut.

I did ask the doctor how it happened that the lines
of the hypnotic poems end where they do. Did the subject interrupt her revery at every six or eight syllables
to indicate the rhythmic break? Is this poetry or a
pseudopoetic collaboration to prove something out of
a textbook?

And where does this leave the real poet?

Maybe a little closer to the pale. The poet re-enters
the city via a county mental hygiene clinic.

A friendly critic who read these notes pointed out
gently that I might be making the same mistake about
psychology as the psychologist made about poetry;
namely, that I have failed to see the poetic import
of Science. I disagree, at least about psychologists.
Modern psychology is the study of the mind *without*
creativity. It is impossible to know the tree except by
its fruits. Psychology studies the Dead and not the
Living.

It seems to me that psychology is one of those sciences that was born out of the ruins of literature, and
we lean upon psychology because literature is no
longer central to our spiritual life. Every success of the
psychologist is a defeat for psychology and a gain for
the great symbolic activity of the mind which we call
poetry. In this sad relationship, the psychologist is
something like a friend of the poet.

The Unemployed Magician

Once in his life, at a time of his own choosing, each poet is allowed to have an interview with the god of letters. He is a real god, I think, and maybe much more than that. He can answer all questions about poetry, especially the ones poets and philosophers have never been able to settle; I suspect that he can answer every other question as well. The poet, unfortunately, cannot return with the answers; as he shakes hands and says good-bye to the god, the visitor is automatically brainwashed. All recollection of the god's wisdom is obliterated and the poet returns home to write—criticism.

Recently I held my meeting with this deity. I am not sure I really remember our talk, but I have a small facility for reconstructing dreams, and I am under the impression that I can recount the most important questions and answers that passed between us.

The god was sitting behind his desk, polite and prepared to listen to questions he had answered thousands of times before. I had a slight temptation to ask *better* questions than others had, but I dropped this pose the moment I saw him slip into his desk a book of mine I had never seen. The cover said *Poems* by Karl Shapiro, 1913 (the date I was born), and it had the *other* date. The sight of this book sobered me somewhat, and the god tried to put me at ease by remarking that poets were usually a little startled by his appearance. I said, on the contrary, his was a rather familiar appearance.

Yes, said the god, I appear to the poets as they think I look. But beyond that my opinions are my own.

I then confided that he bore a remarkable resemblance to T. S. Eliot and, although there was no conceivable connection, to Sigmund Freud. I now noticed that he was holding the perennial cigar that Freud never put down, and which is his emblem. He moved the box in my direction but I declined.

I am not large enough to smoke cigars, I said.

You are taller than Freud, the god replied beneficently. And he added: I have noticed that you are frequently concerned with the appearances of poets. I put this down to your interest in descriptive verse.

That is not quite it, Sir, I answered. Do you mind if I call you *Sir?* I always call critics Sir. [He bowed his head in approval.] I am really interested in the motility of poets; how the poet gets across the street. So many of them don't.

A poet, said the god cryptically, should never be in a position in which he has anything to lose.

But, I said, I am not talking about drunkenness or bawdry, and I am not thinking about rearing a stable of healthy poets.

The deity chuckled, That is just as well. As soon as a man publishes something, people begin to say he drinks too much. You must know by now that it is not the alcohol but the poetry that kills alcoholic poets.

Alcohol is the poetry of the people, as the newspaper is the wisdom of the people. Poetry is a killer. Still [I thought he shrugged] it is a way of life.

More than a way of life, I ventured. It is an affliction.

For those who want it, smiled the god. It is a choice, after all.

I decided not to say poets are born not made, but the god anticipated me by remarking, Anyone, of course, can be a poet.

I gasped painfully and reached for a cigar.

But if what you say is true, I asked, why are there so few poets, and so few good ones?

Statistics is not my strong point, he answered; but the world can tolerate only so many poets at any one time. Frequently the world gathers the first handful of poets it sees and lets genius waste away. To the world, you know, one poet serves as well as another. It is enough for them that a man has chosen to be a poet. Good or bad, he is a poet.

I can't believe that the world has so little regard for literary standards.

Then you are deluding yourself, said the god quietly. But do not be mistaken. The world needs poets and creates a place for them. Your nice sense of discrimination has nothing to do with their need.

Nice! Doesn't it matter if people think Anne Morrow Lindbergh is as good a poet as Shakespeare?

It is unimportant if they do. Bad poetry is as immortal as good. Would you have all men created equal in sensibility and capacity? What a gray world that would be. But the world does give way to the judgments of poets about poetry sooner or later and for better or for worse. The judgments of poets, I might add, are anything but reliable.

Are the judgments of critics any better? (My tone

was a little rude, for his remarks had begun to ruffle me.)

You poets are always putting words in my mouth, the god replied. Why should I judge poetry? It is judged soon enough by men.

But is it judged well?

That is not my affair. Your works of art seek judgment and they find it. I abstain entirely. Why are you troubled about the squabbles of critics? Really, it shouldn't concern you any more than it concerns me. Try to remember that to the world the existence of a poet is the same thing as poetry itself.

I don't understand.

Look at it this way. To the world you are a man set apart because of your occupation, or rather vocation, if you insist on calling it that. You have a responsibility to maintain separateness. It is a simple matter of distance by elevation. Place any man on a stage, a platform or a soapbox, and he is immediately transformed. The angle of declension is what matters. But let this man lose his distance and he is finished. Among savages a magician who loses his hold over the tribe is killed. So with you poets.

Are you putting poets in the same class as politicians and witch doctors?

I did not mean to offend you, said the god; the only difference is the difference of time. A politician is interested in holding you in his spell only until you go to the polls, whereas the poet asks you to elect him for at least a thousand years. Thus the quality of the poetic article is more durable, *aere perennius*, and harder to sell.

You make it sound rather commercial.

Since you have used the word, yes. But the commercialism of poets exceeds the limits of mere words. In short, I have never known a poet who did not

want everything. Partly for that reason he *is* a poet.
From the child in his crib you withdraw bit by bit
the world he thinks he possesses, until the limits are
fixed and he can define what is his and what is not.
To the poet there is no line, no boundary between
subject and object, sleep and waking, intoxication and
sobriety. I am exaggerating but you see my point.

That may be so, I said, but it tells me nothing
about what the poet gives the world.

What does he give the world? the god asked inno-
cently.

But I came to ask you that. I can only give you the
contradictory answers of the past.

The god thought a moment and then said, I am
willing to tell you, on two conditions. One, that you
follow me through an illogical cross-examination and,
two, that you prepare yourself for an unpleasant result.

I will take it on, I said; hemlock and all.

Very well then, he began. Let us confine ourselves
to the poetry of your own time, as that is the most
alive to you and is the poetry that concerns you most.
Who would you say are the best poets of your own
language in your own time?

Well, to take the best known, I would say, Eliot,
Pound, Stevens, Yeats, Auden . . .

That is enough for the moment, interrupted the
god. Now if you will pardon this parlor trick, if you
were allowed to take one book of poems with you to
a desert island, which one would you take?

Why, I answered, I think I would take the poems of
—D. H. Lawrence.

But you didn't even mention Lawrence. Why?

I mean that I enjoy Lawrence more than the
others, but the others are by objective standards
better poets.

What objective standards are you referring to?

The old standards, I said: originality, suitable intensity, applicability, ability to transport, readability, contemporaneity.

Those are nice big terms to hide behind, said the god. Is that what you tell your students?

To tell you the truth, Sir, I am reluctant to tell them what I really think. It would not fit in with the curriculum.

A normal state of affairs, answered the god. But to come back to the point: doesn't your desert-island poet fit the terms you give?

To a degree, but he is too outspoken. Lawrence misses the mystery of language-making in his passion for his own ideas.

I take it then that Lawrence's *ideas* are very close to yours and would keep you good company on your desert island?

No, Sir. I can't swallow a single idea of his.

What! You would carry with you a poet whose ideas you dismiss and whose language lacks great artistry?

I feel [I stammered] that Lawrence in his sincerity, fool that he was, broke through the façade of artistry and literary affectation and stood at the doorway of poetry itself.

Not a very good metaphor, said the god. You are trying to say you don't know what you mean.

I don't know, yet I believe what I say.

You are accusing Eliot, Pound, Stevens, and Yeats of literary affectation. Are they all affected in the same way or do they have different affectations?

The affectation is pretty much the same. Literary affectation always comes when poets have stopped listening to their own voice and try to invent the speech of their contemporaries. Then they become parodists, humorists . . .

One moment, said the god. Do you label this affectation parody and humor?

Parody, I answered, is the literary style of our age. Joyce, Pound, Eliot, whatever else they may be, are all masters of imitation. Or to put it bluntly, copying.

And Stevens also?

Stevens, I said, is a beautiful poet who is really devoid of imagination. He dreams that imagination will come to him, but it does not come. So he becomes a parodist of the imagination.

Perhaps, the god answered, but surely the parodistic—as you say—Eliot and Pound are men of fine imagination.

They are men of fixed ideas, men of programs. They call poetry the dance of ideas. Ideas can't dance.

And these you say are your best poets? Tell me, in what is Yeats a parodist?

Heavens! Yeats is the parodist of belief. Surely you can't deny it. Yeats lived the mask of Yeats for seventy years.

Do you grant the sincerity of Eliot?

Absolutely.

But Eliot, the god said, pleads with us to accept his poetry whether we accept his beliefs or not.

That is the noose in which they all hang, I said.

Yet you accept Lawrence on the grounds of sincerity, although you have no use for his ideas. At the same time you disagree with Eliot's formula for appreciating poetry while keeping the beliefs to one side. And you call Yeats insincere while you profess to admire his craft. Please explain this tangle of contradictions.

I have already admitted, I replied, that I am stopped by a mystery. I am very much concerned about the beliefs of poets. My final opinion of their poetry is colored by what I think of their beliefs. I realize that this is an old-fashioned way to read the poets. As for Lawrence—Lawrence's style is at least true to himself. With the others, the style, the life and all the rest of it are secondary to some fixed idea. Pound's crooked thinking gives him a crooked style. Lawrence is wrong but honest. But this conclusion leaves me nowhere.

I have noticed that you haven't mentioned William Carlos Williams. Surely you cannot call this poet dishonest or insincere or parodistic.

No; I might try to sneak in a copy of Williams to my desert island. And yet . . .

And yet?

Williams, I said, lets me down in another way. He is *too* sincere.

What! So sincerity can be a vice also?

I mean that Williams' refusal to be anything *but* true to the language, as he calls it with a capital L, becomes just another fixed idea.

If I follow your logic then, the god said, you are accusing Williams of insincere sincerity.

Let's call it stylistic obsession, I said; that's the vice we are talking about. It permits poets to be fools without damaging their reputations.

In other words, my friend, you would have poets be true to themselves, you would have them avoid mannerisms, and you would have them entertain ideas with which you agree. At that rate you would have no poetry left to read except your own. But very well, I will accept your terminology in order to get on. You object to the best modern poets, as you call them, on the grounds of stylistic obsessions. You believe they have forced themselves to become insincere in one way or another. Their brilliant artifice you dismiss in favor of the bare prophetic verses of Lawrence. You agree, I think, that Lawrence's beliefs about man and the modern world are savage and atavistic and perhaps childish.

I do.

How then do you account for the greater appeal of Lawrence to your poetic sensibilities than of Eliot or Williams?

I cannot account for it.

Do you think you might possibly agree secretly with Lawrence's harangues about the revival of the blood religions and the lower consciousness?

That is unthinkable, I said.

Would you say that Lawrence had greater writing skill than, say, James Joyce?

I credit them both with great writing genius, but Joyce, that master manufacturer of literary cuckoo clocks—he is the absolute opposite of Lawrence.

Is it the literal nature of Lawrence's verses that appeals to you?

Certainly that is fascinating. But I must remind you, Sir, that I do not class Lawrence as a poet with the others at all.

Then he is something of a prophet or a mystic in your mind?

Something like that, I said.

And since you repudiate his ideas, would you call him a false prophet?

Yes, I suppose so.

Permit me, the god then said, to recite four lines of the song of a cannibal minstrel who is boasting about his chief. This was overheard by an American traveler to the Ivory Coast. Before a huge assemblage the minstrel shouted at the top of his voice:

> My chief Fire Helmet has thirty-nine wives,
> Their necks are like giraffes',
> Their breasts are always full of milk,
> And they are always pregnant!

Do these lines have the literal quality you admire in Lawrence?

They do have the ring of truth, I said, and they make a crude kind of poetry.

Yet, the god went on, the traveler says this is only a spontaneous boasting-song, and he adds that the chief is really impotent.

All the same, I said, it presents a worthy truth, one which the cannibal chief fervently desires, I presume.

The god laughed.

Is it a truth because of the worthiness of the possibility?

Yes, I said stubbornly, I mean worthy in that sense. The truth of so much modern poetry does not seem worthy to me and I reject it.

You are correct in your judgment of the cannibal verses, said the god, except for one thing. They are not poetry.

Why not poetry?

Because there is no poetry or art among savages.

But, my dear Sir, what about the masks, the costumes, the sand paintings, the cave drawings, the epics in verse, the music and all the rest of it?

All of which are so beloved by your twentieth-century writers? Yet, I repeat, they are not poetry, not art.

Now you are quibbling. What are they, then?

I hesitate to say the word, said the god. Have you ever heard the singing of primitive people?

I once listened to some Polynesians singing something to the tune of "Show Me the Way to Go Home." They said it was a hymn.

That will serve, the god answered. Did they seem to take pleasure in the singing?

Now that you mention it, I have never seen such expressions of exquisite pain on anyone's face.

Would you call this a condition of transport?

I would rather reserve the word for higher moments, I answered.

And there you have the basis of the chief error in what you call literary criticism, said the god.

I am completely in the dark.

Let us approach the subject from another angle. What do your chief psychologists have to say about the sources of art?

If you mean Freud and Jung and those people, I replied, they say nothing. They confess that the secret of art is forever a closed book.

That is one interpretation, the god said. But doesn't that strike you as peculiar, coming from men whose specialty is the revealment of secrets?

Yes, I said, I have wondered about it sometimes.

Have you also wondered why both Freud and Jung display poor literary taste when they are trying to explain the cause of a work of art? Not always but on occasion, as when Jung falls back on Rider Haggard's *She* and Freud on Wilhelm Jensen's *Gradiva,* both very inferior works of art?

I have not read these novels, but I accept your opinion.

And can you supply any reason why both Freud and Jung should avoid the issue so important to them concerning the cause and source of works of literature?

I cannot think of any. It is completely unreasonable that they should leave us in the dark.

Would you entertain the possibility that they are hiding something they are afraid to bring to light? the god asked.

Failing any other explanation, I would. But Freud is as much a pioneer as Columbus and has told us the most unpleasant things about ourselves we have ever heard. As for Jung, he has had the courage to revive the despised science of alchemy and apply it to a study of the unconscious mind.

Would you say these two scientists are reverent toward the arts or otherwise?

Most reverent, I said, in the nineteenth-century German fashion.

Do you think their scientific opinions about culture and art are colored by this reverence?

Very likely, but I still do not see what you are driving at.

One moment, said the god. I want you to tell me what you think of these lines of Freud's. You recall Freud's expression, the omnipotence of thought? It is a disturbance in which one's thought produces a false notion of reality. That is, if you are alone and happen to be thinking about your mother who is three thousand miles away, and the door opens and your mother walks in, you are inclined to connect your thinking about her with the actual arrival. Now listen to this:

Only in one field has the omnipotence of thought been retained in our own civilization, namely in art. In art alone it still happens that man, consumed by his wishes, produces something similar to the gratification of these wishes, and this playing, thanks to artistic illusion, calls forth effects as if it were something real. We rightly speak of the magic of art and compare the artist with the magician. But this comparison is perhaps more important than it claims to be. Art, which certainly did not begin as art for art's sake, originally served tendencies which today have for the greater part ceased to exist. Among these we may suspect various magic intentions.

I am beginning to see your point, I said suspiciously. But this means that poetry would be stripped of its civilizing power entirely. I have read that passage several times before and it never appeared to me in that light before.

What about Freud's idea of the sexual basis of neurosis and of everyday acts—do you think they were accepted with open arms?

Not at all, I answered; and in fact I believe that these ideas have already been rerepressed.

Yes, said the god, it seems to be the nature of the mind to sidestep the truth—for instance the truth that poetry is not art and does not civilize. But now we have said the magic word, we can proceed to your main question: what the poet gives the world.

I'm sorry; I am not ready. What is the magic word?

Magic, said the god. Magic itself.

Is this the disappointment you promised me?

Yes. I ask you to consider a singular fact, namely, that when any critic or esthetician or philosopher discusses poetry, he stops on the word *magic* and runs away with his tail between his legs. Their usual dodge is to translate *magic* into *prayer*. These writers say: poetry is prayer; poetry is the Logos; poetry is a form of medicine; poetry is incantation. They will say anything except that poetry is savage magic.

(I tried to think of some who did but could only call to mind a cynical writing of some nineteenth-century critic.)

Peacock, said the god (who was reading my mind), wrote that cynical essay that stung his friend Shelley into writing the awful squeal called *A Defence of Poetry*. Yet Peacock knew that the poet is a semibarbarian in a civilized community. For this reason you do not teach him at school, whereas your students fairly wallow in Shelley. Nor do you learn what Macaulay said: that as civilization advances, poetry almost necessarily declines, that as the philosophizing tendency progresses, generalization takes the place of particularization, and men make better theories and worse poems; that the Greeks fell into convulsions when they heard Homer, as did the Welsh and Germans when they heard their bards; and that, briefly, poetry works best in a dark age, among rude folk, and that the man who aspires to be a great poet in a civilized age must tear to pieces the web of his mind and become as a little child. Here, I think, you have an apt description of the modern poet with his psychoses, his treasons against society, and his egomania.

It seems to me, I said, that you side with the League for Sanity in Writing and other defenders of mediocrity.

On the contrary. At the moment I side with both Plato and Freud, not to mention Macaulay. We were saying that poetry does not exist among savages but that it is something else. Men have finally discovered that the cave paintings of extreme antiquity, those splendid depictions in the darkest recesses of the grottoes, were not meant to be admired or to delight the weary hunter (as Jackson Pollock delights the weary financier); they were meant to produce an effect upon the animal hunted. Nor were they what you call or miscall religious symbols; they were machines of control, a crude method for dominating nature.

Is poetry a crude method for dominating nature?

It is worth considering, the god answered. Soothsaying, bone pointing, love philters, poison brews, Black Masses are all quite at home in poetry and practically nowhere else! Poetry is physical. It is when it begins to talk about the Ideal that it goes to pot. Good poetry is a love potion. I grant its higher forms of stimulation, yet it never gives up the lower. In your time poets have taken refuge in the dream; that is the modern cloak of respectability. Some of you are dishonest enough to claim that poetry is after all *only* an art, only a game. But it is a game in deadliest earnest to anyone who takes it as it is meant.

How is it meant?

It is meant to transform what it touches; it is meant to transform the reader. There is no need to deny it. The poet exists in that ancient state of mind in which everything is living and animate and subject to his spell. Naming is magic; naming, which some call metaphor, is a cage. A literal translation of Genesis says that the Lord brought to the human being each thing to see what he would *cry out* to it, and all that the human being cried out to each living thing, such was its name. This crying out of names is the power of poetry.

You make us medicine men. Druggists!

Precisely. Poems are patent remedies, many of them fakes, some of them poisons. But a surprising number have effected cures. Generally, of course, poets are trying to cure themselves.

Of what?

That depends on the case, he answered. The most common ailment is Love. Age is another. Disbelief is another, and so on. In your time the most common ailment is Reason. Poets have tried to cure themselves of consciousness and they even pride themselves on a certain degree of derangement. Hence their silly masks, as if the uniform of the violent ward will summon the Muse out of time and space.

Well, I said, we don't have much choice with the so-called rational element warring on men of the imagination.

Pure fiction, answered the god. The forms of modern poetic madness are quite boring. Someone once asked Jung what he thought of the Dadaists. He answered: They are too idiotic to be a decent form of insanity. In other words, my friend, your modern poets have been looking for the panacea when they should have been out picking herbs.

But you yourself have said that the community, the tribe, looks to us for inspiration.

That is true, he replied. Wizards are the most ancient class of men. Wizardry belongs to all times. Music, dancing, acting all have their origin in magic. This wizardry is sometimes frightening: it has driven people to mass hysteria, flagellation and even suicide. People are aware of this. They expect you to build a bridge from the unconscious to the conscious and another from the conscious to the heights. They want to come under your power. But they have withdrawn their faith from you.

What would they have, these people you mention?

They would have you perform the primary acts of language and leave off apologetics and sociology. They will permit incomprehensibility but not sleight of hand. They expect detachment and even secrecy, but they do not allow failure. Every sign, every mark of punctuation in every language, is believed by them to be magical. Writing is taboo to most men, you know; they fear it and they put their trust in you. Man has not detached himself from writing magic. The people reject the word even in your so-called literate civilization. How long did it take for them to turn all your books back into pictures? Are you familiar with the final page of that endless story called *The Golden Bough?* Frazer says, "The dreams of magic may one day be the waking realities of science." What do you take that to mean?

It sounds like fuzzy sentimentality to me, I said. Frazer fell in love with his subject and hated to see it come to an end.

No. He meant that even science tends to drift back

to the magical view, not that magic may one day compete with science.

That they will someday have a common ground?

Not really. Because magic is personal as science cannot be. It works well or badly according to the personality of the magician and his power over the audience. Poetry is discontinuous. You cannot take it out of context. Historians like to think of literary progress and literary criteria. They do not exist.

Good heavens! One might as well be a beachcomber if nothing is left of our work but personal will and idiosyncrasy.

All the same, the god went on, the criteria are imaginary and are invented after the fact. There is no universal poetry. Until a poet recognizes this simple fact he will not write his best verses. He will only mouth abstractions.

Then I see no reason to be a poet, I said, today or any other time.

If there is a reason, said the god with a cough, I do not think it could have been stated before your time.

What on earth do you mean?

I mean the twentieth century. Literary philosophy you think is ancient and honorable. You teach the opinions of Plato and Aristotle, thinking you are beginning at the beginning when you are beginning at the end.

I am lost agan. Plato and Aristotle are at the end of what?

When Plato wrote about poetry, the god said, he wrote as a man who had emerged from the darkness of time and had no wish to return man to the shadows. Hence his expulsion of poets from the perfect city. His reason won out over his admiration of the poet; he knew that poetry and civilization don't mix.

Don't forget that the Athenians associated their play-going with Dionysian worship and did not allow the plays to be enacted except during festivals of the god. Plato and his famous student both searched for ways to justify the arts to man, knowing they could not erase them completely.

Do you mean they would have liked to?

Unquestionably. But what I wanted to say was that it is not until your time that man has been in a position to know what art is. Your time, because your contemporaries have rediscovered the jungle of art, the natural undergrowth of art. A century ago and all the centuries before, a man who hung an African mask on his living-room wall would have been sent to Bedlam. Today it is considered the mark of the gentleman.

What you call poetry [he went on] is a modern thing. What reason had Plato, himself one of the greatest writers and also an initiate in the mystery religions, to condemn the poet? Because he recognized in the poet a disguise of the old savagery. The poet is an interloper in civilization. Poetry falls between religion and science and has nowhere to go and nothing to do.

You are only trying to provoke me. You can't make me believe you agree with Voltaire that Shakespeare was a magical savage.

I happen to dislike Voltaire, said the god, but there you have it. Does not Voltaire represent what *you* call civilization?

Shakespeare, I said, is the touchstone of all poetry. Was he a magical savage?

He was the last of the natural poets, said the god. After him it is all increasingly artificial. John Donne is the first of the self-conscious moderns. In his time poetry flees from the stage as from the plague. Milton writes the last epic. The novel is invented; psychology begins in earnest. And poetry is left on the shelf. Am I not right? You must admit that for the past three hundred years poetry has done nothing but engage in a running battle with science. In your own time poets have even come out in the open and have done everything in their power to sabotage civilization.

But if we don't fight against pure consciousness we shall all be snuffed out like so many candles.

It will be your own doing if you are. Poetry has been interfering with the growing light of consciousness but it has only succeeded in drawing the curtains over its own windows. Your jealousy of science is matched only by your dishonest appropriation of religion and your unconvincing revival of antiquated metaphysics. Your interest in Lawrence, of course, reflects this desperation. Lawrence would have no science, no religion, except his own. I grant that times are hard for poets today. That is no reason for poets to run amuck. The trouble with you is that you pretend to be unemployed when you are really too peevish to sit down at your desks. You are so busy trying to impress society, so busy setting yourselves up as referees in the game of value judgments, so busy aping philosophers, so busy jabbing pins into scientists—that your whole lifetime output of verse is thinner than a seed catalogue.

Some of us are voluminous, I muttered.

Voluminous about what? Economic systems, astrological systems, anthropological systems, metaphysical systems, historical cycles, theology . . .

But in this age, I spluttered, this beastly, standardized, reason-ridden, overpopulated, shallow . . .

My friend, said the god, it is not that your age is devoid of poetry or the need for it but that your poets have turned their backs on their own times. The poetry of your age is all war poetry; it has warred on your world. It is dying of peace. Are you historians? What business have you with dates and diagrams? Why must you change the Past, calling it a sacred cow, making it a Tradition? What business have you with the future of man, much less with my future?

You would leave us without human rights, without judgment. We have a social responsibility as well as the next man.

So much and no more, he answered. Your social responsibility will not make your poetry better or worse. And please do not think because you are a poet that your political opinions are better than those of a taxi driver.

Nor moral nor esthetic opinions? I asked weakly.

You force me to say that the moral opinions of poets are of little or no value. As for your esthetic opinions, even those are suspect.

I fail to see that we are good for anything. What is our magic for? What good are our myths if they exist only on paper for antiquarians to read?

Myths, said the god, with a snort. That is the prettiest piece of jargon you poets have come up with. After you lost the battle with consciousness, you sidled up to religion, and when you couldn't compete with religion you invented Myth. Myth would put you back on the map.

But myth is everything to us, I shouted. The beliefs and legends of every age are re-formed in our poems to give them new life and to give life its meaning for those who would live only as human animals. It is metaphysic in its purest form. It is the very protoplasm of poetry!

You sound like Ezra, the god said. He made a move as if to stand up.

Wait. You promised to tell me what the poet gives to the world. I don't see that you have.

It was clever of you poets, I must say, to switch your affections from the church to the university. Now you are playing second fiddle to sociologists you are practically respectable. Next you will be asking for a laboratory to work in. Instead of taking a walk you will go on a field trip. Myth, mythic form, spatial form, the Tradition, theories of the imagination, and all your hundred thousand *isms* are so much bogus philosophy. You have succeeded in fooling yourselves and a few English professors and no one else. But you no longer deserve the name of poet. You pride yourselves on your little aberrations and your upset stomachs. When one of you dies of social life you shout Down with the Industrial Revolution. You look upon a healthy man as a leper. Neurosis, you sing, Mother of the Muses.

What does the poet give the world? I asked again, ignoring his insults.

The god looked at me over his spectacles.

One thing and one thing only. The present. Others give the past. Still others give the future. The poet gives this moment and that is all. Poetry is humanizing, not civilizing. It allows men to survive in the only world they know—the world of themselves. Not outside the law but in spite of it. Why is the law-breaker or the man of passion a hero? Because in him the drama of the human predicament comes to life. Why is Odysseus a hero? Because he is both loyal and treacherous. Why is Oedipus a hero? Because he committed instinctively the most terrible crime against nature. Why is Hamlet a hero? Because he is weak in his nobility. Every schoolboy knows Milton's sympathy for Satan, that prince of exiles upon whom you model yourself. But the perfect man or the perfect devil puts you to sleep. He has no reality, no presence.

Then the poet is humanity's apologist?

Please don't use words like that. The poet is not trying to prove anything. Beware of the poet who tries to bring you over to his side; he is a confidence man and power hungry. The next time you read a poet whose opinions disturb you, ask yourself whether he is on the side of his characters or on the side of the law—any law. If he is on the side of the law then you may call him an apologist and begin to doubt him as a poet.

I began to quote Hopkins: Wert Thou my enemy, O Thou my friend.

Precisely. Or as Yeats put it: Poetry is made out of the quarrel with oneself.

It is curious to hear you quote Yeats while I quote Hopkins.

But I like poetry, answered the god, I take it where I can find it. Religious poets may use flattery; unfortunately the most effective hymns are nearly always literary trash. The art that leads to consequences is bad art. Art comes back to the artist. *He* is the standard.

Surely you aren't saying that the artist considers himself a god?

Ah, you are close to a marvelous truth. Don't you think it splendid that almost nothing is known of Shakespeare and that scholars still wonder if there ever was such a person?

It is splendid. I hope and pray that no one will ever be able to solve the mystery.

Yes, said the god. It is a great tribute to him that he did not care to leave the world strewn with his laundry bills, love letters, and canceled checks. In your country, I understand, there are libraries devoted to such collections.

Then you are saying that the greatest poet not only did not consider himself a god but hardly even a man worthy of leaving his signature?

The artist who considers himself a god is either a madman or a criminal or both. The true poet is the village practitioner, a Ramakrishna, so to speak. The Greeks pictured the seer as blind; that was a way of putting it. In the end, the true poet is awed by what he sees and by what he has done. But he does not thank himself. He disappears, sometimes name and all, and sometimes his works. Do you know the highest compliment that can be paid the poet?

No, I asked eagerly, what is it?

For a man to travel thousands of miles to a strange land, to stand in a certain spot and say: So this is where Thomas Hardy got his hair cut.

I started to protest but it was too late. Someone came forward with a blackboard eraser which he held over my head. I shook hands with the god, who smiled and winked to the attendant. As the door closed quickly behind me I managed one more glimpse over my shoulder. The man in the chair—I still can't believe it—was D. H. Lawrence.

What Is Not Poetry?

THIS CHAPTER is divided into two parts; the first part is autobiographical and the second is theoretical. The first part tells the story of how I became a critic and the second part is an outline of my poetics, such as they are. These are two views of the same subject and I hope each section will throw light on the other.

The present essays are intended to be the last criticism I shall ever write. In this book I am getting together those few essays which I think worth keeping and which I hope will be of some help to young poets and would-be critics. It is the small mass of my own discarded criticism which I want to mention here before going on to my ideas of the theory and practice of poetry.

Whenever I meet a young poet I ask him among other things how much he knows about criticism. If he says he knows nothing I breathe a sigh of relief for both of us; if he begins to talk about criticism instead of poetry I know the conversation will soon grind to an embarrassing halt. On the other hand,

263

whenever I meet a young critic I quickly confide to him that I am what he calls an *impressionistic* critic —an expression that has some of the overtones of "up from the city streets"—and we can then chat politely and patronizingly with each other. With full-grown and famous critics my experiences have been briefer and sometimes bristling, but I have not cultivated many friendships of this kind.

As long as I can remember I have had an instinctive dislike for criticism of almost every description, whether it is Freud's on Dostoyevsky, Jones' on *Hamlet*, Richards' on theory, or for that matter Aristotle's, and nearly all the moderns. I once enjoyed the *Biographia Literaria*, at least the parts that deal with Wordsworth or *Venus and Adonis* (the sections about the imagination always struck me as being either unintelligible or unconvincing). One of the things I like best about the book is that it is a scrapbook, not a full-scale esthetic. Critics like Sainte-Beuve have held my attention for a while but I have never really learned anything from them. Among modern critics I like to read Edmund Wilson—especially when he is not talking about literature—George Orwell, Van Wyck Brooks and other "impressionistic" writers. I have never been able to make sense out of a history of criticism, primarily because I do not believe that criticism has a history. My favorite essay is Longinus' "On the Sublime," but philosophical essays in general are beyond me. I cannot retain a philosophical concept in my head for more than five minutes and I suspect any poet who can. If poetry has an opposite it is philosophy. Poetry is a materialization of experience; philosophy the abstraction of it.

In spite of the few names I have mentioned I have tried consistently to avoid reading criticism all my life. But life has pushed criticism under my nose. I discovered to my horror when I began to teach modern poetry that it was not really poetry I was teaching for the most part, but criticism. It was only about ten years ago that it began to dawn on me that the poetry called Modern is little more than a façade for various philosophies of criticism, literary maneuvers and cultural propaganda for one or another persuasion. As my acquaintance with this vast literature grew I began to understand the poetry anthology of our time, the university textbook of modern poetry, the purpose of the literary quarterly, the existence of great international prize committees, the strange political pronouncements of certain poet-critics, the public anger at modern poetry, and the innocence of my own bits and pieces of criticism. And, like most poets of our time, the deeper I became involved in criticism the less desire I had to write poetry or even read it. The chill fell on my soul. Finally, I began to understand the criticism of my poems which people had spoken about from time to time and which I could never make sense of. One thing that had puzzled me greatly was the disaffection of certain critics who originally praised my poems far out of proportion to their merit and who later condemned the same poems. It was because they now understood my "critical position" that they disliked poems which had previously appeared to them of a high order of work!

For five years I edited *Poetry* magazine and was forced to read a great deal of book-review criticism for publication. My only aim as editor of this famous magazine was to keep its reputation what it was reputed to be. Because of the intensity of modern critical activity I had no difficulty getting well-known writers to give us reviews. The one famous piece of criticism I solicited was W. C. Williams' review of Sandburg's *Collected Poems*. Sandburg never forgave this essay by Williams and my part in it; but it is the best essay on Sandburg ever written; unfortunately for everybody concerned it was quite negative.

The poetry, by and large, I printed in this magazine was mostly "critical" poetry, or academic poetry. It was the kind of poetry that came; it was the official poetry, the poetry à la mode, and I printed it. Had I been editing a magazine of my own making I would probably have published an entirely different sort of verse. Editing *Poetry* was a job for me, not a vocation, certainly, and I let the magazine coast as it had for forty years. I was afraid to tamper with its respectability. The critics invariably complimented me on my editing; I was not aware of what they meant until I knew their criticism. They meant that I was holding the line for them.

It is still a mystery to me that I was chosen to edit this magazine. My first poems of any worth had been printed in *Poetry* ten years before I became editor. Immediately upon acceptance of the poems, the editor asked if I would undertake to write a review. Thinking it some kind of obligation or perhaps *honor* I accepted and wrote my first review; the books were by Edmund Blunden and Siegfried Sassoon, I think, and I struggled with the piece. At about the same time the *Partisan Review* asked me to write them a letter for publication about the army camp I had become a member of. These were my initiation into criticism. From then on I took it for granted that I was expected to write essays or reviews when asked and I almost never refused. By the time I was discharged from the army several years later, my poetry had become sufficiently well known for me to be invited to lecture before literary audiences. Thus I took the final plunge and became a bona-fide critic. My lectures evidently sat well with the listeners, for

I was shortly offered a job as Associate Professor at an excellent university. This was a great honor for me because I had left that university as a sophomore and was still a sophomore. It is not uncommon for poets to leave the university before they get a degree and I sometimes advise young poets to do the same. The scholarly profession is the one I respect above all others (I do not consider literature a profession), but the poet who can also be a good scholar is a very rare beast. And literary scholarship has been so contaminated by modern criticism in our time that it is dangerous for the poet to attempt to become a scholar, unless he can keep his wits about him.

I am not going to render an account of all the essays and reviews I have published. I don't know what I have written myself; I have no records, no clippings, no bibliography. Now and then someone will ask me about a certain article or poem I wrote and I do not even remember writing it, much less where it appeared. Much of my criticism has been written for publication in a foreign language and I have no original of the thing I penned. The only reason for this slovenliness is my lack of ambition as an essayist or critic or littérateur. Several of my lectures, however, have been published in *Poetry*, the only place I ever attempted to print them. On one occasion three lectures of mine were printed as a small book called *Beyond Criticism;* a few copies were sold and the rest remaindered. Generally, these essays tried to state the same opinions I offer here, but in a more general fashion.

My chief venture into criticism, however, was with the verse *Essay on Rime*, which I wrote in New Guinea to amuse myself. Reviewed on the front page of the *New York Times Book Review*, it sold about ten thousand copies and brought down upon me the wrath of all the gods of criticism. For saying what I thought of Modern poetry and naming names I was henceforth on the intellectual blacklist. Even William Carlos Williams felt called upon to rap my knuckles.

Lest this recital become completely pointless, I want to mention the drift of my previous lectures. Nearly all of them have in one way or another dealt with the need for the poet to dissociate himself from criticism. Only on one occasion did I depart from this principle: that was after the Bollingen Prize controversy when, like other writers, I was shocked at the accusations of the *Saturday Review of Literature* against all of us who were members of that literary jury, and I went to the defense of the jurors. I voted against giving Pound that prize, but I believed all the same that the jurors acted in good faith. Since then I have boned up on their criticism, and I no longer believe that they acted in good faith. The methods used by the *Saturday Review* were unspeakable (calling the prize a Fascist plot), but it now seems to me that the jurors, led by Eliot himself, acted in a distinctly underhanded manner. The journalistic outburst in the *Saturday Review* against our Bollingen committee drove me to write a defense of—the New Criticism, of all things! My first act on becoming editor of *Poetry* was to publish that silly essay. A New York publicist who was trying to raise money for *Poetry* said to me: "I see you have joined the T. S. Eliot covered wagon." He knew more about criticism than I did.

That was my chief lapse of critical sense. On one other occasion—to conclude this *mea culpa*—I jumped on Robert Graves for lumping together all modern poets and throwing them into limbo. It was particularly his criticism of Dylan Thomas that upset me, but I also said the usual mealy-mouthed words about

Eliot, Pound, and Auden. This was before I had read *The White Goddess*, which immediately became one of my favorite books, one which can stand in place of all the New Criticism ever written. Graves has a world-view, which is part of a tradition older and deeper than any tradition employed by the Modernists; of his part in this great stream of criticism I was unaware.

Every poet of my generation grew up in the shadow of the criticism of T. S. Eliot. Whether he read this criticism or not, he was influenced by it. Every vestige of opposition to Eliot had been erased by the mid-thirties, when I began to write verse in earnest. How could a young writer not admire Eliot when even a radical highbrow publication, not to mention all the highbrow right-wing magazines, fell to their knees before this strange puritanical American? Those who didn't, like Williams or Hart Crane, were considered rustics. My tastes and affections had always been with Hart Crane and Williams, but the intellectuals told me otherwise. It took me years of teaching and editing and poring over modern criticism to see the light. It was not poetry the big pontifical magazines wanted: it was Culture. Poetry was only a handy tool of culture. I firmly believe that whatever good poetry I have written was written because of my ignorance of criticism; I just as firmly believe that every poet of our age who has been too close to criticism has either given up poetry completely or has ruined his work because of it. There is no question that Hart Crane was driven to distraction by the niggardliness of his critics, and that poets with the great gifts of Ransom and Tate and Warren have cut their poetry to fit the cloth of the critic. The greatest freedom poets can hope for in the twentieth century is freedom from critical theorizing and a return to the *laissez faire* amateur criticism of the audience. The remarks that follow, although they are not consecutive or logical, will attempt to point the way back to a poetry which is not restrained or informed by Modern Criticism or the poetry that has been written out of this criticism.

It has always seemed to me that everyone except the critic knows what poetry is—I am not trying to be facetious—and that poets and other artists must from time to time remind the audience that the criticism stands between them and poetry. There is one extraordinary fallacy which lies at the bottom of most literary criticism and which is such an obvious fallacy to the ordinary reader and the poet that it seems a profundity when anyone mentions it. The fallacy is that of meaning, the treatment of poetry as language. One might, in the jargon of the age, call it "the understanding fallacy" or "the semantic fallacy." Poetry is not language; its raw material is language, but from this point on the poet goes in one direction, while the critic goes in the opposite direction. The *word* in poetry is not a word in any already existing sense; and I call it a not-word.

The most obvious and salient fact about the natural separation of poetry from criticism is that in the greatest ages of poetry there has been little or no criticism. Criticism comes, if at all, after the art.

Criticism is a department of philosophy, not of literature. The function of criticism is not to "correct taste," as Eliot would have it, but to understand the nature of art. This kind of inquiry is of no interest whatever to the audience or to the artist. Once the artist begins to puzzle about the nature of poetry he moves into the realm of philosophy, his language takes on the gray cast of abstraction, and he ceases to experience that unity with the world which is the poet's characteristic quality. All "philosophical" poetry, whether in Dante, Blake, Lucretius, Milton, Shelley, Bridges, or Eliot is weak to the extent that it philosophizes. This is pointed out by critics themselves at times when criticism is honest and regards itself as a branch of philosophy.

There is an accidental similarity between philosophy and poetry: neither takes language seriously. Philosophy is suspicious of language; poetry sees language as one of the manifestations of nature (the one closest to the poet). To the poet, as to the philosopher, language is in a constant state of flux. The philosopher tries to arrest this flux; the poet only tries to keep up with it.

When critics remark upon poetry as a kind of game, they are naming the wrong object. Poetry is never play to the poet; language is. In trying to follow the play of language the poet is trying to follow the play of nature. The painter follows nature through color, the composer through harmony, the poet through the squawks of the human voice box.

The relationship between poetry, Nature, and mysticism is something like this: the poet substitutes Language for Nature. Everything he knows he knows through the medium of language. The poet has a natural affinity with Nature, whether trees and daffodils or armadillos and scarabs or human beings. (In intellectual, self-conscious times the poet tries to see the "nature" of societies and civilizations, as Yeats, Auden, and Pound and Eliot do. This is the ragged edge of poetry that soon breaks out into politics and theology.) The poet's natural affinity with Nature makes him contiguous to all forms of mysticism, good and bad. The weak poet is magnetized toward some popular *mystique* or even religion. The strong poet is always the heretic and the saint. Even in weak poets like Eliot and Pound there are traces of "religious heresy."

All the great scriptures were probably penned by poet-mystics. Mysticism is not an aim of art (nor is it an aim of mystics!): mysticism is a pejorative used by critics in a rational age to denote a departure from the established meanings of words. Every good poet is a "mystic"; that is, he departs from the dictionary, as the painter departs from the straight line and the perfect circle.

The departure from the Dictionary is not intentional but natural. In the great ages of poetry and the other arts there are no dictionaries or encyclopedias. Shakespeare didn't know how to spell. We know how to spell and have no Shakespeare. Classicism is the attempt to write the dictionary of forms. In our time the Classicism of Eliot, Pound, and Yeats has attempted to arrest the forms of poetry via the amazing stratagem of arresting the forms of society.

The meaning of poetry, as far as language is concerned, is the meaning of *hey-nonny-nonny*. To the poet, *hey-nonny-nonny* means what the other words in the poem failed to say.

It was a lover and his lass
    With a hey and a ho and a hey nonny-no
That o'er the green corn-field did pass

> In the spring time, the only pretty ring time
> When birds do sing, hey ding a ding a ding,
>   hey ding a ding a ding, hey ding a ding a ding
> Sweet lovers love the spring.

The critic will pipe up and chirp: Onomatopoeia!

Living in an age of literacy, we have lost contact with the sources of poetry and see everything through books. The modern poet has turned his back on modern life and views it with undisguised hostility. This psychological provincialism gives modern poetry its tone, whether in Eliot or in Robinson Jeffers. In fact, *The Waste Land* and the *Cantos* have all the characteristics of a hillbilly poetry: broken dialect, broken tradition, a desperate desire to hold on to a half-forgotten past, and a provincial viciousness involving a fundamentalist interpretation of scripture, and tar and feathers.

The rational person is least able to understand poetry. Or rather, it is his understanding of it that prevents him from seeing it as anything but a series of words in meters, with various rhetorical devices and "levels" of meaning. He does not perceive, as all other people perceive, including children and savages, that poetry is a way of seeing things, not a way of saying things. Poetry is "different," not because of meters and figures of speech and symbols (these things exist in advertisements), but because it is a way of seeing a thing differently. The reaction of an audience to good poetry is laughter—the laughter of delight and discovery, not of derision. In fact, the basic emotion aroused by any work of art, however somber or tragic, is joy, even hilarity.

The poet really does see the world differently, and everything in it. He does not deliberately go into training to sharpen his senses; he is a poet because his senses are naturally open and vitally sensitive. But what the poet sees with his always new vision is not what is "imaginary"; he sees what others have forgotten how to see. The poet is always inadvertently stripping away the veils and showing us his reality. Many poets, as we know, go mad because they cannot bear the worlds of illusion and falsehood in which most human beings spend their lives.

The mystic condemns what is called loosely the Imagination. The imagination is the fool in the house, says St. Teresa. The poet thinks in terms of reality, not in terms of the imagination. Reality in his mind is not very far from what the mystics and ecstatics mean by reality. Most uses of imagination in poetry indicate a forcing of one's way toward reality. And in times when the poet theorizes about the imagination, poetry moves dangerously close to rationalism. Notice the mechanistic, highly rational Poe forcing the imagination to create "effects."

The poet never says this to himself, but in effect this is what he means when he begins a poem: he is asking "what is the poetry of . . ." whatever he happens to be dealing with. By poetry, he means the reality of, the totality of. What is the poetry of love at first sight? What is the poetry of desperate ambition? What is the poetry of myself, my consciousness? And the poet with his peculiar way of seeing breaks down each particle of the experience into "the poetry of." "Landscape plotted and pieced." The turtle is "large and matronly and rather dirty." But this is silly: one could go on to quote every poem ever written; and it would be a poem because it created the reality of whatever it happened to be about. Whenever the poet is not "oned" with the experience we can always detect the forcing, the insincerity.

When we hear critics talk about paradox, ambiguity, conceit and so forth, we should be on guard. They are talking about forced poetry, poems in which the author has tried by violence to break through the habitual delusions into reality. The violence of much modern poetry stems from this cold-blooded forcing of reality.

Critics are inclined to misinterpret the poet or artist's use of the ugly; they think either he is making a social statement or a paradox. In good poetry and painting that use the ugly, the poet and painter are, on the contrary, writing about the beauty of ugliness.

There is no borderline between poetry and prose. Even verse (meter) is no distinction. There is only greater or lesser heat. The novel is simply the narrative poem in extension. The novel deals with the poetry of character, the poetry of situation, the poetry of history. It is possible to speak of more or less poetry in a writer, meaning more or less vision-of-reality. Everyone is part poet; it is the poet in each of us that responds to the whole poet. The poet may be a biological sport or a freak. The prose man is the man of average sensibilities, the man who limits his experience of life. The most common universal experience of reality is love. The prose man falls in love once or twice, or according to some psychologists, thrice. If he keeps it up he is in danger of becoming a poet.

Critics frequently speak of rhymes, stanzas, meters and so on as a kind of ritual in which the poet "objectifies" experience. This is nonsense. The forms are not rituals at all but realities. The Greek meters, for instance, were dance steps: the rhythms so produced expressed a mode of thought. On the other hand, when meters are used arbitrarily we get faked poetry. "Iambic pentameter" represented the poetry of English rhythm for a thousand years. This was not "ritual"; it was "the poetry of" the rhythm of our language. The situation in America demanded a new rhythm which we are still trying to find the poetry of.

Keats noted that the poet is generally without "character"; he is a fluid, open and vulnerable character, much like a child. Everyone has observed this about poets. In general, the chief characteristics of any poet are his honesty, his self-acceptance, and his vulnerability.

Poetry is no more language than the landscape is paint. Poetry is a version of language, a reading of it. But poetry, as a version of language is also a version of nature and of human nature. Most human transactions are carried out without language, without speech or writing, language being employed as an aid to more direct forms of communication. As everyone knows, more can be conveyed by the language of glances than poetry can tell; Proust speaks of the language of clothes, and so forth. Buying a ticket at a station window, one reveals more by tones of voice, pace, dress, facial expression, and so on, than any passage by a great novelist can convey. The poet recognizes the limitations of human language and is always slightly outside language. He sees that language is in a state of becoming and cannot be arrested; poetry is rhythmic because the poet takes language at flood and goes with it. He senses the wave of language.

There is usually no criticism during ages of great poetry because at such times it is understood that poetry is not language pure and simple. In our time, when rationalism is world-wide and the intellectuals are the chief spokesman for everything, the tendency is to think of poetry as language, or language treated in a particular way. Actually, poetry is the "poetry of" language, just as painting is the "poetry of" line, color and mass, sculpture is the poetry of solids, and so on. Poetic, picturesque, sculpturesque are all derogatories denoting the failure to penetrate the realities of the material.

The association between poetry and religion is always tenuous; both are emotionally centered modes of behavior and as such they sometimes meet. Poetry seems to have a natural aversion for religion, however, as it does for all form of organization. There is some reason to believe that most scriptural poetry (poetry admitted to bibles) is not "religious" to begin with but is the work of some particular poet or of some folk. This poetry may have a basis in secular experience or it may be "the poetry of" revelation of one kind or another. The best example of the first is The Song of Songs, very likely a collection of Semitic marriage poems, later given theological or allegorical interpretations by the Hebrews, the Catholics, and the Protestants. The Psalms, on the other hand, are God-poetry, the poetry of worship, thanks, supplication, etc.

It is idle to claim that poetry is either a secular art or an art of the supernatural. These are critical dualisms: secular and supernatural—which solve nothing. The poet does not distinguish between them. The natural poet, the primitive poet, the "lyrical" poet, cannot make any such distinctions, because they do not exist for him. The poet is always "one" with his experience; to that extent he does inhabit the realm of the supernatural. All artists search for a unification of the elements of a particular experience, the photographer cropping a negative no less than the painter choosing his landscape or model, or the poet looking for the poetry of the thing that engages him at the moment. The artist is different from other people in that he is in a constant state of "oneness" with his experience. When he is not, he is out of Paradise; he has fallen into the world of rationality where all dualisms run riot. It is a fact, I think, that to most poets the ordinary world seems insane; and quite naturally the poet seems mad to the pedestrian or rational mind. Pure science bears most of the characteristics of art; chiefly what is different about the work of abstract science is the absence of the emotional center of motivation; but scientists are, in the popular rational mind, also considered mad.

Modern criticism has waged war against science in the same way that it has waged war against poetry. Modern criticism is really a branch of what is called Social Science—a better name would be Moral Science—the hybrid science which includes such dubious sciences as economics, political science, psychology, sociology, and even history. History, which used to be a true literary art like poetry, has been debased in our time to a pseudoscience. Criticism tries to debase science and subvert poetry. The removal of this criticism and its pseudosciences should be a primary aim of educators. Sociology is a poetry substitute, not a science. Most sociologists are poets who are working in the wrong medium. I mean this literally.

The great men of science in our time are not honored by the poets. Why is this? Because Modern Criticism in a war against positivistic thinking lumps all science under materialism. This jealousy of Science, whether abstract or practical, comes from the puritanical critics such as Eliot and Pound who know or care nothing about the aims or achievements of science, and is only one of many criticisms of contemporary life. In poetry it has been a fad, since Eliot, to condemn every aspect of contemporary life, with Science as the enemy. The other arts are free of these shallow hates and envies. Whitman's love of science is one of the reasons for his condemnation by modern criticism. It is notable that the culture poets and other Ideocrats make free use of the pseudosciences but ignore true science. Sociology is the poetry of the twentieth century. It writes about such things as Car Culture, etc.

All true poetry is absolutely amoral. What is the moral of *Hamlet?* What is the moral of Mozart's Twentieth Piano Concerto? These are nonsense questions. Even when a work of art becomes "literary," like much Renaissance painting, using biblical subject matter, it lies beyond the reach of religion. Poetry is eternally out of favor with all forms of authority, not because it is antagonistic to authority (only inferior poetry battles against society) but because it does not recognize the reality of authority as it is practiced in society. All art is polarized toward some humanistic point of view, on the one hand, and toward some nonauthoritarian *mystique* on the other. Thus it is always close to "the people" and always slightly beyond the reach of the authorities. Poetry dedicated to the "elites," the authorities, is degenerate, moralistic, authoritarian poetry.

It is true that poetry represents not only the periphery of language but the periphery of a certain kind of consciousness. The poet or artist explores this consciousness constantly until it becomes habitual with him. Robert Graves puts it this way: "The function of poetry is religious invocation of the Muse—its use is the experience of mixed exaltation and horror that her presence excites."

As everyone is aware, poetry exists among the most ancient and primitive peoples as well as among the most civilized. It is one of the first forms of communication among children, that is, one of the primary manifestations of the sense of joy. There is probably no other form of art which is universal in the way poetry is. The uses of poetry are always self-limiting, however, and bear no relationship to history or to society. Modern poetry's attempt to interpret poetry as a refined or pure form of language or as an implement of civilization violates all the known facts about poetry. Poetry exists in a dimension outside civilization, as Plato said or seemed to say.

Everything shows progress except poetry. The reason is that the poet exists in past, present, and future together. History to the poet is a fairy tale. Nor does the poet recognize Literature; he sees this poem and that poem, but not in time, in sequence. The poet understands also that the events of one's own time rarely touch the poet or artist. His knowledge of the present is not a knowledge of wars, what's in the newspaper, and the latest highbrow opinion, but of how his contemporaries talk.

All good poetry has an immediate impact upon its audience. This is proved simply by the existence of the greatest poetry in the form of drama or narrative. Nearly all Modern poetry fails in impact, immediate or otherwise. Even Dante, a poet enmeshed in theology, sought out the common language, the language of the street, for his epic poem. By modern standards, he should have chosen Latin for his poem. If there is only one law of art it is that the work must be capable of apprehension as a whole and at once. This is the nature of art, that it is wholly and immediately apprehended, like a tree or a woman.

The question of the low taste of the audience is always the chief argument for criticism. Actually there is no way to determine the taste of audiences except on the spot. What we know of "taste" is always interpreted by critics and is thus merely a written record of learned opinion. The famous gaffs in literary taste are made by critics, not by audiences.

What modern criticism does not take into account, respecting the audience, is that there is not one audience but innumerable audiences. It seems painfully obvious to point out—but there is a difference between the Punch and Judy audience and the opera audience. There is a different audience for ballad poetry than for epic and tragic poetry. All appreciation, however, rises from the bottom and does not descend from the top. The sickness of modern poetry is the sickness of isolation from any living audience. There is no healthy literature that does not grow out of naïve, folk, and "primitive" art. It is notable that every art in the twentieth century except poetry has drawn richly from jazz, the movies, advertising, the comic strip, commercial design, and even radio and TV. Poetry is somehow deprived of its contact with contemporary art on the popular and even commercial levels. It is only poetry in its rebellious aspects that has tried to regain contact with popular art, without which there can be no sophisticated art. We should write off Modern Poetry, the poetry of the American expatriates of 1915, as a failure to seize power, or as a temporary counterrevolution. If someone would draw up a tentative list of the true poets of our time, those who have abstained from culture bolshevism and who have maintained their touch with popular art, we would find that nearly all those poets lie outside the English language, that is, outside the influence of the poetry-criticism of our time.

Probably the most profound idea in the writings of T. S. Eliot is that of the split between the rational functions of the mind and the creative functions. (He does not use these terms and his dating of the "split" is a very late one.) The extraordinary thing about Eliot's recognition of this process was the use he made of it; instead of aiming at some process for reunifying sensibility, as he called it, he deliberately chose the nostalgic prescientific path of religion. Thus there is no place in Eliot's system for modern science, out of which the split had grown. This contempt for objective science has crippled modern poetry and made it incapable of dealing with our world. The schizophrenic spiderweb of the *Cantos* shows where the antiscience prejudice leads. Pound's rejection of the modern world of science has a purely esthetic motive—art over all. Yeats' rejection of science also destroys any possibility of a reunified sensibility in his work.

But the poet should not be the creator of Unified Sensibility in the first place, but only one of the expressions of it. Poetry cannot change or influence history; or if it can, it is only by example. A good poem or any true work of art is a projection of a whole, organic, "biopsychic" personality. Most of our so-called great modern poems are sick poems, poems split either against Reason or against the Supernatural or against Society. Whereas a poem such as "Song of Myself" is a demonstration of man's unity with Nature and with man's condition.

A "solution through poetry" is therefore a misnomer, and all modern poetics fall apart at this point. The problem of a true twentieth-century criticism must be to separate out all rationalistic poetry (the poetry of social criticism, culture propaganda, all poetry that is sectarian or based upon idea systems) from truly unified poetry. Such poetry lies in a different dimension from politics, religion, or philosophy. It accepts all these things, without being dominated by them.

Art with consequences is by definition bad art. Poetry can do no more than affirm the unification of human with nonhuman nature. If God enters the poet's work, religion cannot. Morality cannot. "Sin" cannot. The Baudelairean travesty upon man's wholeness is seen in his hatred of society and his involvements with historical ideas. All such poetry—which is the model for Modern poetry—ends up as Idealism, the rejection of the whole for the part. Poe's idealization of Beauty ends up as the worship of the beautiful female dead body and the invention of the Whodunit.

The poet is not, in the vulgar saying, either a dreamer or an idealist, but a realist in the highest sense of the word. Modern poetry has given us schemes and blueprints, nightmares, analyses, programs, politics, and metaphysics. Where true poetry is benign and liberating to the human psyche, Modern poetry is a dangerous psychological evil, reinforcing every form of split between man and his world.

All forms of this split in man's consciousness begin with the cynical impudent question, What is Art? The moment this question is posed the split appears and critics begin to talk about form and content, prose and poetry, image and idea, body and soul, innocence and guilt, anxiety and felicity, and good and evil. To the poet none of these dualisms represent reality. Poetry says of all such dualisms—they do not exist.

Poetry has not been taken seriously since the Renaissance (Eliot's date) because it has been considered an art. We consider it ornamentation, recreation, a higher amusement for leisure time and for the educated. Yet modern painting has found its way to every level of our world; music also; architecture especially. Primitive painting is encouraged all over the world, but we cannot name a single primitive poet or child poet of our time. Painters and sculptors have rediscovered the great works of the Etruscans, Minoans, of Mohenjo-Daro, of the African. Literature has rediscovered nothing. Poetry is literally buried alive today; where it exists it is virtually unheard of. It is, as I have reiterated *ad nauseam*, the fault of no one but the poets themselves and their arty self-consciousness that we have evolved an Alexandrian, Byzantine, Neo-Classical art, and not poetry. But the world will have poetry at any cost. *The real poetry of the modern world is advertising*, probably the most debased form of poetry in history but the only authentic poetry we have. Advertising is pure poetic activity—debased to the nth degree, dishonest in intention, vulgar past all imagination, but poetry, the true poetry of modern commerce. Advertising is the poetry of the American masses; sociology is the poetry of the educated middle class; and academic poetry the poetry of cultural officialdom. The aim of advertising is not to sell things (nobody believes the claims of advertisers) but to convince the defenseless victim that he is happy. It is not necessary to own the latest gadget or patent medicine but only to know that the manufacturer loves us. Russia has successfully stamped out poetry because propaganda is a good substitute for it; propaganda is national advertising and it is rapidly becoming the poetry of our masses, too. I think people accept sociology in the same way that they accept advertising and propaganda—as a poetic version of our life. But where is the authentic American poetry of our century? Probably in hiding, if anywhere. Or under our noses, if we really want to find it.

Poets of the Cosmic Consciousness

THERE IS SUPPOSEDLY a conflict between poets and scientists, artists and rationalists. No doubt there is and will be for a long time to come. In one version this conflict dates back to the Renaissance, when modern science really got going. In another version it goes back to the old dichotomy between Plato and Aristotle, with the poet-philosopher on one side and the maker of definitions on the other. Platonists and Aristotelians oppose each other down the years; mystics and Thomists do battle; and in modern criticism we have debates over imagination versus reason, and intuition versus intellect, or whatever the terms happen to be from time to time.

None of this has ever been very enlightening. It is very much like Tweedledum and Tweedledee. If only we could recognize that this altercation is pure theoretical debate, then we might be able to get somewhere. We must recognize that the so-called quarrel between the rationalists and the intuitionalists (or whatever high-sounding names we want to give them) is not a quarrel between scientists and poets but between critics and other critics, intellectuals and other intellectuals, even theologians and other theologians. Left alone, this conflict resolves itself into nothing, but there are always new Tweedledums and Tweedledees appearing on the scene, with R for Romantic marked on one helmet and C for Classicist on the other. Philosophy itself seems powerless to stop this quarrel, although as the philosopher Whitehead says: "In (formal) logic, a contradiction is the signal of defeat: but in the evolution of real knowledge it marks the first step in progress toward a victory." Poets are disinclined to believe in contradictions in the first place.

It is not the poet who gives battle to the scientist, nor the scientist to the poet; it is our old friend the intellectual, the middleman of literature. In the argumentative world of criticism there is plenty of literary bloodshed but it doesn't amount to much, either in the real world of poetry or in the real world of science.

Yet there seems to be a life-and-death struggle between science and poetry. Poets of a critical turn of mind accuse scientists of esthetic insensitivity; scientists supposedly accuse poets of living in a dreamland which has no relation to life. But as far as I can determine, the scientist is a whole-hearted devotee of the arts! He loves the arts and even practices them; he goes to them with the gusto of a man whose mind is alive, whose senses are athirst for the supersensations which arts can provide. In contrast to the scientist, who takes to the experiences of art freely and healthily, there is the critic and (all too often) the literary specialist, who is interested in the arts only if they happen to touch upon his "field." The critic and the specialist tend to engage in the pursuit of literature not because they have an affinity for it, not because they love poetry or fiction, but for secondary reasons.

The curious literary phenomenon of science-hatred

stems from a few poets, many pseudopoets, and almost all literary critics. It is a basic literary convention of the twentieth century, and it is disgusting. It is a very recent "tradition," if I may use the word. Science-hatred got into poetry only about a generation ago, with the rise of Eliot, Pound, and Yeats and the New Critics to authority. The Romantics and Victorians a century ago were elated by what they called progress and even technical invention—most of them, at least. Whitman's perceptions about science and his frank admiration for it was used as evidence against him when the modern poets came to power. Even the early twentieth-century poets adored science. Marinetti, the Italian Futurist, tried to found a school of poetry based on exaltation of the machine. Sandburg and Ezra Pound (in his more innocent days) looked with respect upon science and the technological revolution. More recently, the poets who followed Eliot (Auden, Spender, Day Lewis) held up the scientific ideal as a panacea for the condition of modern man. But evidently this ideal was tied too closely to Marxism in their minds, because all these poets gave up their love of science when they lost faith in—Russia! This is typically the way of the intellectual, or what D. H. Lawrence called the Idealist. The intellectual has no real affinities except to ideas. When the idea dies his loyalty dies. Auden has become a puppet of T. S. Eliot, Spender some kind of indefinable cultural idealist, and so on. We are forced to conclude that the interests of these poets in science was either insincere or that it was not science at all but Society they cared about. And here lies the rub.

Science-hatred stems from those writers who feel that art has been displaced or abolished in the modern world. Looking about for a scapegoat they seize upon what they think of loosely as Science. I doubt whether these poets or critics know much about Science. Actually, I have never known or heard of a poet who could pass a high-school examination in any science of any description. The detestation of the sciences is pure bigotry, pure ideology, prejudice on a schoolboy level. But these prejudices are highly decorated with ideological criticism. Fortunately, this condition applies only to poetry; it does not apply to painting (which has profited happily from technological discovery), or music, which makes use of everything science can put in its hands. It does not even apply to fiction, which has no science-hatred to speak of, and has even developed a thing called science fiction, which promises more than "classical" poetry can to open out in new directions. Nor does this condition of science-hatred apply as much to all modern poetry as it does to modern English-American poetry! This is something worth examining: we are dealing with a very local, very narrow tendency. There are poems in the modern anthology in English condemning Einstein (by Cummings and MacLeish); Einstein is blamed for upsetting the moral order and for perhaps helping to make our world hideous with industrialism, standardization, and so on.

At a deeper level, however, we find D. H. Lawrence criticizing the destruction of the instinctual functions of man. Lawrence had some science-hatred of his own, but we should remember that Lawrence was a deep admirer of Whitman and of America. In Eliot and Pound science-hatred is really a shallow America-hatred, a petty longing for the grand old days when knowledge was not a free commodity but a property of the "elites." Rilke himself, probably the best poet the twentieth century has produced, wrote: "All we have gained the machine threatens . . ." but he added, "so long as it makes bold to exist in the spirit instead of obeying." He speaks without bitterness of the "playing of pure forces that no one touches who does not kneel and marvel." But most of the fashionable moderns see nothing good whatever in the machine, although they tend to live in the largest cities and have the intellectuals' horror for the open spaces.

Let me repeat what I have so far said.

There is supposedly a deep and irreconcilable division between Science and Art, between Reason and Imagination.

This conflict is an ideological conflict with no basis in reality. It is perpetuated and restated from time to time, not by artists or scientists but by theoreticians, literary critics, and cultural opportunists.

Certain culture opportunists of our own time have declared war upon scientific objectivity, experimentation, and even technological progress. They have done so for personal reasons or in the mistaken view that they were helping to preserve various esthetic or spiritual "values" of the past.

By the process of guilt-by-association they have blamed Science with a capital S for the ills of society, for the general spiritual malaise (assuming there is such a thing), and even for the historical situation.

This cultural antiscientism is today a very local phenomenon: it came into existence only about a generation ago, through the self-styled Classical revolution of T. E. Hulme, Pound, Eliot, Yeats, and their followers, most of whom are members of a school of criticism called the New Criticism. It exists outside Anglo-American poetry and criticism only insofar as this critical infection has spread. It flourished in France a century ago but seems to have died out.

Thus far I will have retained most of the readers, everyone except followers of Modern Criticism and modern Classicist poetics. But from this point on I will be working in the dark and am liable to lose everybody, including myself. I am going to attempt to show that the science versus art conflict is fictitious. More than that, I will attempt an inquiry into the "cosmic consciousness" of the poet or artist; the object being to show a certain unity of aim between poetry, mysticism, and science. (When I use the word science I exclude all sciences of man: social sciences—especially psychology. Our inquiry into cosmic consciousness *is* in fact psychology, but it is psychology based upon the works of poets, mystics, ecstatics and those writings which are incorporated into the scriptures of every people. This kind of psychology also touches all those forms of protoscience such as alchemy, astrology, and magic.)

I choose the term "cosmic consciousness" because it was used in the nineteenth century in reference to Walt Whitman. It is as good a name as any. By cosmic consciousness is meant the capacity of the individual consciousness to experience a sense of total unity with all Nature, or the universe, or some degree of that experience. Whether this capacity is "pathological" or "normal" makes no difference; what is important is the fact of its existence and its significance. The literature of "cosmic consciousness" is, as I have suggested, very wide and is possibly the largest body of written matter in the world—or was before the age of mass printing. In a sense, all literature of any kind before Modern Science is related to the literature of cosmic consciousness, whether poetry or magic (early experimental science or consciousness psychology). The works at the center of this literature are, however, those usually classed as mystical writings.

There is a basic relationship between poetry, mystical writings, and science—namely, the expression of the principle of unity in all things. I know nothing about science but it is apparent that underlying all scientific inquiry is the *belief* in this unity. It is belief in precisely the same way that the mystic believes in his perception of unity. Without this belief in a total interrelationship of things science would be powerless to add one construct to another. Psychologically it would have no motive. Mystical writings, however, are not a search for this unity but a record of it. And poetry, all art, is a more formal and immediate expression of the same principle.

Neither science, mysticism, nor poetry need articulate this principle. It is taken for granted; it is a kind of intuitive knowledge which can be erased only by the more rigid forms of thought, those in which a sterile logic is allowed to operate at the expense of experiential or subjective knowledge.

The poet does not know the difference between subjective and objective knowledge. He is a poet partly because he doesn't. Nor does he know the difference between sacred and secular knowledge: that is a theological distinction which lies outside his sphere of interest. As far as one can tell, poetry is not a metaphorical or symbolic version of the world but an actual representation of reality. Given the conditions of art, that it materializes from the emotional centers of the mind, it yet belongs to the same world of reality as the mathematical formula. We are all under the influence of the mechanistic psychologies of the nineteenth and twentieth centuries and our terminology is clumsy to begin with. But as far as poetry is concerned, objective and subjective do not exist. (Modern poetry succeeded in destroying the natural poetic impulse in our time by evolving a theory of "objective" poetry and even a theory of personality to go along with it. Naturally, this objectivity theory used Whitman and Blake as the first points of attack.)

Our education tells us that the reasoning faculties are the highest faculties of man. Poetry tells us that the reasoning faculties are only equal to and perhaps even inferior to the emotional and instinctual faculties as powers of perception. The kind of consciousness I am talking about does not appear in Freud or in measurement psychology; it appears in all those works I mentioned, those of the mystics, illuminati, poets, and magicians (premodern psychologists), certain philosophers, and, I am sure, scientists.

Higher consciousness, in fact, results from a unification of the reasoning centers with the other centers of the mind and body. A purely reason-bound science shortly finds itself confronted with disturbing and inexplicable phenomena, or with contradictions which upset the applecart. In speaking of the unification of other "centers" in the mind and body I am paraphrasing certain of the ancient psychologies which are far more sophisticated than any we know in our time and which are rejected by contemporary psychology—the official psychologies in our schools and hospitals. Most, but not all, of these psychologies I am speaking of are Oriental and are just beginning to make their way into the West.

I would like to give one example of a Freudian view of certain phenomena of consciousness known as Psi phenomena. It is very interesting to see how Freud, the mechanistic psychologist, approaches such material and what his reaction to it is. Psi phenomena is a term that refers to such data as extrasensory perception, telepathic communication, mediumism, etc.

In 1933, Freud published a paper on "Dreams and the Occult." I use the date to show that it was a lecture from Freud's mature years, after all his major work had been done. In this paper Freud admitted

from his own clinical experience the existence of telepathic and thought-transference phenomena. Freud
did not follow up these Psi data; his concern, as he
said, was not the occult but whether the existence of
occult manifestations would in any way threaten his
theory of psychoanalysis! He went further and com-
forted himself with the thought that these phenomena
"would seem actually to favor the extension of the
scientific [or, as opponents would say, mechanistic]
way of thinking onto the elusive world of the mind."
He then suggested—mechanistically—that man may
have some atrophied capacity for communication
without language, like the ants and the bees.

The transit of Freud's reason-inhibited mind is interesting. He observes the Psi phenomena and immediately looks about for the mechanism. The poet,
mystic, occultist, and perhaps the visionary scientist
would look for the context instead. Freud could see,
of course, that there was a connection between the
appearance of Psi phenomena and extreme emotional
states; his interest in Dostoyevsky's epilepsy is one
example of his curiosity about the mental states of
artists. Freud decided that Dostoyevsky, however, was
not a true epileptic but a pseudoepileptic. (It reminds
us of the old-fashioned accusations against the mystical experience: that it is not real but somehow halluci-
nated.) Freud tries to dispose of the occult by saying
that one of the secret motives of occultism is to come
to the aid of religious belief. This is a good insight
from the founder of psychoanalysis, but the emphasis
is peculiar, as it must be in any Freudian discussion
of religion. Far from enforcing religious belief, the
occultist tries to rise above it. Nearly all the great
mystics ("occultists") have been treated as heretics
by their own religions, nor have they been founders
of new sects.

This is not meant to be a protracted anti-Freudian footnote, but Freudianism is one of the stumbling blocks between us and an understanding of the wider psychologies. We recall that Freud fainted dead away when he discovered that Jung had finally deserted him. Jung's recognition of the importance of mysticism in the study of psychology was and still is the chief threat to the whole Freudian system.

Jung is far from being an occultist or poet, but he is less of a rationalist than his teacher. Jung recognizes in all mystical systems not what Freud would think of as personal neurosis, but the presence of consciousness disciplines and a vast interrelationship between minds and their contents. Freud's ignorance of mysticism and even of religion is that of the typical nineteenth-century rationalist, about what was thought to be superstition or "poetry." His ingenious theory of the creation of Christianity (that those Jews who "confessed" to the murder of Moses became the Christians and the "unmentionable crime" of killing the father of Judaism became "original sin")—this kind of thing is basically frivolous. Freud prefers the Christians because they release "the repressed material" and so on; that is, they are good psychoanalytical subjects.

In rejecting Freudian mechanics and Freud's causal logic, Jung has performed one of the great scientific and creative acts of our time. For the first time, perhaps since the Middle Ages, a trained scientist and scholar has examined occult texts of the past, not as superstition and protoscience but as living insights into man's relation to the cosmos. I will give one example.

The chief authority on magic at the present time (Lynn Thorndike) mentions a Chinese work called the *I Ching* (*Book of Changes*) as an ancient work of divination. Thus he gives the typical rationalist view of what is thought by other scholars to be one of the world's most important books. Jung, in writing an introduction to this work, notes first that both branches of Chinese philosophy, Confucianism and Taoism, are rooted in it. Hence its historical importance, if nothing else. The *I Ching* or *Book of Changes* is at least three thousand years old, in all likelihood much older. To Western eyes it has always appeared as a collection of spells for the purpose of fortunetelling, and in a sense that is precisely what the *I Ching* is! When writing his introduction to the book Jung himself asked the *I Ching* (as one asks a human being) its judgment about its present situation—that is, Jung's intention to present the book to the Western world.

I want to quote a few observations of Jung's about this book and its relation to "consciousness" psychology.

"It is a curious fact," says Jung, "that such a gifted and intelligent people as the Chinese has never developed what we call science. Our science, however, is based upon the principle of causality, and causality is considered to be an axiomatic truth. But . . . the axioms of causality are being shaken to their foundations [by modern physics] . . . we know now that what we term natural laws are merely statistical truths and thus must necessarily allow for exceptions . . . we need the laboratory with its incisive restrictions in order to demonstrate the invariable validity of natural law. If we leave things to nature, we see a very different picture: every process is partially or totally interfered with by chance, so much so that under natural circumstances a course of events absolutely conforming to specific laws is almost an exception."

Here I may interject the commentary that poetry and all art is natural in precisely this manner, the staggering phenomenon of individuation (chance) being the starting point of poetry. Western science is unable to cope with the fact, for instance, that every biological event is unique. Notice how the poet, D. H. Lawrence, says the same thing: "There is in the nature of the infant something entirely new, underived, underivable, something which is, and which will forever remain *causeless*." Lawrence underlines "causeless."

Jung goes on to say that the Chinese mind as seen through the *I Ching* is exclusively preoccupied with the *chance* aspect of events and not the causal aspect. Causality is hardly noticed. "While the Western mind carefully sifts, weighs, selects, classifies, isolates, the Chinese picture of the moment encompasses everything down to the minutest nonsensical detail, because all the ingredients make up the observed moment."

This "upside-down" Chinese view Jung calls "synchronicity," the opposite of our law of causality. In synchronicity there is "a peculiar interdependence of objective events among themselves as well as with the subjective (psychic) states of the observer . . . The ancient Chinese mind contemplates the cosmos in a way comparable to that of the modern physicist, who cannot deny that his model of the world is a decidedly psycho-physical structure."

I will leave the *I Ching* at this point except to add that the *I Ching* "fortunetelling" method follows upon a throw of coins or a throw of a bundle of yarrow sticks, the configurations of which are interpreted in the text of the book in answer to a question asked. Only one throw is permitted. As Jung says: "If a handful of matches is thrown to the floor, they form the pattern characteristic of the moment. But such an obvious truth as this reveals its meaningful nature only if it is possible to read and to verify its interpretation, partly by the observer's knowledge of the subjective and objective situation, partly by the character of the subsequent events."

The "one chance" is similar to Lawrence's "one chance" of being born in a particular form. And "reading the pattern" of events is, of course, a fair definition of the creative act of the artist. The *I Ching* is thus an oracular interpretation of reality based on the actual observation of the subjective-objective event.

I am not trying to make a parallel between the *I Ching* and the poetic process; I mean only to point out the similarity between "synchronicity" in this ancient system of thought and in all creative activity. The psychological process is the same; the awareness of chance on a cosmic scale is the same. We get this awareness in all great Western literature. Tolstoy, writing of the Napoleonic wars says: "Nothing is the cause."

The difference in attitude toward Nature or the cosmos in the East and in the West is best seen in Zen Buddhism. (The present interest of poets in this Japanese "way of life" is a reaction against the rationalistic poetry and criticism of the whole Modernist school.) The exercises, quips, and disciplines of Zen attempt to abolish dualities of every description. It opposes symbolism and draws the attention to what it calls "direct pointing" to the truth. Immediacy in Zen is not unlike synchronicity in the *Book of Changes*. A Zen saying goes:

> No thought, no reflection, no analysis,
> No cultivation, no intention;
> Let it settle itself.

The high aim of Zen is a perfect awakening of consciousness without ignoring the immediate situation: "to enter into awakening without exterminating the

defilements" (that is, without ignoring what is unpleasant to recognize—this is the poetic of William
Carlos Williams). Zen instruction is a maze of paradoxes all designed to destroy the false rationalism of
logic, classification, and symbol. Zen sayings and Zen
"problems" belong to nothing comparable in Western
thinking except poetry, writings of the mystics, and,
it may be, certain phases of modern science. Even the
dualism of good and evil is eradicated in Zen, just as
it is in all successful works of art. "The conflict between right and wrong / Is the sickness of the mind,"
says one of the oldest Zen epigrams. Zen also gets rid
of the distinction between "me" and "my experience."
This entire philosophy or way of life claims that it
has nothing to teach, that its truth is self-evident and
so obvious that it is, if anything, concealed by explaining it. But this truth is self-evident only to the awak-
ened, to the absolutely conscious. Its object is to
waken higher consciousness.

Zen Buddhism has had a profound impact upon the
arts as well as upon the social life and history of the
Japanese people. The Noh drama, one of the highest
reaches of dramatic art, is founded upon the Zen paradox of naturalness in extreme control. The terrific formality of Japanese art is not based upon the false
dualism of form-content but upon the noncausal idea
of immediacy and spontaneity in all works of nature—
Lawrence's "immediate present." To be able to perceive the formality in chance and the chance in
formality calls for a conditioning of consciousness
which is familiar to artists everywhere, as well as to
mystics and to the great scientific discoverers. Western scientists are fully aware of the play of "intuition"
in discovery and the phenomenon of coincidental discovery, recognized even by Freud as a manifestation
of Psi activity.

It is quite obvious that causal science has achieved all its successes independent of these synchronistic psychologies of the Orient and of the European past. Similarly, all the failures in Western science occur in the realm of human events (social science). Science seems incapable of dealing with problems of civilization. But the question whether science is a deterrent to civilization is absurd. Science claims no such ambition in one direction or the other. Once it does it ceases to be science.

It appears that in the twentieth century we have reached the point at which Oriental "ways of life" are about to penetrate the West. At the same time it appears that science has reached that frontier at which it meets up with art and what is called mysticism. We can see this in the reaction of Jung against Freud (cosmic versus rationalistic psychology), in the tremendous spurt of creative activity the world over, and in the speculations of cosmic scientists—which I know about mostly from rumor. Civilization is no more the concern of the poet than it is of the scientist and the mystic. "Civilization" is, in fact, a word, like "culture," which means nothing. Civilization is an invention of the sociologist and of the politician.

Nature consciousness or cosmic consciousness is being forced upon the attention of the world from every side; the deep vein of mysticism has been opened again and the age of pure rationalism seems to be on the wane. In this there can be little advantage to science except on those shadowy borders where knowledge of the mind can help the scientist to apprehend his own material. "Science," says the religious philosopher Von Hügel, "is but part of a whole, but a function, a necessary yet preliminary function, of the whole of man . . . Crush out, or in any way mutilate or de-autonomize, this part, and all the rest will suffer." A tremendous synthesis is in the making between modern science, the ancient psychologies of the past, and what we call poetry or art. The good will is all on the side of the scientists; and the rapprochement must come from the artists. The artist seems to be the nexus between the scientist and the mystic.

The modern physicist has a much greater tolerance for the mystical view than the nineteenth-century scientist. The Austrian physicist Erwin Schrödinger, in a book called *Mind and Matter*, discusses the modern scientific idea of what Jung calls synchronicity: he calls it "potential simultaneity." Because of the discoveries of Einstein, Lorentz, Poincaré, Gibbs, and others, the physicist no longer takes causality as the basic mechanical law. Event A causes event B is no longer the rule; A and B may occur together or even in reverse, as in the events in *Through the Looking-Glass*. (Lewis Carroll was, of course, a mathematician who was dealing with what we call relativity.) Schrödinger says this of the modern physicist's conception of time: "To be allowed to play about with such a master's programme believed unassailable . . . seems to be a great relief, it seems to encourage the thought that the whole timetable is probably not quite as serious as it appears at first sight. And this thought is a religious thought, nay I could call it *the* religious thought." And this scientist even points to the reason for the obscurity of such a notion to most people, namely that language is so imbued with the idea of time that we cannot use a verb *without using it in one or another tense.*

(Here, incidentally, Pound and William Carlos Williams come to our aid: both were looking for the verb without tense, so to speak. The substantive quality of the Chinese verb is what attracted Pound to

Chinese; the timelessness of the object is what attracted Williams. Imagism was an unsuccessful experiment in this direction.)

I maintain, through this fog of references, that modern science, mysticism, and poetry occupy the same ground, which may be called, for want of a better phrase, cosmic consciousness.

I offer a new expression—science-mysticism. There is, in fact, such a thing as science-mysticism, which should be the concern of every scientist and every poet, if only as bedside reading. Poets gravitate toward this kind of literature in the same way that Yeats gravitated toward medieval magic—partly in revulsion against religion but still searching for the truth lying back of religion. I will cite two modern "science-mystics": P. D. Ouspensky and Wilhelm Reich, whose names will never sully the pages of the culture journals. I first came upon Ouspensky through reading about the American poet Hart Crane. Reich came to my attention through a personal friend, a Freudian psychologist who became a Reichian. Reich himself died in a prison after the police ordered his books burned in New York City. A truckload of Reich's works were destroyed by court order; nearly all of his books are under ban of publication in the United States. Reichian psychologists, doctors, and technicians have been driven from hospitals and persecuted mercilessly.

Ouspensky's interest was consciousness discipline. His aim was to discover such a discipline suitable for modern twentieth-century man. Previous disciplines of consciousness meant renunciation of the world. The Hindu fakir undergoes fantastic physical suffering in order to rise to a higher stage of consciousness; in so doing, his emotional and intellectual faculties atrophy. The monk follows a path of faith and religious sacrifice in order to expand consciousness; in his case the physical and intellectual centers tend to atrophy. The yogi follows a way of knowledge at the expense of the body and of the emotional faculties. Ouspensky posits a fourth method to attain superior consciousness which will not exclude any of the psycho-physical "centers" nor the day-to-day element of chance. The object, as with all mystics, is to rise above the confused states of consciousness and living sleep which characterize nearly all men. According to Ouspensky, there are three types of men we know of: the lowest type, motivated by the physical centers; the second, by the emotional centers; and man number three, by the intellectual centers. But four other higher types can be hypothesized, the seventh or highest being the one which can account for such figures as Jesus and Gautama, the founders of religions. These men did not intend to found religions; it is the misinterpretations of their teachings to their students which were eventually written down and turned into systems of action which we know as Hinduism, Buddhism, Christianity, and so on. According to this view all religions are debasements of esoteric teaching and mystical instruction. Ouspensky calls them pseudoreligions. For instance, Ouspensky and Gurdjieff, one of his teachers, expound the New Testament as a system of consciousness knowledge in which the expression "the Kingdom of Heaven" is a gloss for "esoteric knowledge" or higher consciousness. The entire Testament suddenly becomes intelligible according to a few such glosses. (A glimmering of this knowledge creeps through in the recent discussion of the Dead Sea Scrolls and the Essenes. Mystics have always been familiar with the Essenes and their relation to esoteric Judaism and Christianity; in rational scholarship it is something new. Whether Jesus and the

Buddha were "divine" is a matter of terminology; both had attained the "seventh" stage or "heaven" of consciousness. "The Kingdom of Heaven is at hand" does not mean the end of the world but final illumination. It is a parallel to the Hindu saying: "When the student is ready the master arrives."

Religion, in short, is debased psychology, just as psychoanalysis is debased religion. Freudianism tries to displace the old pseudoreligions; but it is itself a pseudo-pseudoreligion.

Ouspensky's system is only a modern version of dozens of ancient consciousness systems; he was certainly not trying to start a cult. His objectivity repels me considerably; he has nothing to say about art or literature and his works are full of mathematical formulas and diagrams which I cannot understand. Yet when he explains the phenomenon of the Gothic cathedral not from the "history of art" but as the geometrical model for the occult teaching of cosmic consciousness, I begin to understand these fantastic monuments. The science-mystic is always looking for the context, the wider context, the still wider context, *ad infinitum*. This is good "poetry"; I assume it is good science as well.

The objective scientific validity of the findings of Wilhelm Reich is not for me to decide. If you mention the name of Reich to anyone at random, he will dig around in his memory and perhaps come up with a terrified leer. "Oh, Reich. The orgone-box man." Reich broke with official psychoanalysis and founded a school of his own based upon the concept (according to him, the physical existence) of a universal cosmic energy which he named "orgone" energy. Evidently Reich was highly respected in some circles before his crash; even the Atomic Energy Commission backed him and his laboratories in experimenting with this energy, medically and theoretically. During the Korean War, Reich and his workers experimented with the effects of radioactive fissionable matter on orgone-active materials. The clash of the two "energies" produced its own kind of radiation sickness with such dangerous consequences that the experiments were abandoned and the AEC withdrew its support.

Orgone energy (or cosmic energy) was originally used by Reich for medical therapy and psychotherapy. Later it was used for cancer treatment, and Reich gave evidence of achieving favorable results. Reich, however, was ostracized from the medical profession; at present, he is considered as evil as those anatomists who robbed graves in the Dark Ages under pain of death.

The basis for the hatred of Reich is, of course, his use of sex therapy and his theory of the orgasm, which were as offensive to psychological "science" as to the police and the clergy. Reich nevertheless speaks to the poet and the mystic as well as to the scientist. The feeling of having one's roots in nature, he says, is common to all great poets and writers, thinkers and artists, just as it is always felt in true religion though never completely realized. And because this sense of being rooted in nature either has been experienced mystically or attributed to the eternally unknowable regions beyond human ken, the search for knowledge, according to Reich, has always turned into superstitious, irrational, metaphysical beliefs.

Reich observes that modern man as chemist will regard his writings as a return to (the "phlogiston theory" or) alchemy, while the religious fanatic will regard him as a criminal blasphemer. To the poet and mystic it will be evident that what Reich calls the cosmic-energy ocean in which all things exist is indeed what others call God.

Another recapitulation is in order at this point.

"Cosmic consciousness" was a term used to refer to the poetry of Whitman in the nineteenth century and is a fair definition of a kind of poetry which lies at the center of the creative activity, whether in poetry, mysticism, or in science itself.

It is the belief in or the principle of the natural unity of all things which motivates human knowledge and human art.

The rationalization of this principle leads to pseudo-art and pseudoscience. Religion itself is a derivative of the knowledge given us by mystics (usually called "heretics"), occultists, magicians, poets, science-mystics, and scientists themselves.

Carl Jung's scholarly investigation of the Occult is one of the most important scientific and esthetic events of our age.

"Synchronistic" philosophies such as are embodied in the *Book of Changes* and in Zen Buddhism are in no wise contradictory to Western "causal" science but supplement our science. To quote Von Hügel: "Western science is part of a whole, a necessary function of the whole of man; we cannot mutilate our science without mutilating the whole man."

What I choose to call "science-mysticism" is a bridge, perhaps a flimsy one, between the great knowledge of Western science and the great knowledge of the old psychologies and *mystiques* of the past. Science-mystics like Ouspensky and Reich point the way to consciousness disciplines which may be the next stage in human evolution. If not theirs, then similar disciplines.

There is no place for religion in a discussion of this kind; nor is there any place for sociology; nor for rationalistic poetry and esthetics.

I return to Whitman, the chief modern exponent of

cosmic consciousness, as Blake was a half-century before him. We must admit at once that we cannot know
Whitman through modern criticism. Eliot called
Leaves of Grass claptrap; Pound, the rationalist poet,
could see only politics in Whitman; Williams was
steered carefully away from Whitman by his contemporaries. The scholar and historian F. O. Matthiessen, writing in the thirties and forties, saw in Whitman only a political visionary, but politics were only
a minute fraction of Whitman's vision. Recently, the
scholar James E. Miller has published perhaps the
first full-scale study of *Leaves of Grass* as a mystical
document; this book may mark a turning point in our
attitude toward Whitman. It ignores the rationalist
sociological view of Whitman and plunges into the
central mystical experience of Whitman's poetry, even
outlining the stages of the revelation or psychological
breakthrough in Whitman's case.

I would like to refer back, however, to an older
book, one written at the turn of the century, the book
called *Cosmic Consciousness*, by Richard M. Bucke.
Bucke was a doctor and medical superintendent of
an asylum for the insane in London, Ontario. He
was a friend of Whitman's and once had to write a
defense of Whitman's sanity. (One of the contemporary views of Whitman was that he was mad.) I am
not recommending Bucke's book as any sort of defini-
tive work or even as a good study, but as an example
of the kind of interpretation which lies closer to the
meaning of this kind of poetry than our criticism can
deal with. Bucke's book is only partly about Whitman
and it is in most respects a very quaint study.

Bucke gives the following instances of cosmic consciousness: Gautama, Christ, Paul, Plotinus, Moham-
med, Dante, Las Casas (the sixteenth-century Span-
iard who fought against Indian slavery in the New

World); St. John of the Cross, Jakob Behmen, Blake, Balzac (on the basis of *Séraphita*); and Whitman. Among imperfect instances of cosmic consciousness he treats Moses, Isaiah, Socrates, Pascal, Spinoza, Swedenborg, Wordsworth, Pushkin, Emerson, Tennyson, Thoreau, Ramakrishna, and a score of persons identified by initials (more or less contemporary case histories). It might clarify matters if we said that Bucke today would probably place Mahatma Gandhi in the first category as a true case of cosmic consciousness and Dylan Thomas in the second as a doubtful case.

Cosmic consciousness differs from human consciousness in that human consciousness is ordinarily consciousness of oneself as distinct from all other objects and beings in the universe. In cosmic consciousness there is a sense of identification with the universe, an intellectual enlightenment or illumination which may last only briefly but which (according to the testimony of all illuminati) places the individual on a new plane of existence. According to Bucke and other commentators, the man of cosmic consciousness is in effect a member of a new species of the race. He is characterized by a state of moral exaltation, enhanced intellectual power, a feeling of elevation, elation, and joyousness, and a conviction of immortality. In mysticism (which is the ordinary name for this kind of consciousness) the world and the universe are indeed paradise; this is in direct opposition to the religious view that the world is an illusion, a vale of tears, or perhaps Hell itself. There is an incurable optimism in this position which is repellent both to the rational and the religious mind. The Americanism of Whitman is neither political nor philosophical, though it implies a philosophical optimism, perhaps. To the man of cosmic consciousness all things are purposeful, innately and extrinsically perfect. "Divine am I, inside and out," says Whitman, which is usually misconstrued as an egotistical poeticism whereas it is something quite different.

Having gone so far with the mention of esoteric, unknown, and even disreputable books, I will close with a mention of one more. This is the recent "grammar of poetic myth," as its author calls it, the book being Robert Graves' *The White Goddess*. This work is based on the belief that true poetry is a magical language bound up with popular religious ceremonies in honor of the Moon-Goddess or Muse. This magical poetry was rejected by the early Greek philosophers, who substituted the religion of logic and a rational poetic (Classicism) for the poetry of poetic myth. Graves' book, in short, is a bible of "Romanticism," encompassing the secret mystery cults of Eleusis, the ancient poetic colleges of Ireland and Wales, and the witch covens of Western Europe. This poetic tradition survived until the close of the seventeenth century, after which it was driven so far underground that true poetry from that time on results only from inspired or even pathological states. According to Graves, nineteenth-century poetry is melancholic and degenerate on the whole, with notable exceptions. Throughout European history, we can trace the inner struggle of the poet between worship of the Goddess and worship via the official religions. In the ancient rite the poet and priest were one; in modern Europe the poet must choose between poetry and religion, as we know from the works of Skelton, Donne, Crashaw, Herbert, Herrick, Swift, Crabbe, Kingsley, and Hopkins. "The poet survived in easy vigour only where the priest was shown the door; as when Skelton, to signalize his independence of Church discipline, wore the Muse-name 'Calliope' embroidered on his cassock in silk and gold, or when Herrick proved his devotion to poetic myth by pouring libations of Devonshire barley-ale from a silver cup to a pampered white pig. With Donne, Crashaw and Hopkins the war between poet and priest was fought on a high mystical level; but can Donne's *Divine Poems* . . . be preferred to his amorous *Songs and Sonnets?* or can the self-tortured Hopkins be commended for humbly submitting his poetic ecstasies to the confession-box?"

John Clare worshiped the White Goddess, as did Keats in the *"Belle Dame sans Merci,"* and Coleridge in the *Ancient Mariner.* Blake was a "poetic college" unto himself. The Goddess, among other things, is a lovely, slender woman who may suddenly transform herself into sow, mare, bitch, vixen, she-ass, weasel, serpent, owl, she-wolf, tigress, mermaid or loathsome hag. She is, of course, the Moon, the object of all fertility ritual. But the poet concerned with this theme cannot draw distinctions between "sacred history" and "profane myth," says Graves. To this extent, worship of the White Goddess is a phase of the poetry of cosmic consciousness.

I have chosen, more or less at random, about ten examples of works of cosmic psychology from the "poet's library." Another poet would provide ten or twenty or a hundred other studies, perhaps from astrology or alchemy. Poe was a phrenologist, Hopkins a Scotist, but these particular beliefs signify nothing. Whether the poet becomes a student of flying saucers or of the mystical doctrine of correspondences is all one; so long as he steps across the line from Reason to Intuition he is safe. Dr. Bucke's old-fashioned work of cosmic consciousness is as valid for the poet as Professor Schrödinger's account of noncausality, or Jung's explanation of Oriental "synchronicity." Psi phenomena and Rilke's angels, Lawrence's blood religion or Graves' ritual of goddess worship are not, to the poet's mind, categorically different from Reich's theory of the orgone energy of the universe. And the psychological disciplines of Ouspensky, based upon Hindu and Christian exercises, point to the same phenomena we find in Bucke or in Whitman, and so forth. All of this literature is "poetry," that is, irrationally true. And were all such literature lost to the world overnight it would almost immediately reappear of itself, because it exists outside time and beyond reason. That is the meaning of Wordsworth's line: "Enough of Science and Art." I ran across this quotation from Wordsworth in a strange and wonderful book called *Zen in English Literature*, by a British scholar, R. H. Blyth (The Hokuseido Press, Tokyo, 1942).

> Our meddling intellect
> Mis-shapes the beauteous forms of things:—
> We murder to dissect.
>
> Enough of Science and Art;
> Close up those barren leaves;
> Come forth, and bring with you a heart
> That watches and receives.

The Greatest Living Author

I CALL Henry Miller the greatest living author because I think he is. I do not call him a poet because he has never written a poem; he even dislikes poetry, I think. But everything he has written is a poem in the best as well as in the broadest sense of the word. Secondly, I do not call him a writer, but an author. The writer is the fly in the ointment of modern letters; Miller has waged ceaseless war against writers. If one had to type him one might call him a Wisdom writer, Wisdom literature being a type of literature which lies between literature and scripture; it is poetry only because it rises above literature and because it sometimes ends up in bibles. I wrote to the British poet and novelist Lawrence Durrell last year and said: Let's put together a bible of Miller's work. (I thought I was being original in calling it a bible.) Let's assemble a bible from his work, I said, and put one in every hotel room in America, after removing the Gideon Bibles and placing them in the laundry chutes. Durrell, however, had been working on this "bible" for years; I was a Johnny-come-lately. In fact, a group of writers all over the world have been working on it, and one version has just come out.

There is a commonplace reason why this volume is very much needed. The author's books are almost impossible to obtain; the ones that are not banned are stolen from libraries everywhere. Even a copy of one of the nonbanned books was recently stolen from the mails en route to me. Whoever got it had better be a book lover, because it was a bibliography.

I will introduce Miller with a quotation from the *Tropic of Cancer:* "I sometimes ask myself how it happens that I attract nothing but crackbrained individuals, neuroesthenics, neurotics, psychopaths—and Jews especially. There must be something in a healthy Gentile that excites the Jewish mind, like when he sees sour black bread." The "healthy Gentile" is a good sobriquet for Miller, who usually refers to himself as the Happy Rock, Caliban, "just a Brooklyn boy," "Someone who has gone off the gold standard of Literature" or—the name I like best—the Patagonian. What is a Patagonian? I don't know, but it is certainly something rare and *sui generis.* We can call Miller the greatest living Patagonian.

How is one to talk about Miller? There are authors one cannot write a book or even a good essay about. Arthur Rimbaud is one (and Miller's book on Rimbaud is one of the best books on Rimbaud ever written, although it is mostly about Henry Miller). D. H. Lawrence is another author one cannot encompass in a book "about" (Miller abandoned his book on Lawrence). And Miller himself is one of those Patagonian authors who just won't fit into a book. Every word he has ever written is autobiographical, but only in the way *Leaves of Grass* is autobiographical. There is not a word of "confession" in Miller. His amorous exploits are sometimes read as a kind of Brooklyn Casanova or male Fanny Hill, but there is probably not a word of exaggeration or boasting to speak of—or only as much as the occasion would call for. The reader can and cannot reconstruct the Life of Henry Miller from his books, for Miller never sticks to the subject any more than Lawrence does. The fact is that there isn't any subject and Miller is its poet. But a little information about him might help present him to those who need an introduction. For myself, I do not read him consecutively; I choose one of his books blindly and open it at random. I have just done this; for an example, I find: "Man is not at home in the universe, despite all the efforts of philosophers and metaphysicians to provide a soothing syrup. Thought is still a narcotic. The deepest question is *why*. And it is a forbidden one. The very asking is in the nature of cosmic sabotage. And the penalty is—the afflictions of Job." Not the greatest prose probably, but Miller is not a writer; Henry James is a writer. Miller is a talker, a street-corner gabbler, a prophet, and a Patagonian.

What are the facts about Miller? I'm not sure how important they are. He was born in Brooklyn about 1890, of German ancestry, and in certain ways he is quite German. I have often thought that the Germans make the best Americans, though they certainly make the worst Germans. Miller understands the German in himself and in America. He compares Whitman and Goethe: "In Whitman the whole American scene comes to life, her past and her future, her birth and her death. Whatever there is of value in America Whitman has expressed, and there is nothing more to be said. The future belongs to the machine, to the robots. He was the poet of the body and the soul, Whitman. The first and the last poet. He is almost undecipherable today, a monument covered with rude hieroglyphics, for which there is no key . . . There is no equivalent in the languages of Europe for the spirit which he immortalized. Europe is saturated with art and her soil is full of dead bones and her museums are bursting with plundered treasures, but what Europe has never had is a free, healthy spirit, what you might call a MAN. Goethe was the nearest approach, but Goethe was a stuffed shirt, by comparison. Goethe was a respectable citizen, a pedant, a bore, a universal spirit, but stamped with the German trademark, with the double eagle. The serenity of Goethe, the calm, Olympian attitude, is nothing more than the drowsy stupor of a German bourgeois deity. Goethe is an end of something, Whitman is a beginning."

If anybody can decipher the Whitman key it is Miller. Miller is the twentieth-century reincarnation of Whitman. But to return to the "facts." The Brooklyn Boy went to a Brooklyn high school in a day when most high schools kept higher standards than most American universities today. He started at CCNY but quit almost immediately and went to work for a cement company ("Everlasting Cement"), then for a telegraph company, where he became the personnel manager in the biggest city in the world. The telegraph company is called the Cosmodemonic Telegraph Company in Miller's books, or in moments of gaiety the Cosmococcic Telegraph Company. One day while the vice-president was bawling him out he mentioned to Miller that he would like to see someone write a sort of Horatio Alger book about the messengers.

I thought to myself [said Miller]—you poor old futzer, you, just wait until I get it off my chest . . . I'll give you an Horatio Alger book . . . My head was in a whirl to leave his office. I saw the army of men, women and children that had passed through my hands, saw them weeping, begging, beseeching, imploring, cursing, spitting, fuming, threatening. I saw the tracks they left on the highways, lying on the floor of freight trains, the parents in rags, the coal box empty, the sink running over, the walls sweating and between the cold beads of sweat the cockroaches running like mad; I saw them hobbling along like twisted gnomes or falling backwards in the epileptic frenzy . . . I saw the walls giving way and the pest pouring out like a winged fluid, and the men higher up with their ironclad logic, waiting for it to blow over, waiting for everything to be patched up, waiting, waiting contentedly . . . saying that things were temporarily out of order. I saw the Horatio Alger hero, the dream of a sick America, mounting higher and higher, first messenger, then operator, then manager, then chief, then superintendent, then vice-president, then president, then trust magnate, then beer baron, then Lord of all the Americas, the money god, the god of gods, the clay of clay, nullity on high, zero with ninety-seven thousand decimals fore and aft . . . I will give you Horatio Alger as he looks the day after the Apocalypse, when all the stink has cleared away.

And he did. Miller's first book, *Tropic of Cancer*, was published in Paris in 1934 and was immediately famous and immediately banned in all English-speaking countries, and still is. It is the Horatio Alger story with a vengeance. Miller had walked out of the Cosmodemonic Telegraph Company one day without a word; ever after he lived on his wits. He had managed to get to Paris on ten dollars, where he lived more than a decade, not during the gay prosperous twenties but during the Great Depression. He starved, made friends by the score, mastered the French language and his own. It was not until the Second World War broke out that he returned to America to live at Big Sur, California. Among his best books several are banned: the two *Tropics* (*Tropic of Cancer*, 1934, and *Tropic of Capricorn*, 1939); *Black Spring*, 1936; and part of the present trilogy *The Rosy Crucifixion* (including *Sexus*, *Plexus*, and *Nexus*).

Unfortunately for Miller he is a man without honor in his own country and in his own language. When *Tropic of Cancer* was published he was even denied entrance into England, held over in custody by the port authorities and returned to France by the next boat. He made friends with his jailer and wrote a charming essay about him. But Miller has no sense of despair. At the beginning of *Tropic of Cancer* he writes: "I have no money, no resources, no hopes. I am the happiest man alive."

George Orwell was one of the few English critics who saw his worth, though (*mirabile dictu*) T. S. Eliot and even Ezra Pound complimented him. Pound in his usual ungracious manner gave the *Tropic of Cancer* to a friend who later became Miller's publisher, and said: Here is a dirty book worth reading. Pound even went so far as to try to enlist Miller in his economic system to save the world. Miller retaliated by writing a satire called *Money and How It Gets That Way*, dedicated to Ezra Pound. The acquaintanceship halted there, Miller's view of money being something like this (from *Tropic of Capricorn*): "To walk in money through the night crowd, protected by money, lulled by money, dulled by money, the crowd itself a money, the breath money, no least single object anywhere that is not money, money, money everywhere and still not enough, and then no money, or a little money or less money or more money, but money, always money, and if you have money or you don't have money it is the money that counts and money makes money, *but what makes money make money?*" Pound didn't care for that brand of economics.

But all the writers jostled each other to welcome Miller among the elect, for the moment at least: Eliot, Herbert Read, Aldous Huxley, John Dos Passos and among them some who really knew how good Miller was: William Carlos Williams, who called him the Dean, Lawrence Durrell, Paul Rosenfeld, Wallace Fowlie, Osbert Sitwell, Kenneth Patchen, many painters (Miller is a fanatical water colorist). But mostly he is beset by his neuresthenics and psychopaths, as any cosmodemonic poet must be. People of all sexes frequently turn up at Big Sur and announce that they want to join the Sex Cult. Miller gives them bus fare and a good dinner and sends them on their way.

Orwell has written one of the best essays on Miller, although he takes a sociological approach and tries to place Miller as a Depression writer or something of the sort. What astonished Orwell about Miller was the difference between his view and the existential bitterness of a novelist like Céline. Céline's *Voyage au Bout de la Nuit* describes the meaninglessness of modern life and is thus a prototype of twentieth-century fiction. Orwell calls Céline's book a cry of unbearable disgust, a voice from the cesspool. And Orwell adds that the *Tropic of Cancer* is almost exactly the opposite! Such a thing as Miller's book "has become so unusual as to seem almost anomalous, [for] it is the book of a man who is happy." Miller also had reached the bottom of the pit, as many writers do; but how, Orwell asks, could he have emerged unembittered, whole, laughing with joy? "Exactly the aspects of life that fill Céline with horror are the ones that appeal to him. So far from protesting, he is *accepting*. And the very word 'acceptance' calls up his real affinity, another American, Walt Whitman."

This is, indeed, the crux of the matter and it is unfortunate that Orwell cannot see past the socio-economic situation with Whitman and Miller. Nevertheless, this English critic recognizes Miller's mastery of his material and places him among the great writers of our age; more than that, he predicts that Miller will set the pace and attitude for the novelist of the future. This has not happened yet, but I agree that it must. Miller's influence today is primarily among poets; those poets who follow Whitman must necessarily follow Miller, even to the extent of giving up poetry in its formal sense and writing that personal apocalyptic prose which Miller does. It is the prose of the Bible of Hell that Blake talked about and Arthur Rimbaud wrote a chapter of.

What is this "acceptance" Orwell mentions in regard to Whitman and Henry Miller? On one level it is the poetry of cosmic consciousness, and on the most obvious level it is the poetry of the Romantic nineteenth century. Miller is unknown in this country because he represents the Continental rather than the English influence. He breaks with the English literary tradition just as many of the twentieth-century Americans do, because his ancestry is not British, and not American colonial. He does not read the favored British writers, Milton, Marlowe, Pope, Donne. He reads what his grandparents knew was in the air when Victorianism was the genius of British poetry. He grew up with books by Dostoyevsky, Knut Hamsun, Strindberg, Nietzsche (especially Nietzsche), Elie Faure, Spengler. Like a true poet he found his way to Rimbaud, Ramakrishna, Blavatsky, Huysmans, Count Keyserling, Prince Kropotkin, Lao-tse, Nostradamus, Petronius, Rabelais, Suzuki, Zen philosophy, Van Gogh. And in English he let himself be influenced not by the solid classics but by *Alice in Wonderland,* Chesterton's *St. Francis,* Conrad, Cooper, Emerson, Rider Haggard, G. A. Henty (the boy's historian—I remember being told when I was a boy that Henty had the facts all wrong), Joyce, Arthur Machen, Mencken, John Cowper Powys, Herbert Spencer's *Autobiog-*

raphy, Thoreau on "Civil Disobedience," Emma
Goldman—the great anarchist (whom he met)—
Whitman, of course, and perhaps above all that com-
panion piece to *Leaves of Grass* called *Huckleberry
Finn.* Hardly a Great Books list from the shores of
Lake Michigan—almost a period list. Miller will introduce his readers to strange masterpieces like
Doughty's *Arabia Deserta* or to the journal of Anaïs
Nin which has never been published but which he
(and other writers) swears is one of the masterpieces
of the twentieth century. I imagine that Miller has
read as much as any man living but he does not have
that religious solemnity about books which we are
brought up in. Books, after all, are only mnemonic
devices; and poets are always celebrating the burning
of libraries. And as with libraries, so with monuments,
and as with monuments, so with civilizations. But in
Miller's case (*chez* Miller) there is no vindictiveness,
no bitterness. Orwell was bothered when he met
Miller because Miller didn't want to go to the Spanish
Civil War and do battle on one side or the other.
Miller is an anarchist of sorts, and he doesn't especially care which dog eats which dog. As it happens,
the righteous Loyalists were eaten by the Communists
and the righteous Falangists were eaten by the Nazis
over the most decadent hole in Europe; so Miller was
right.

Lawrence Durrell has said that the *Tropic* books
were healthy while Céline and D. H. Lawrence were
sick. Lawrence never escaped his puritanism and it is
his heroic try that makes us honor him. Céline is the
typical European man of despair—why should he not
despair, this Frenchman of the trenches of World War
I? We are raising up a generation of young American
Célines, I'm afraid, but Miller's generation still had
Whitman before its eyes and was not running back to

the potholes and ash heaps of Europe. Miller is as good an antiquarian as anybody; in the medieval towns of France he goes wild with happiness; and he has written one of the best "travel books" on Greece ever done (the critics are unanimous about the *Colossus of Maroussi*); but to worship the "tradition" is to him the sheerest absurdity. Like most Americans, he shares the view of the first Henry Ford that history is bunk. He cannot forgive his "Nordic" ancestors for the doctrines of righteousness and cleanliness. His people, he says, were painfully clean: "Never once had they opened the door which leads to the soul; never once did they dream of taking a blind leap into the dark. After dinner the dishes were promptly washed and put in the closet; after the paper was read it was neatly folded and laid away on a shelf; after the clothes were washed they were ironed and folded and then tucked away in the drawers. Everything was for tomorrow, but tomorrow never came. The present was only a bridge and on this bridge they are still groaning, as the world groans, and not one idiot ever thinks of blowing up the bridge." As everyone knows, Cleanliness is the chief American industry. Miller is the most formidable anticleanliness poet since Walt Whitman, and his hatred of righteousness is also American, with the Americanism of Thoreau, Whitman, and Emma Goldman. Miller writes a good deal about cooking and wine drinking. Americans are the worst cooks in the world, outside of the British; and Americans are also great drunkards who know nothing about wine. The Germanic-American Miller reintroduces good food and decent wine into our literature. One of his funniest essays is about the American loaf of bread, the poisonous loaf of cleanliness wrapped in cellophane, the manufacture of which is a heavy industry like steel.

Orwell and other critics tend to regard Miller as a kind of hedonist and professional do-nothing. And morally, they tend to regard him as one of that illustrious line of Americans who undermine the foundations of traditional morals. Miller quotes Thoreau's statement, which might almost be the motto of the cosmic writer: "Most of what my neighbors call good, I am profoundly convinced is evil, and if I repent anything, it is my good conduct that I repent." One could hardly call Thoreau a criminal, yet he had his runins with the law, just as Miller has, and for the same reasons. The strain of anarchism and amorality is growing stronger in American literature, or that branch of it that I am talking about, and Miller is one of its chief carriers. It is not only Emma Goldman, Thoreau, Mark Twain, Whitman, and perhaps Salinger, but that whole literature of Detachment from political hysteria and overorganization. I am influenced enough by these people and by Miller to tell my students, the poets at least, to cultivate an ignorance of contemporary political and military events because they do not matter. I tell them not to vote, to join nothing. I try to steer them toward their true leaders and visionaries, men almost unknown in the polite literary world, Reich for instance. Wilhelm Reich furthered a movement in Germany called "Work Democracy"; not machine politics, no politics at all, but democracy within one's immediate orbit; democracy at home. America is still the only country where social idealism and experimentation have elbow room; there are still communities that practice primitive Christianity, such as the Catholic anarchists; and just plain little homemade gardens of Eden such as Miller's cliff at Big Sur. The life he describes in *Big Sur and the Oranges of Hieronymus Bosch* is a far cry from the little fascist dreams of the New Classicists. And it is a far cry from the bitter isolationism of Robinson Jeffers or even of Lawrence. Morally I regard Miller as a holy man, as most of his adherents do—Gandhi with a penis.

Miller says in a little essay on Immorality and Morality: "What is moral and what is immoral? Nobody can ever answer this question satisfactorily. Not because morals ceaselessly evolve, but because the principle on which they depend is factitious. Morality is for slaves, for beings without spirit. And when I say spirit I mean the Holy Spirit." And he ends this little piece with a quotation from ancient Hindu scripture: Evil does not exist.

Whitman, Lawrence, Miller, and even Blake all have the reputation of being sex-obsessed, Miller especially. Whereas Whitman writes "copulation is no more rank to me than death is," Miller writes hundreds of pages describing in the minutest and clearest detail his exploits in bed. Every serious reader of erotica has remarked about Miller that he is probably the only author in history who writes about such things with complete ease and naturalness. Lawrence never quite rid himself of his puritanical salaciousness, nor Joyce; both had too much religion in their veins. It is funny to recollect that Lawrence thought *Ulysses* a smutty book and Joyce thought *Lady Chatterley* a smutty book. Both were right. But at least they *tried* to free themselves from literary morality. Miller's achievement is miraculous: he is screamingly funny without making fun of sex, the way Rabelais does. (Rabelais is, of course, magnificent; so is Boccaccio; but both write against the background of religion, like Joyce and Lawrence.) Miller is accurate and poetic in the highest degree; there is not a smirk anywhere in his writings. Miller undoubtedly profited from the mistakes of his predecessors; his aim was not to write about the erotic but to write the whole truth about the life he knew. This goal demanded the full vocabulary and iconography of sex, and it is possible that he is the first writer outside the Orient who has succeeded in writing as naturally about sex on a large scale as novelists ordinarily write about the dinner table or the battlefield. I think only an American could have performed this feat.

We are dealing with the serious question of banned books, burned books, and fear of books in general. America has the most liberal censorship laws in the West today, but we have done no more than make a start. I have always been amused by the famous decision of Judge Woolsey who lifted the ban on *Ulysses,* although it was certainly a fine thing to do and it is a landmark we can be proud of. Woolsey said various comical things, such as that he could not detect the "leer of the sensualist" in Joyce's book, and that therefore (the logic of it escapes me) it is not pornographic. In excusing the use of old Saxon words he noted that Joyce's "locale was Celtic and his season Spring." And, in order to push his decision through, Judge Woolsey stated that *Ulysses* "did not tend to excite sexual impulses or lustful thoughts," and he closed his argument with the elegant statement that although the book is "somewhat emetic, nowhere does it tend to be an aphrodisiac." Emetic means tending to produce vomiting and I doubt that Joyce savored that description of his masterpiece. The implication, of course, is that vomiting is good for you, and lustful thoughts not. Now everyone who has read *Ulysses* knows that the book is based largely on the lustful thoughts and acts of its characters and that Joyce spared no pains to represent these thoughts and deeds richly and smackingly. *Ulysses* is, since the Judge used the word, a pretty *good* aphrodisiac, partly because of

Joyce's own religious tensions. Miller, on the other hand, is no aphrodisiac at all, because religious or so-called moral tension does not exist for him. When one of Miller's characters lusts, he lusts out loud and then proceeds to the business at hand. Joyce actually prevents himself from experiencing the beauty of sex or lust, while Miller is freed at the outset to deal with the overpowering mysteries and glories of love and copulation. Like other Millerites I claim that Miller is one of the few healthy Americans alive today; further, that the circulation of his books would do more to wipe out the obscenities of Broadway, Hollywood, and Madison Avenue than a full-scale social revolution. But I very much doubt whether any Judge Woolsey will ever admit Miller's banned books to legal publication. They are too intelligible. Even an innocuous little book like Allen Ginsberg's *Howl* had to fight its way through the San Francisco courts. Miller was one of his adherents, as was Professor Mark Schorer of the University of California. Schorer is one of our best critics, the author of a fine study of Blake, and the man who helped to get *Lady Chatterley* taken off the banned list.

Miller has furthered literature for all writers by ignoring the art forms, the novel, the poem, the drama, and by sticking to the autobiographical novel. He says in *The Books in My Life* (one of the available works), "The autobiographical novel, which Emerson predicted would grow in importance with time, has replaced the great confessions. It is not a mixture of truth and fiction, this genre of literature, but an expansion and deepening of truth. It is more authentic, more veridical, than the diary. It is not the flimsy truth of facts which the authors of these autobiographical novels offer but the truth of emotion, reflection and understanding, truth digested and assimilated. The being revealing himself does so on all levels simultaneously." Everything Miller has written is part of this great amorphous autobiographical novel and it must be read not entirely but in large chunks to make sense. Many of the individual works are whole in themselves, one dealing with his life in Paris, one with his life as a New Yorker, and there is, in fact, a definite span of years encompassed in the works. But the volumes of essays are also part of the story and there is no way to make a whole out of the parts. Miller is easy to quote if one quotes carefully; the danger is that one can find massive contradictions, unless there is some awareness of the underlying world and the cosmic attitudes of the author. These views are by no means unique, as they are the same as those of all those poets and mystics I referred to in a previous essay. What makes Miller unique is his time and place; he is the only American of our time who has given us a full-scale interpretation of modern America, other than the kind of thing we find in the cultural journals. Incidentally, we do not find Miller in these journals, which, presuming an interest in letters and art, are really organs of social and political opinion.

Readers of Whitman recall that Whitman was blistering about the materialism of this country a century ago, and its departure from the ideals of the founding fathers. Miller is worse. Now it is a commonplace of modern poetry that the poet dissociates himself from life as it is lived by the average American today. Whitman and Miller heap abuse on the failure of the country to live up to its promise. Miller writes as a poet about the demonic hideousness of New York City, Chicago, the South, or he rhapsodizes when there is anything to be rapturous about. But it is not Art that he cares about; it is man, man's treatment of man in America and man's treatment of nature. What we get in Miller is not a sense of superiority but fury, even the fury of the prophet of doom.

Miller knows America from the bottom up and from coast to coast. In the same way he knows Paris as few Frenchmen do. But when Miller describes slums it is usually with the joyous eye of the artist, not with the self-righteous sneer of the social reformer. Here, too, one might describe his psychology as "Oriental" rather than modern. The cultural situation is a matter of complete indifference to him. Miller frequently immerses himself in such modern Indian mystics as Krishnamurti and Ramakrishna, but without any of the flapdoodle of the cultist. He is himself one of the foremost of the contemporary men of Detachment. His influence (like that of Lawrence) comes as much from his life as from his writings. Here it is better to quote. This is Myrtle Avenue in Brooklyn:

But I saw a street called Myrtle Avenue, which runs from Borough Hall to Fresh Pond Road, and down this street no saint ever walked (else it would have crumbled), down this street no miracle ever passed, nor any poet, nor any species of human genius, nor did any flower ever grow there, nor did the sun strike it squarely, nor did the rain ever wash it. For the genuine Inferno which I had to postpone for twenty years I give you Myrtle Avenue, one of the innumerable bridlepaths ridden by iron monsters which lead to the heart of America's emptiness. If you have only seen Essen or Manchester or Chicago or Levallois-Perret or Glasgow or Hoboken or Canarsie or Bayonne you have seen nothing of the magnificent emptiness of progress and enlightenment. Dear reader, you must see Myrtle Avenue before you die, if only to realize how far into the future Dante saw. You must believe me that on this street, neither in the houses which line it, nor the cobblestones which pave it, nor the elevated structure which cuts it atwain, neither in any creature that bears a name and lives thereon, neither in any animal, bird or insect passing through it to slaughter or already slaughtered, is there hope of "lubet," "sublimate" or "abominate." It is a street not of sorrow, for sorrow would be human and recognizable, but of sheer emptiness: it is emptier than the most extinct volcano, emptier than a vacuum, emptier than the word God in the mouth of an unbeliever.

This is a man describing his own neighborhood, but the street is a type that runs from the Atlantic to the Pacific, with variations:

The whole country is lawless, violent, explosive, demoniacal. It's in the air, in the climate, in the ultra-grandiose landscape, in the stone forests that are lying horizontal, in the torrential rivers that bite through the rocky canyons, in the supranormal distances, the supernal arid wastes, the over-lush crops, the monstrous fruits, the mixture of quixotic bloods, the fatras of cults, sects, beliefs, the opposition of laws and languages, the contradictoriness of temperaments, principles, needs, requirements. The continent is full of buried violence, of the bones of antediluvian monsters and of lost races of man, of mysteries which are wrapped in doom. The atmosphere is at times so electrical that the soul is summoned out of its body and runs amok. Like the rain everything comes in bucketsful—or not at all. The whole continent is a huge volcano whose crater is temporarily concealed by a moving panorama which is partly dream, partly fear, partly despair. From Alaska to Yucatan it's the same story. Nature dominates, Nature wins out. Everywhere the same fundamental urge to slay, to ravage, to plunder. Outwardly they seem like a fine, upstanding people—healthy, optimistic, courageous. Inwardly they are filled with worms. A tiny spark and they blow up.

The passages on Times Square repeat and catalogue, like Whitman; they are a little too painful to read out of context. Here is a bit of Chicago; Miller is wandering in the Negro slums with a fellow visitor:

We got into the car, rode a few blocks and got out to visit another shell crater. The street was deserted except for some chickens grubbing for food between the slats of a crumbling piazza. More vacant lots, more gutted houses; fire escapes clinging to the walls with their iron teeth, like drunken acrobats. A Sunday atmosphere here. Everything serene and peaceful. Like Louvain or Rheims between bombardments. Like Phoebus, Virginia, dreaming of bringing her steeds to water, or like modern Eleusis smothered by a wet sock. Then suddenly I saw it chalked upon the side of a house in letters ten feet high:

GOOD NEWS! GOD IS LOVE!

When I saw these words I got down on my knees in the open sewer which had been conveniently placed there for the purpose and I offered up a short prayer, a silent one, which must have registered as far as Mound City, Illinois, where the colored muskrats have built their igloos. It was time for a good stiff drink of cod-liver oil but as the varnish factories were all closed we had to repair to the abattoir and quaff a bucket of blood. Never has blood tasted so wonderful! It was like taking Vitamins A, B, C, D, E in quick succession and then chewing a stick of cold dynamite. Good news! Aye, wonderful news—for Chicago. I ordered the chauffeur to take us immediately to Mundelein so that I could bless the cardinal and all the real estate operations, but we only got as far as the Bahai Temple . . .

Or, again—in explanation:

Oh, Henry, what beautiful golden teeth you have! exclaimed my four-year-old daughter the other morning on climbing into bed with me. (That's how I approach the works of my confreres.) I see how beautiful are their golden teeth, not how ugly or artificial they are.

Combating the "system" is nonsense. There is only one aim in life and that is to live it. In America it has become impossible, except for a few lucky or wise

people, to live one's own life; consequently the poets
and artists tend to move to the fringes of society.
Wherever there are individuals, says Miller (like
Thoreau) there are new frontiers. The American way
of life has become illusory; we lead the lives of prison-
ers while we boast about free speech, free press, and
free religion, none of which we actually do enjoy in
full. The price for security has become too great;
abundance has become a travesty. The only thing for
nonenslaved man to do is to move out to the edge,
lose contact with the machines of organization which
are as ubiquitous in this country as in Russia. "Instead
of bucking your head against a stone wall, sit quietly
with hands folded and wait for the walls to crumble
. . . Don't sit and *pray* that it will happen! Just sit and
watch it happen!" These sayings the culture litera-
teur condemns as irresponsible. Miller follows through
with the complete program of nonparticipation in our
machine society, which is organized from the cradle
to the grave. "Just as Gandhi successfully exploited
the doctrine of nonresistance, so these 'saints of the
just' practiced non-recognition—non-recognition of
sin, guilt, fear and disease . . . even death." Whitman
also believed in nonrecognition of death. His view of
death as part of life is one of the many reasons for
his unpopularity in America, where death is considered a crime against society. "Why try to solve a
problem? *Dissolve* it! [says Miller]. Fear not to be a
coward, a traitor, a renegade. In this universe of ours
there is room for all, perhaps even need for all. The
sun does not inquire about rank and status before
shedding its warmth; the cyclone levels the godly and
the ungodly; the government takes your tax money
even though it be tainted. Nor is the atom bomb a
respecter of persons. Perhaps that is why the righteous
are squirming so!"

All of this is about modern America and the high cost of security. Do we really have a high standard of living? Miller says not, as most poets do. If living means appreciation of life we have the lowest standard of living in the world, in spite of the fact that it costs more to live in America than in any country in the world. Miller says "the cost is not only in dollars and cents but in sweat and blood, in frustration, ennui, broken homes, smashed ideals, illness and insanity. We have the most wonderful hospitals, the most fabulous prisons, the best equipped and highest paid army and navy, the speediest bombers, the largest stockpile of atom bombs, yet never enough of any of these items to satisfy the demand. Our manual workers are the highest paid in the world; our poets the worst . . ."

And Miller gives this answer, letting Krishnamurti say it:

The world problem is the individual problem; if the individual is at peace, has happiness, has great tolerance, and an intense desire to help, then the world problem as such ceases to exist. You consider the world problem before you have considered your own problem. Before you have established peace and understanding in your own hearts and in your own minds you desire to establish peace and tranquillity in the minds of others, in your nations and in your states; whereas peace and understanding will only come when there is understanding, certainty and strength in yourselves.

To place the individual before the state, whether the Russian state or the American state, is the first need of modern man. To interpret Miller, man is like the common soldier on the battlefield; he can know nothing of the battle at large or of its causes; he can know only the fifty feet or so in his immediate vicinity; within that radius he is a man responsible for himself and his fellows; beyond that he is powerless. Modern life, having made everyone state conscious, has destroyed the individual. America has as few individuals today as Russia, and as many taboos to keep the individual from coming to life as the USSR. First, we have contaminated the idea of society; second, we have contaminated the idea of community. Miller writing about his little community at Big Sur frowns on the idea of community itself. "To create community—and what is a nation, or a people, without a sense of community—there must be a common purpose. Even here in Big Sur, where the oranges are ready to blossom forth, there is no common purpose, no common effort. There is a remarkable neighborliness, but no community spirit. We have a Grange, as do other rural communities, but what is a 'Grange' in the life of man? The real workers are outside the Grange. Just as the 'real men of God' are outside the Church. And the real leaders outside the world of politics."

"We create our fate," says Miller. And better still: "Forget, forgive, renounce, abdicate." And "scrap the past instantly." Live the good life instantly; it's now or never, and always has been.

Miller is "irresponsible" as far as official and popular politics go, or as far as common church morality goes, and as far as literary manners go. But he is not a poseur, he has no program, yet he has a deep and pure sense of morality. I would call him a total revolutionary, the man who will settle for nothing less than "Christmas on earth." In his remarkable study of Rimbaud, a prose-poem of one hundred and fifty pages called *The Time of the Assassins*, Miller discourses on the spiritual suicide of modern youth.

I like to think of him as the one who extended the boundaries of that only partially explored domain. Youth ends where manhood begins, it is said. A phrase without meaning, since from the beginning of history man has never enjoyed the full measure of youth nor known the limitless possibilities of adulthood. How can one know the splendor and fullness of youth if one's energies are consumed in combating the errors and falsities of parents and ancestors? Is youth to waste its strength unlocking the grip of death? Is youth's only mission on earth to rebel, to destroy, to assassinate? Is youth only to be offered up to sarifice? What of the *dreams* of youth? Are they always to be regarded as follies? Are they to be populated only with chimeras? . . . Stifle or deform youth's dreams and you destroy the creator. Where there has been no real youth there can be no real manhood. If society has come to resemble a collection of deformities, is it not the work of our educators and preceptors? Today, as yesterday, the youth who would live his own life has no place to turn, no place to live his youth unless, retiring into his chrysalis, he closes all apertures and buries himself alive. The conception of our mother the earth being "an egg which doth contain all good things in it" has undergone a profound change. The cosmic egg contains an addled yolk. This is the present view of mother earth. The psychoanalysts have traced the poison back to the womb, but to what avail? In the light of this profound discovery we are given permission . . . to step from one rotten egg into another. . . . Why breed new monsters of negation and futility? Let society scotch its own rotten corpse! Let us have a new heaven and a new earth!—that was the sense of Rimbaud's obstinate revolt."

Miller calls for an end to revolt once and for all. His message is precisely that of Whitman, of Rimbaud, of Rilke: "Everything we are taught is false"; and "Change your life." As a writer Miller may be second- or third-rate or of no rating at all; as a spiritual example he stands among the great men of our age. Will this ever be recognized? Not in our time probably.

The Rimbaud book ends with a Coda, a little recital of the literature of despair which has surrounded us for a hundred years. Listen to it. It is a fitting close to the present book.

Rimbaud was born in the middle of the nineteenth century, October 20th, 1854, at 6:00 A.M., it is said. A century of unrest, of materialism, and of 'progress,' as we say. Purgatorial in every sense of the word, and the writers who flourished in this period reflect this ominously. Wars and revolutions were abundant. Russia alone, we are told, waged thirty-three wars (mostly of conquest) during the 18th and 19th centuries. Shortly after Rimbaud is born his father is off to the Crimean War. So is Tolstoy. The revolution of 1848, of brief duration but full of consequences, is followed by the bloody Commune of 1871, which Rimbaud as a boy is thought to have participated in. In 1848 we in America are fighting the Mexicans with whom we are now great friends, though the Mexicans are not too sure of it. During this war Thoreau makes his famous speech on Civil Disobedience, a document which will one day be added to the Emancipation Proclamation. . . . Twelve years later the Civil War breaks out, perhaps the bloodiest of all civil wars. . . . From 1847 until his death in 1881 Amiel is writing his *Journal Intime* . . . which . . . gives a thoroughgoing analysis of the moral dilemma in which the creative spirits of the time found themselves. The very titles of the books written by influential writers of the 19th century are revelatory. I give just a few . . . *The Sickness unto Death* (Kierkegaard), *Dreams and Life* (Gérard de Nerval), *Les Fleurs du Mal* (Baudelaire), *Les Chants de Maldoror* (Lautréamont), *The Birth of Tragedy* (Nietzsche), *La Bête Humaine* (Zola), *Hunger* (Knut Hamsun), *Les Lauriers Sont Coupés* (Dujardin), *The Conquest of Bread* (Kropotkin), *Looking Backward* (Edward Bellamy), *Alice in Wonderland, The Serpent in Paradise* (Sacher-Masoch), *Les Paradis Artificiels* (Baudelaire), *Dead Souls* (Gogol), *The House of the Dead* (Dostoiefsky), *The Wild Duck* (Ibsen), *The Inferno*

(Strindberg), *The Nether World* (Gissing), *A Rebours* (Huysmans). . . .

Goethe's *Faust* was not so very old when Rimbaud asked a friend for a copy of it. Remember the date of his birth is October 20th, 1854 (6:00 A.M. Western Standard Diabolical Time). The very next year, 1855, *Leaves of Grass* makes its appearance, followed by condemnation and suppression. Meanwhile *Moby Dick* had come out (1851) and Thoreau's *Walden* (1854). In 1855 Gérard de Nerval commits suicide, having lasted till the remarkable age of 47. In 1854 Kierkegaard is already penning his last words to history in which he gives the parable of "The Sacrificed Ones." Just four or five years before Rimbaud completes *A Season in Hell* (1873), Lautréamont publishes privately his celebrated piece of blasphemy, another "work of youth," as we say, in order not to take these heartbreaking testaments seriously. . . . By 1888 Nietzsche is explaining to Brandes that he can now boast three readers: Brandes, Taine, and Strindberg. The next year he goes mad and remains that way until his death in 1900. Lucky man! From 1893 to 1897 Strindberg is experiencing a crise . . . which he describes with magisterial effects in the *Inferno*. Reminiscent of Rimbaud is the title of another of his works: *The Keys to Paradise*. In 1888 comes Dujardin's curious little book, forgotten until recently. . . . By this time Mark Twain is at his height, *Huckleberry Finn* having appeared in 1884, the same year as *Against the Grain* of Huysmans. . . . By the fall of 1891 Gissing's *New Grub Street* is launched. It is an interesting year in 19th century literature, the year of Rimbaud's death. . . .

What a century of names!. . . Shelley, Blake, Stendhal, Hegel, Fechner, Emerson, Poe, Schopenhauer, Max Stirner, Mallarmé, Tchekov, Andreyev, Verlaine, Couperus, Maeterlinck, Madame Blavatsky, Samuel Butler, Claudel, Unamuno, Conrad, Bakunin, Shaw, Rilke, Stefan George, Verhaeren, Gautier, Léon Bloy, Balzac, Yeats. . . .

What revolt, what disillusionment, what longing! Nothing but crises, breakdown, hallucinations and visions. The foundations of politics, morals, economics, and art tremble.

The air is full of warnings and prophecies of the debacle to come—and in the 20th century it comes! Already two world wars and a promise of more before the century is out. Have we touched bottom? Not yet. The moral crisis of the 19th century has merely given way to the spiritual bankruptcy of the 20th. It is "the time of the assassins" and no mistaking it. . . .

Rimbaud is indeed the symbol of the death of modern poetry. This seer, this visionary deserts poetry at the age of eighteen to make money, by gunrunning, even by slave-trading, ending with a death-bed conversion. His is a life of slander, beginning with the motto "Death to God" chalked on the church door and ending with extreme unction and the money belt under the bed. I think the message of Rimbaud to Miller is the death of poetry, the death of history. The whole romantic agony of the nineteenth century is summed up in this adolescent genius, a curse laid on us. Miller obliterates the curse; he pronounces the benediction over Rimbaud, over the death of poetry, over the death of civilization itself but with a sidesplitting laugh without an iota of animosity in it. Miller leads us away from the charnel house of nineteenth-century poetry; he does not even recognize the existence of twentieth-century poetry. For poetry has lost its significance, its relevance, and even its meaning in our time. To begin again it must repair to the wilderness, outside society, outside the city gates, a million miles from books and their keepers. Almost alone of the writers of our time Henry Miller has done this; I would guess that his following is enormous and that it is just beginning to grow. Like Nietzsche, like Lawrence, his word somehow spreads abroad and somehow cleanses the atmosphere of the mind of its age-old detritus of tradition, its habits of despair, its hates.

One word more: at the close of his beautiful clown story, "The Smile at the Foot of the Ladder," Miller talks about the clown, the hero of so much of the best contemporary literature.

Joy is like a river [says Miller], it flows ceaselessly. It seems to me that this is the message which the clown is trying to convey to us, that we should participate through ceaseless flow and movement, that we should not stop to reflect, compare, analyze, possess, but flow on and through, endlessly, like music. This is the gift of surrender, and the clown makes it symbolically. It is for us to make it real.

At no time in the history of man has the world been so full of pain and anguish. Here and there, however, we meet with individuals who are untouched, unsullied, by the common grief. They are not heartless individuals, far from it! They are emancipated beings. For them the world is not what it seems to us. They see with other eyes. We say of them that they have died to the world. They live in the moment, fully, and the radiance which emanates from them is a perpetual song of joy.

And Miller is certainly one of these who have died to the world, like the clown. The ponderous absurdities of modern literature and the world it perpetuates dissolve in the hilarities of this almost unknown American author; this poet who dissociates himself from the so-called modern age and whose one aim is to give literature back to life. There are not many of these emancipated beings left in our world, these clowns and clairvoyants, celebrants of the soul and of the flesh and of the still-remaining promise of America. And of these few great souls the greatest is— the Patagonian.

ABOUT THE AUTHOR

KARL SHAPIRO was born in Baltimore, Maryland, on November 10, 1913, and attended the University of Virginia and Johns Hopkins University. In 1946 he was appointed Consultant in Poetry at the Library of Congress, and then, in 1947, he joined the faculty of Johns Hopkins University, where he taught writing courses. In 1950 he became editor of *Poetry: A Magazine of Verse*. Mr. Shapiro is now Professor of English at the University of Nebraska, and is editor of the *Prairie Schooner*. He is a member of the National Institute of Arts and Letters.

Mr. Shapiro's poems, essays and reviews have appeared in leading literary magazines. His second volume of verse, *V-Letter and Other Poems*, was awarded the Pulitzer Prize in 1945.